GROWING UP NISEI

THE ASIAN AMERICAN EXPERIENCE

Series Editor

Roger Daniels, University of Cincinnati

A list of books in the series
appears at the end of this book.

GROWING UP NISEI

Race, Generation, and Culture among
Japanese Americans of California, 1924–49

DAVID K. YOO

Foreword by Roger Daniels

University of Illinois Press
Urbana and Chicago

© 2000 by the Board of Trustees of the University of Illinois
All rights reserved
Manufactured in the United States of America
∞ This book is printed on acid-free paper.
Library of Congress Cataloging-in-Publication Data
Yoo, David K.
  Growing up Nisei : race, generation, and culture among
  Japanese Americans of California, 1924–49 / David K. Yoo ;
  foreword by Roger Daniels.
    p. cm. — (The Asian American experience)
  ISBN 0-252-02508-3 (alk. paper)
  ISBN 0-252-06822-X (pbk. : alk. paper)
  1. Japanese Americans—California—History—20th century.
    2. California—History—20th century. 3. California—
  Race relations. I. Title. II. Series.
F870.J3Y66   2000
305.895'6073'0904—dc21   99-6263
CIP

1 2 3 4 5 C P 5 4 3 2 1

CONTENTS

FOREWORD

Roger Daniels

The historical literature about the Nisei in California is dominated by the traumatic wartime incarceration that disrupted the lives of virtually the whole generation and those of their foreign-born parents. Dozens of books, beginning with Carey McWilliams's *Prejudice: Japanese Americans, Symbol of Racial Intolerance* (Boston, 1944), have used the Nisei prewar experience as simply a prelude for the wartime atrocity that followed.[1] Such a literature, quite naturally, tends to focus on what was done to Japanese Americans rather than on what they did and said in the past, to use Carl Becker's stripped down definition of history.

The great strength of David Yoo's *Growing Up Nisei* is that he has avoided this trap. He first examines and analyzes the lives of the more active older members of the Nisei generation in the two decades *before* Executive Order 9066 made them what I have called "prisoners without trial." While Yoo never forgets or ignores the pervasive discrimination that Nisei and other persons of color faced in pre–World War II America, his focus enables him to avoid the victim syndrome and look at the Nisei of the 1920s and 1930s as "ordinary" people with prosaic, everyday concerns about how to cope with the world around them. Then, and only then, does he examine how the Nisei reacted to their wartime ordeals.

In three probing chapters Yoo explores the education of the Nisei and their search for careers, looks at Nisei religion with analysis of both Christian and Buddhist organizations, and provides an extensive treatment of the ethnic press and some of its more able young practitioners. Most of his protagonists are members of the older cohorts of the Nisei generation, persons born between 1900 and 1920. Yoo shows how the more articulate members of those cohorts tried, with some success, to create niches for themselves in Issei-dominated communities.

Growing Up Nisei does not, of course, ignore the concentration camps. The trauma of exile and incarceration are covered well in the later chapters. Yoo provides a new perspective on that much-studied experience—what he calls "The Firestorm of War and Incarceration." In subsequent chapters he analyzes, in some detail, how a few skilled Nisei journalists who remained at liberty wrote and argued about the meaning of what was happening to the shattered wartime community, and he explores interviews done in Chicago by Charles Kikuchi, an atypical Nisei. A brief epilogue indicates how the trauma of the wartime experiences was a continuing factor for the community even after the closing of the camps and the rescission of other restrictive measures.

Much of *Growing Up Nisei* thus explores an uncharted landscape in which there are still important features to be discovered and described. Although Yoo looks almost exclusively at Japanese Americans, his book can be used by other scholars not only as a model for studying the lives of Japanese Americans who lived outside of California but also for the lives of the citizen generations of those other, less-numerous Asian American groups—particularly Chinese and Filipinos—who had established sizable communities in mainland American cities in the decades before World War II.

Note

1. John Modell's book *The Economics and Politics of Racial Accommodation: The Japanese of Los Angeles, 1900–1942* (Urbana: University of Illinois Press, 1977) is the most outstanding exception to this generalization.

PREFACE

This book is about American identity, about that complicated process by which people come to identify their sense of self and group in relation to the United States. In a nation comprised largely of immigrants and their descendants, the story of "becoming Americans" is one that extends from our founding to the very present. Despite the centrality of migration, settlement, and identity formation, however, the variations on this general trend are as numerous as those who have ventured to these shores. Moreover, factors such as region, time period, and class make it difficult to generalize about American identity. Patterns and shared themes begin to fade and blur as one pushes below the surface.

Such was the case in this narrative—a study of second-generation Japanese Americans who came of age in California during the second quarter of the twentieth century. Like so many others, these men and women forged their identities within the tangle of immigrant and native contexts. Yet what emerges from delving into their worlds are glimpses of how issues like race, generation, and culture uniquely shaped their experiences. That Japanese Americans contended with such themes within a crucible of time marked by racial subordination, economic depression, a world at war, and mass incarceration makes their story even more extraordinary.

The documentation and analysis of the times and spaces that Japanese Americans occupied represent an effort to reclaim a generation and a group that has often gone unnoticed, lost, as it were, within assumptions of assimilation and insignificance. Though most American historians today would suggest a middle ground between wholesale assimilation and ethnic retention, the fact remains that we know too little about the actual lives of second-generation groups such as Japanese Americans. Perhaps more than their parents, the lives of the children of immigrants hold important clues about the complexities, conflicts, and contradictions of "becoming Americans." Because racial concerns played such a major role in their experiences, studying Japanese Americans provides an opportunity to ask how the distinctive and enduring marker of "race" has been part of U.S. immigration history—a component that is often missing. More than filling "gaps," this narrative account examines how Japanese Americans created their own cultures even as they negotiated the larger contexts of which they were a part.

While the individuals, communities, and institutions that appear in these pages are a reflection of Japanese America, I will be the first to suggest that this story represents only one angle of vision. I might list numerous caveats, but perhaps two will suffice. The first is that Kibei Nisei, children of immigrants who were sent back to Japan at an early age and raised there, are not featured much in this book. In part, this had to do with availability of sources, but it also involved the issue of language. Although English was clearly dominant among the second generation, fully incorporating Japanese-language sources would have enabled a more nuanced rendering of Nisei experiences. Second, in terms of region, the urban outweighs the rural, which again largely reflected the types of sources available and employed.

As for terminology, I have relied heavily on the generational words in the Japanese language that immigrants and their successive generations have used. Not surprisingly, "Issei" (immigrants, or first-generation) and "Nisei" (children of immigrants, or second-generation) are peppered throughout the book, but I have also used "Nikkei" (Japanese people) to refer inclusively to Japanese Americans. The terms employed for wartime experiences have their own history, starting with the federal government's euphemism: "relocation center." Although "relocation" has historical significance, "concentration camp" much more accurately reflects what took place, though not to be mistaken for the death camps of Nazi Germany. Much of the literature on the camps has used "internment," but technically the internment camps were restricted to the centers run by the Department of Justice rather than the camps administered by the War Relocation Authority (WRA), which housed the majority of Japanese Americans. Hence, I have followed the lead of others in using "incarceration" to denote the experiences of those who spent time in the WRA camps.

✿ ✿ ✿

While research and writing are often solitary endeavors, I am fully aware that many people and institutions have guided and assisted me over the years. Although acknowledgment here is hardly sufficient, I am glad for the opportunity to offer my thanks. This book began as a dissertation at Yale University, and a number of historians helped shape this project in its early stages. It has been a privilege to work with Howard Lamar, who set high scholarly standards infused with a gracious humanity. Bill Cronon has taught me much about history and writing, and I've appreciated his counsel. I am thankful for the encouragement of many others in New Haven, including Jon Butler, Harry Stout, David Montgomery, Robert Stepto, and fellow students in American studies and history.

At UCLA, I learned a great deal about Asian American history over the course of two academic years of dissertation research and writing. Don Nakanishi, director of the Asian American Studies Center, deserves much thanks for making my stay possible. I was fortunate to have Yuji Ichioka serve as my sponsor, and ever since our first meeting he has given generously of his time and considerable expertise. A number of people at UCLA helped me to think through this project: Eiichiro Azuma, Stacey Hirose, Glen Kitayama, Lon Kurashige, Marjorie Lee, Russell Leong, Valerie Matsumoto, Brian Niiya, Glenn Omatsu, and Steffi San Buenaventura.

My academic home since graduate school has been in Claremont, and I have had the good fortune of being a member of the history faculty at Claremont McKenna College. My thanks to Arthur Rosenbaum and Gaines Post, who have served as department chairs. The college, via Dean Anthony Fucaloro, has supported work on the manuscript through summer grants and subvention funding. Within the Claremont Colleges consortium, conversations with colleagues in American history and Asian American studies have helped in sharpening my focus. My work also was ably assisted by talented student research assistants: Sarah Stauffer, Rita Lin, Valerie Makino, and Wendy Wang.

In the course of writing and revising this project, I have had a number of opportunities to present my work at conferences and in other settings. Along the way, many people have offered helpful comments and suggestions, including Michael Kimura Angevine, Hal Barron, Philip Gleason, Arthur Hansen, Alice Yang Murray, Joe Parker, Rita Roberts, Vicki Ruiz, Beth Schweiger, Jere Takahashi, Dana Takagi, Timothy Tseng, K. Scott Wong, and Judy Yung.

The support of archivists, research libraries, and funding institutions has been a key to the completion of this project. Much of the archival work was done at the Bancroft Library at the University of California at Berkeley; the Department of Special Collections at UCLA; the Huntington Library; the Hoover Institution at Stanford University; the Institute of Buddhist Studies; the Graduate Theological Union; the Japanese American National Museum; and the Los Angeles Public Library. My thanks to staff members at those institutions. Fellowships from the Rockefeller Foundation, UCLA, the Huntington Library, the Louisville Institute, the Haynes Foundation, and Yale University enabled me to do the research and also provided time for writing.

At the University of Illinois Press, I met Executive Editor Karen Hewitt early on, when the book manuscript was far from a reality. I've appreciated her interest in my project as well as her guidance since then. Likewise, I have been able to work with Roger Daniels, the editor of The Asian American Experience series. His insightful and copious comments on the entire manuscript have helped me immensely. Valerie Matsumoto did a thorough as well as an open reading of the manuscript, and I thank her for her thoughtful and helpful comments.

Portions of chapter 2 appeared as "Enlightening Identities: Buddhism and Japanese Americans of California, 1924–41" in *Western Historical Quarterly* 27 (Autumn 1996): 281–301. Portions of chapter 3 appeared as "'Read All about It': Race, Generation, and the Japanese American Ethnic Press, 1925–41" in *Amerasia Journal* 19 (1993): 69–92. I am grateful to the editors of those journals for permission to include here revised versions of those articles.

Friends and family have given much of their time and resources to help me in this project. I cannot name everyone, but I would be remiss if I did not recognize a few people. Tadashi Fujita and Ryo Munekata connected me to a host of other Nisei in northern and southern California who granted interviews and provided access to personal papers. Bill Ng and Arleen de Vera offered their hospitality, enabling me to complete much of my research in northern California. I owe the most to my family, especially my parents, Chin Hyong and Dong Myong Yoo. Their love and support over the years have been gifts that I try not to take for granted. My brother Eugene and his family adopted a poor and struggling graduate student in a time of need. Nathaniel and Allison, my nephew and niece, don't fully realize how much they gave to their uncle in providing fun opportunities to step outside the dissertation. Similarly, one of the joys of being in southern California has meant being surrounded by my immediate and large extended family. My in-laws, S. W. and Grace Chung, have offered encouragement and have been generous in helping us care for our son. Sharing the journey with my wife, Ruth, and our son, Jonathan, is a daily reminder of what is good and most important in life. Negotiating family and dual careers can be crazy at times, but rarely a day goes by when I am not thankful for our lives together.

Only in completing this manuscript has it become clearer to me how this history is entangled with my own. The questions that drive this narrative, while steeped in my study of American history and Asian American studies, also emanate from my experiences of growing up within a Japanese American enclave in southern California. Little did I know that one day I would examine the worlds linked to my Sansei (third-generation) and Yonsei (fourth-generation) friends and their Nisei parents or grandparents. As a child of immigrants, I often sensed an affinity with these older Nisei— an affinity that I attribute to some extent on a shared second-generation experience even while recognizing real differences. My hope is that the story presented here conveys a sense of the richness of their legacy.

GROWING UP NISEI

INTRODUCTION

Hiro and the unnamed narrator strolled the fairgrounds on Treasure Island in San Francisco Bay for one last time before the lights went out at midnight. The closing of the fair signaled the end of the summer; and, as they had done on so many nights, the second-generation Japanese Americans (or Nisei[1]) enjoyed the bustle of the crowds and the cool evening air that enveloped them. Their unhurried, winding walks took on the form of an evening ritual marked by lengthy discussions that spilled over from one day to the next: "I knew what was coming next. All summer long we had argued about ourselves . . . the problem of the second generation of Japanese ancestry. 'I tell you. We're not getting anywhere. We haven't a chance.' . . . 'You're wrong Hiro,' I would say. 'We'll climb and make ourselves heard. We have something to express in us and we will be heard.' Hiro would shake his head. 'You write stories and sing in the clouds. You dream too much.'" So the conversation went, interspersed with moments of silence when the disagreement between friends became too much. Despite their differences, however, both agreed that it would take time for Japanese Americans to work their way through the barriers that they faced in the United States.[2]

Toshio Mori's genius in capturing the everyday sights, sounds, and feel of Japanese America included a 1941 short story, "Sweet Potato," about the dilemmas that young Nisei encountered as they came of age in California. Like so many before and after them, Nisei struggled with the process of becoming Americans, a central motif in the story of the United States. Unlike other immigrants, however, Japanese Americans forged their sense of self and their group identity amid the enduring hardships of race—especially the mass incarceration during World War II. *Growing Up Nisei* takes up the theme of identity formation, asking how the particular journeys of Japanese Americans address issues of race, generation, and culture. Three main themes intertwine throughout the narrative presented here. The first has to do with the pressing need to analyze the actual experiences of the children of immigrants to better understand the complexities of American identity. As self-evident as this may seem, the second generation, by and large, have been overlooked within the historical literature. The neglect has primarily stemmed from assumptions of their supposed seamless assimilation into American society—a view, ironically, shared even by scholars who have championed ethnic retention among immigrant groups. The move toward grounding inquiry within particular historical contexts and away from static models of acculturation suggests how identity formation involved *both* accommodation and resistance.

The focus on Nisei experience girds the second theme—a case both for historical agency and for the broadening of the scope of Japanese American history. The dominance of World War II has scripted Japanese Americans into a cameo appearance within narratives of U.S. history. They enter and exit a lone scene, confined in barbed-wire compounds. Isolating the war years does violence to the integrity of Japanese American history, for continuity and divergence are lost. In particular, the spotlight on incarceration has obscured the creation of a rich Nisei subculture during the 1920s and the 1930s that represented a vital, alternative space between immigrant and native contexts. That subculture is critical in understanding identity formation among the second generation before and during the war, as well as the connections between the two periods. Placing the war in a larger context reminds us that Japanese Americans should not be viewed merely as victims but as historical agents who directed the course of their lives within given circumstances.

Among those circumstances, perhaps no factor played as fundamental a role as race; and this third theme underscores its significance as a category of historical interpretation. The increasing tendency to view American identity in terms of ethnicity has subtly masked the persistence of race in the United States. The stories of Nisei provide an opportunity to trace how race translated into the lives of Japanese Americans not as some immutable entity but as a socially constructed and highly variable social force. Paying attention to the multiple meanings and uses of racial terms, categories, and attitudes not only uncovers a Nisei world heavily marked by race but also offers insight into a chapter of race relations in California.

The events chronicled in these pages are framed on one end by the Immigration Act of 1924—which effectively curtailed further migration from Japan to the United States—and on the other by the sensational "Tokyo

Rose" treason trial of 1949. In the first half of the book, case studies of education and schooling, racial-ethnic churches, and the immigrant press detail the emergence of a Nisei subculture during the interwar years. The war years are the focus of the second part of the narrative, in which Nisei inside and outside the camps continued the process of identity formation under extreme conditions. Much of the discussion involves the Los Angeles and the San Francisco metropolitan areas, since they served as the principal sites for California Nisei organizations and as the cultural centers of Japanese America. As the second generation struggled to find their place in America, they were part of a remarkable period of U.S. history punctuated by immigrant and racial politics, economic depression, a world war, incarceration, and the cold war.

The Nisei Era

In delving into the world of Japanese Americans, *Growing Up Nisei* extends the scope of migration to include the second generation, a generation that historian Rudolph Vecoli has called the terra incognita of American immigration history.[3] A generational approach is especially appropriate for Japanese Americans because of their discrete migration and birth patterns. Japan's decision to allow migration, coupled with U.S. exclusion policies, meant that the vast majority of immigrant (Issei) males came to America between 1890 and 1908, the year the Gentlemen's Agreement went into effect. Under this agreement, Japan discontinued the issuing of passports to laborers for the United States and Hawaii, but a provision enabled wives, children, and parents to join current residents (until 1924, when exclusion effectively ended all further immigration). The presence of women enabled families to form, and a steady increase in births took place in California between 1908 and 1924 (see table 1). Given the concentration of births, it makes sense to speak of a Nisei generation.

By 1940, American-born Japanese (60,148) in California (see table 2) well outnumbered foreign-born Japanese (33,569). The bulk of the Nisei population consisted of those from the ages of ten to twenty-four. Much of the second generation attended public schools, and 1940 attendance figures for California and Washington state suggest that a greater percentage of Japanese Americans were in school than their peers.[4] Of the 39,095 Nisei in California fourteen years old and older, 17,207 persons (44 percent) had found employment; of that number, 6,951 individuals (40 percent) worked in agriculture, and 10,122 people (59 percent) labored in nonagricultural fields. Far more males (11,898) had entered the workforce

Table 1. Nisei Births in California, 1910–30

Year	Number	Japanese American Births as a Percentage of All Births in California
1910	719	2.2
1911	995	2.6
1912	1,467	3.7
1913	2,215	5.0
1914	2,874	6.2
1915	3,342	7.0
1916	3,721	7.3
1917	4,108	7.9
1918	4,218	7.6
1919	4,458	8.0
1920	4,971	7.4
1921	5,275	7.3
1922	5,066	6.9
1923	5,010	6.2
1924	4,481	5.2
1925	4,016	5.4
1926	3,597	4.4
1927	3,241	3.8
1928	2,833	3.4
1929	2,353	2.9
1930	2,230	n.a.

Source: Edward K. Strong, *Japanese in California* (Stanford, Calif.: Stanford University Press, 1933), 62.

than females (5,309). Women's work in agriculture consisted primarily of unpaid family labor, while the majority of men toiled as farmers, managers, or paid laborers. In the nonagricultural fields, clerical and sales represented the largest category for both men and women, but low-paying domestic work for women and unskilled labor for men ran a close second. Nisei in San Francisco (90 percent) and Los Angeles (94 percent) overwhelmingly found jobs in the ethnic economy, either working for their families or for Japanese employers.[5]

Nisei, because of their temporal affinity, experienced much of life together and clearly had a sense of generational consciousness despite variation based on factors such as gender, class, and region. In other words, while not discounting salient differences, many Nisei had a sense of their shared status as a generation—in large part because of a shared history that reinforced that identity. As research on life course has shown, experiencing such major historical events as the Depression and World War II deeply affect-

Table 2. Nisei Population in California, 1900–1940

Year	Male	Female	Total	Total Japanese American Population in California
1900	87	56	143	10,151
1910	1,619	1,553	3,172	41,356
1920	10,864	9,950	20,814	71,952
1930	25,689	23,290	48,979	97,456
1940	31,932	28,216	60,148	93,717

Source: Dorothy S. Thomas, Charles Kikuchi, and James Sakoda, *The Salvage* (Berkeley: University of California Press, 1952), 575–79.

ed the identity process of a given cohort or generation. Being Nisei served as a main filter for many Japanese Americans who came of age during this period. As John Modell's recent study has suggested, American youth built subcultural and institutional structures that were instrumental in setting patterns for coming into one's own. For Nisei, generational identity was significant, steeped in common experiences and historical circumstances that infused self-identity and group identity within an immigrant-centered and racially circumscribed environment.[6]

In their day-to-day lives, Nisei moved between many spheres and occupied multiple identities; hence, it makes little sense to argue for an authentic self that somehow was either Japanese or American. The more compelling question, although more difficult, is to ask how Nisei negotiated the complexities of identity formation in the toss and tumble of their times. The result is a less uniform and authoritative (and, for some, less satisfying) picture, but the highly varied nature of what it meant to be Nisei more accurately reflects the actual historical experiences of Japanese Americans. As Deborah Dash Moore's fine study has shown, there were many ways to be Jewish in America that had much more to do with the urban milieu of New York City than some fixed, immutable notion of Jewish culture. In creating their own spaces, the second generation not only navigated life in at least two worlds but struggled to make sense of their multiple selves. The tendency to dismiss an "assimilated" second generation has meant that many scholars have missed the opportunity to explore how identity formation developed in the lives of second-generation immigrants. Similarly, historian Donald Weber has called for an overhaul of the "apostate" second generation, arguing that, instead of "a thoroughgoing compulsion to forget, the children of immigrants found numerous ways to mediate the burden of their hyphenated status."[7]

Mapping the Past

Reclaiming the second generation enlarges the scope of Japanese American history beyond its most distinctive feature: the saga of the concentration camps. The tragic nature of this episode makes its prominence understandable, and yet, missing is the ebb and flow of change and continuity over time. Consequently, it is easy to forget that Nisei identity formation was well underway before Pearl Harbor. This study's anchoring of the war years in the larger sweep of the past causes the camps to appear less as an isolated, wartime mistake than as the culmination of a racial legacy that dated to the late nineteenth century. Historian Yuji Ichioka has suggested that the 1920s and the 1930s, rather than being some mere backdrop to the war, merit attention for what these years tell us about the interconnectedness of Japanese American history.[8] This book sheds light on a period rendered opaque by the long shadow cast by World War II.

While Nisei have not gone completely unnoticed by scholars, the need remains for sustained historical documentation and analysis of Nisei identity formation.[9] Social scientific, generation-based studies, relying largely on survey and interview research, have been limited in their ability to reconstruct the contexts in which Nisei lived.[10] Sociologist S. Frank Miyamoto regretted not having studied the emergent Nisei society of the 1930s more carefully in his pioneering study of Japanese Americans in Seattle, *Social Solidarity among the Japanese in Seattle*. While *The Nisei: The Quiet Americans*, written by journalist Bill Hosokawa, provides much information, it is largely a popular account. Two important studies have been published recently: Eileen Tamura on the Nisei in Hawaii and Jerrold Takahashi on second- and third-generation political styles.[11] While *Growing Up Nisei* draws from these works, it also joins them in providing a fuller account of the Nisei. The distinction between Hawaii and California, for instance, is an important one. As one scholar has noted, Hawaii constitutes a special case, since it has been so strikingly different from the mainland. The largest single ethnic group on the islands, Nikkei ("Japanese people") have exercised a political and social influence in the state that has not been replicated elsewhere. In addition, the vast majority of Hawaiian Japanese Americans were not incarcerated during the war; thus, the camps factor much less in their history.[12] Furthermore, the institutional and social history in this study complements Takahashi's careful attention to politics within Japanese America.

An important access point to the Nisei past in California has been the documentary base generated by studies conducted with Japanese Americans before and during World War II. In the interwar years, researchers from Stanford University and the University of Southern California administered intelligence tests, engaged in fieldwork, and compiled information in the greater San Francisco and Los Angeles areas.[13] During the war, the concentration camps served as living laboratories for social scientists who gathered data, kept field notes, and engaged in participant observation.[14] While these sources collectively represent thousands of pages of information, they are problematic in that the researchers rarely questioned their own assumptions that guided their research design as well as the interpretation of their findings. Not surprisingly, many social scientists merely confirmed their preexisting biases. Because Japanese Americans were treated as a problem and/or as a deviant people, their humanity and agency rarely emerged, nor did the historical contingencies of their lives. Instead, Nisei served as subjects for flawed social scientific research that was bent on proving the validity of some measure (e.g., intelligence tests) or that viewed their incarceration as an opportunity to experiment with social engineering. While the documents produced by these studies contain valuable data, Ronald Takaki has reminded us that Asian Americans should not be studied primarily in terms of statistics or of what was done to them but "as men and women with minds, wills, and voices."[15]

Accordingly, primacy is given to Japanese Americans as historical agents. The result, to borrow the words of Roger Daniels, is a move from the excluders to the excluded.[16] In the process, not only is a buried past reclaimed, but it is realized through a humanizing angle of vision. Rather than being viewed as a people whose historical significance stemmed from their assimilation (or lack thereof) or their victimization, Nisei are portrayed as women and men who exercised decision-making power in their lives, interpreting and acting out their own history. Recent developments in U.S. immigration history have shown greater sensitivity to the malleability of identity formation. Nevertheless, research on the children of immigrants has not flourished and this generation continues to be tied to older, problematic paradigms.[17]

Subcultural Foundations

Moving into the worlds that Nisei inhabited reveals the subculture they founded during the 1920s and the 1930s that helped them to negotiate their times, including the storm of war and incarceration. Education, racial-ethnic churches, and the immigrant press constituted vital elements in the experiences of the second generation, influencing as well as bearing the signature of those affiliated with them. The schools served as an early and formative introduction to the world outside the immigrant community. Nisei encountered the American ideals of freedom, equality, and justice even if such notions were contradicted in their actual lives. In contrast, the churches and especially the newspapers helped American-born Japanese build their own structures that catered to their generational and sociocultural needs. In examining the institutional life of Japanese Americans, the complexities of "generation" and "race" emerge. Both markers set Nisei apart in a racial-ethnic community adapting to a new social environment and in a society divided by color. Ethnic neighborhoods and institutions afforded these women and men opportunities to shape the direction and content of their lives.

Students formed Japanese clubs in high schools and colleges. Churches sponsored the Young Buddhist Association (YBA) and the Young People's Christian Conference (YPCC). English-language sections in the immigrant daily newspapers provided a network of news, opinion, and information written for and by the second generation. As a rule, Nisei organized and led their own groups and activities that contributed to the development of leadership skills. These venues offered a wide range of educational, cultural, social, religious, and athletic programs that addressed the concerns of Japanese Americans. Rather than serving as mere way stations en route to assimilation, Nisei organizations, experiences of prejudice, and the immigrant community actually reinforced the generational and racial-ethnic identities of American-born Japanese.[18] While racial barriers affected the quality of life that Japanese Americans experienced, they also provided the impetus for Nisei to develop their own networks. As Lisa Lowe has pointed out, distance from the American cultural sphere, instead of reflecting a failed integration, preserved Asian American culture "where the palimpsest of lost memories is reinvented, histories fractured and retraced."[19] The spaces that Nisei helped create facilitated their struggle with what it meant to be "Japanese American." Rather than a simple choice between two alternatives, identity formation entailed a negotiation of multiple meanings related not only to race, gender, and class but also to such themes as generation, the economy, politics, and international relations.

Because of the relative youth of the second generation, especially in the years prior to World War II, it is easy to dismiss the contexts within which Nisei developed their sense of self and group. Historians Elliot West and Paula Petrik have commented on the tendency to view the history of children and adolescents as "cute" or "nice" rather than seeing it as instructive of human experience.[20] This study takes seriously the fragments of evidence found in student publications, church newsletters, oratorical contests, and other outlets that existed for Japanese Americans. What is clear from written documents and subsequent oral histories is that many Nisei expended a considerable amount of energy over the issues of generational and racial identity. No other second-generation group has had to face the questions of its place in America under the extraordinary conditions that the Nisei encountered.

The Significance of "Race"

A social context heavily colored by racial politics made the issue of race, like generation, equally unavoidable in the negotiation of Japanese American identity. Nisei clearly occupied a racially subordinate position in America, whether that subordination was codified in law or a part of social norms. Race influenced access to public facilities, options for housing and employment, and movement within spatial boundaries. A recent study on youth in America noted that race represented the most powerful single variable for the socialization of Americans of African, Latino, and Asian descent, despite the considerable weight of other factors such as class.[21] In this regard, Nikkei have been subject to distinctive treatment that has been reserved for racial-ethnic minorities in the United States. While incarceration during World War II represented the most blatant form of discrimination, Japanese Americans have been set apart by race throughout their past.

The significance of race, so clearly borne out by history, has faded in contemporary debates in which ethnicity has often supplanted the discussion of race. On the surface, such a move appears to be an inclusive one. Nearly all Americans have undergone the process of migration to the United States and, by extension, the movement from the status of "ethnic" to "American." The problem with focusing on ethnicity at the expense of race is that the acculturation process in America has been far from uniform. Despite the changing nature of racial politics, the problem of the color line has been and continues to be a reality in the United States. Though Asian Americans have been part of the nation for approximately 150 years, they remain perpetual foreigners—strangers in their own country—in public perceptions. A related phenomenon, just as problematic, is that European Americans, by virtue of their "whiteness," occupy an unmarked category that privileges it as normative. The shift to ethnicity, moreover, attributes new meanings to terms such as "diversity" and "pluralism" that speak not so much to real differences between peoples but to aspects of ethnic "invention" that are held in common. In a subtle turn, "cult of ethnicity" proponents have reasserted the virtue of Anglo-American assimilation as the American way, reinscribing the past to reflect one nation, indivisible. In this schema, St. Patrick's Day, Columbus Day, and Oktoberfest are really celebrations of ethnicity more than they are about being Irish, Italian, or German American. Hence, all Americans can become "ethnic" and embrace these festivals. The troubling question that lingers, however, is why these celebrations (and groups) and not others have become part of the national culture.[22]

Undermining race as a distinct analytical category dismisses the ways in which peoples of color have had far fewer choices and a more difficult time in shaping their identities. Historical amnesia can result in a forgetfulness of how the color line has divided us as a nation even as it has been so central to our collective past. In the case of Japanese Americans, racial markers created legal and social barriers that dramatically influenced life chances and the quality of life. Nisei hardly saw their reflection in the mirror of America; thus, a racial lens is critical in understanding their relationship to the larger social contexts of their times.[23] Toward this end, this study relies on a racial formations perspective developed by sociologists Michael Omi and Howard Winant that places race at the center of an analytical framework: "racial categories themselves are formed, transformed, destroyed and re-formed. We use the term 'racial formations' to refer to the process by which social, economic and political forces determine the content and importance of racial categories, and by which they are in turn shaped by racial meanings. . . . [Race is] an unstable and 'decentered' complex of social meanings constantly being transformed by political struggle."[24]

A "racial formations" perspective underscores the importance of translating the ways that race has operated in specific historical circumstances rather than treating race as a fixed entity that can itself obscure other sets of social relations, including the internal differences within a given group like Japanese Americans.[25] Although biologically determined notions of race have long been discredited by social science, such notions persist because most people at some level still experience race in terms of biology. The meanings given to phenotypical difference reveal how race is always culturally conditioned. According to historian Peggy Pascoe, Americans have understood race "as an indivisible essence that included not only biology but also culture, morality, and intelligence." Matters have been even further complicated by the emergence of a dominant modernist racial ideology, cultivated in the period between the 1920s and the 1960s, that envisioned the end of racism as dependent on the deliberate nonrecognition of race. Consequently, the contemporary emphasis on "color blindness" has often shrouded the ideologies that gird racial thinking.[26] Sifting through the complexity of race will require attention, as one scholar has noted, to its particularities found in local contexts with political processes, social change, and human differences sharing the interpretive stage.[27]

The discussion of race among Japanese Americans also reveals (among other things) the need to move beyond the traditional black-white framework that is still dominant in the United States. California's multiracial landscape historically has included significant American Indian, Asian American, and Mexican American populations, and narratives must do more than simply include these groups; they must ask how their histories alter the assumptions embedded in a binary racial model. Tomas Almaguer takes up the task in his study of the origins of white supremacy in California, narrating the commonalities as well as the differences of how race influenced each of the three groups mentioned. He also makes a persuasive case against those who would relegate racial politics to class issues, documenting an "elective affinity" between the material interests of Euro-Americans of varied classes and the racial ideologies that simultaneously structured the new Anglo-dominated society in California after statehood.[28]

Growing Up Nisei

Institutions that deeply affected Nisei during the interwar years are the subject of chapters 1, 2, and 3. Chapter 1 is concerned with how schooling and education factored into the socialization of Japanese Americans. The second generation attended schools in California during an era when progressive education found expression through efforts to Americanize immigrant children. Sources, including printed pieces from oratorical and essay contests and newspaper articles, underscore the importance of examining how Japanese Americans interpreted their own school experiences.

The second chapter highlights the role of ethnic Buddhist and Christian churches and documents how they offered important niches to Nisei who participated in religious life. Along with the rites, religious holidays and festivals, and other meanings vested in religion, church-sponsored organizations enabled Nisei to socialize and to explore their identities. Church newsletters and magazines demonstrate that Buddhists and Christians, while valuing their religious affiliations, did not limit their concerns to faith but often discussed the future more generally as Japanese Americans. The ties that bound Nisei together did not eradicate real religious differences but did illustrate how adherents of both traditions shared much in common.

The richness of the second-generation world as it appeared in the English-language sections of the immigrant press is the subject of chapter 3. In the mid-1920s, portions of the newspapers devoted to the second generation appeared and paralleled the growth of the Nisei. The papers acted as road maps during the prewar years, when a tightly organized Nisei culture flourished. The press not only provided an important network of information but also created an outlet for Nisei journalists, artists, writers, and editors. In particular, the chapter explores how the press presented issues pertaining to race and generation.

The narrative moves into the war years in chapters 4, 5, and 6. Because so much has been written on the camps, *Growing Up Nisei* is selective in its treatment of this period. An emphasis is placed on the central theme of generational and racial-ethnic identity formation to provide a link to earlier chapters. Although forced removal shut down much of the Japanese American institutional life that had existed prior to the war, Nikkei created variations of the groups that they had been a part of before the war— the subject of chapter 4. Schooling continued in the camps. Administrators may have seen camp education as a prime opportunity to speed the assimilation of students in American society, but the absurdity of lessons on democracy and freedom behind barbed wire was all too apparent. Nevertheless, students who did attend class found a measure of order. The schools in camp also enabled a large corps of Japanese American teachers and teacher assistants to gain work experience. As they had before the war, makeshift temples and churches and their attendant groups continued to serve their constituencies in the new and desolate landscapes. Although sources of comfort, religious institutions also served as sites of resistance. Buddhists and Christians found in their religion a means of processing the swirl of events that surrounded them and, in some cases, used religious platforms to speak out against their plight. Despite a radical change in circumstances, threads of continuity connected wartime chaos to the past.

Chapter 5 traces how Japanese Americans during the war found familiar voices in the newspapers that served the readership of a dislocated and captive audience. In particular, the focus is on the wartime editorials of journalists who used their vantage point outside the camps to interpret unfolding events to their readers. Among these journalists were veteran reporters Larry and Marion Tsuguyo Tajiri, who edited the *Pacific Citizen,* the in-house organ of the Japanese American Citizens' League (JACL) in Salt Lake City. The Tajiris utilized their experience and skill to craft a progressive racial vision that drew on the past to encourage readers to work for improved race relations in the present and the future. James Omura of the Denver-based *Rocky Shimpo* provided an alternative voice to the

JACL leaders who fashioned themselves as spokesmen for Japanese America. Through his fiery columns, Omura critiqued unquestioning loyalty to the United States and urged readers to exercise their rights as citizens.

Chapter 6 bridges the war and the immediate postwar period and relies heavily on the life histories recorded as part of the Japanese [American] Evacuation and Resettlement Study (JERS), headed by demographer Dorothy Swaine Thomas of the University of California at Berkeley. Charles Kikuchi, a JERS field investigator and Nisei, interviewed fellow Japanese Americans who had resettled in Chicago. Although not representative of the entire Nikkei population, the life histories provide a rare opportunity to access detailed accounts of how Japanese Americans, in the midst of the war, reflected on their individual, family, and community history.

The epilogue offers a glimpse of what Nisei faced in the aftermath of war. Doors once closed slowly began to open within a revitalized California economy and a less-restrictive racial climate. As Nisei continued their education, entered careers, married, and started families of their own, many focused their energies on the future. In the midst of this recovery came the 1949 trial of Iva Toguri d'Aquino. This Nisei woman from Los Angeles, marooned in Japan during the war, found herself caught within the federal government's cold war web as the infamous "Tokyo Rose." Tried for treason in San Francisco, d'Aquino and her case are especially suggestive in thinking about the twists and turns that Nisei faced in coming to terms with their identity as Japanese Americans.

Inheriting a Legacy

Writing just before Pearl Harbor, even the insightful Toshio Mori could not have predicted the cataclysmic changes that were in store for Japanese Americans. In addition to a world at war, Mori and his fellow Nisei would witness firsthand the forced removal of the entire West Coast Japanese American population. Although what happened during the war seemed inconceivable, portents of the internment were embedded in Japanese American history. Members of the second generation inherited a racial legacy and needed only to look to their parents to glimpse what might lie ahead.

Since their arrival in America in the late nineteenth century, Japanese immigrants had experienced much hardship and heartbreak. The courts upheld naturalization laws in effect since 1790 that entitled only "free, white" immigrants access to U.S. citizenship.[29] Based on such laws, legislators passed measures to prevent Issei from owning the California agricultural lands that they had made fabulously fertile. Restrictive housing

Abiko Family (*left to right*): Yonako, Yasuo, and Kyutaro. San Francisco, California, c. 1920. (Gift of the Yasuo William Abiko Family, Japanese American National Museum [92.127.3])

Keep
California
White

RE-ELECT
James D. Phelan
United States Senator

 147

Campaign poster of Senator James Phelan of California, c. 1921.
(Japanese American National Museum [94.285.5])

covenants, antimiscegenation laws, and other forms of racial discrimination added to the woes of Japanese Americans.[30] Despite such harsh conditions, many Issei raised families, formed communities, and helped build the American West. Immigrant leaders such as publisher Kyutaro Abiko advocated permanent settlement and assisted Issei in finding a foothold through farming. Community organizations offered a measure of support and relief and also enabled Japanese Americans to challenge the efforts of those who worked against them.[31] While Issei struggled to combat anti-Japanese activity, they found themselves outside the body politic by virtue of their permanent alien status, underscoring their vulnerability within the social and political setting. An especially bitter defeat came with the passage of the Immigration Act of 1924, which effectively excluded all further migration from Japan.[32]

Those who had lobbied for exclusion did not rest on the laurels of their success. Even if future migration had been blocked, the Japanese who remained posed problems. The formation of families meant there would be another generation of Japanese Americans. By birthright, however, Nisei were U.S. citizens and represented a different and, to some, a graver threat. Several years before exclusion, James D. Phelan, U.S. senator from California, proposed a constitutional amendment that would grant citizenship only to persons whose parents were eligible to citizenship. His rationale was that "Japanese do not lose their racial identity, but . . . it perseveres through all generations." Phelan was not ultimately successful in his bid, but such efforts illustrated the determination of those opposed to the Japanese to push for their agenda at the highest levels of government.[33]

Although subject to the racial politics that had infused the experiences of their parents, the second generation, according to historian Yuji Ichioka, represented the remaining hope for Japanese America. Immigrant leaders interpreted the failure to avert exclusion in 1924 as the culmination of their rejection by the United States and pinned their hopes increasingly on the second generation: "the Nisei's future, however precarious it appeared in 1924, suddenly loomed all-important to them. The future of the Japanese in the United States now depended on how their children would grow up and fare in their own native land."[34]

As Nisei came of age in the aftermath of exclusion, they followed in the footsteps of immigrants who had sunk their roots in largely inhospitable soil. The second generation, native and yet strangers, discovered that their connections to the past would have profound implications in the creation of their own history.

THE ABCS OF A NISEI EDUCATION

In the winter of 1925, a Pullman car rolled along, transporting Kazuo Kawai home to Los Angeles after a visit to the East Coast. Kawai, a student at Stanford University, recalled several discussions with an African American porter, who upon "seeing that I was not a white man, but a Japanese . . . beckoned me to come into his inner sanctuary by the washroom several times during the long, monotonous journey." As the two sat in close quarters, the unnamed porter mentioned that he attended college but had taken time off to earn money to support his education. Kawai heard doubt in the porter's words. The porter mentioned that some coworkers held college degrees, but their status did not differ from his or from those who had not gone to school, since "the Negro is looked upon as a servant, and the white man will not recognize him as anything else."[1] Kawai recalled:

> That statement surprised me then, and I thought proudly to myself: "Thank goodness, we Japanese in America are not like the Negroes. We are not a servile people." I listened to the porter's story with a detached, condescending sympathy. But since then I have been thinking and observing and recently in my own experience, I have come across incidents which are forcing me to reluctantly wonder very seriously if the new generation of American-born Japanese on the Pacific coast is not facing the same problem as the Negroes in finding suitable vocations.[2]

Schooling represented a key site of socialization for Nisei in California during the years between the world wars. Students encountered administrators and teachers who viewed education as a primary instrument in bringing immigrant children into the "mainstream" of American society.

Much of the effort to mold students fell under the umbrella of Americanization. Although much attention has been paid to the program and policy dimensions of the movement, Americanization is of particular interest for our purposes because it underscores how schooling was a value-laden process.[3] In short, the schools were institutions vested with multiple meanings by all parties involved. For researchers who conducted fieldwork among Japanese Americans during the 1920s and the 1930s, initial confidence in the powers of assimilation gave way to lingering doubt as they documented the persistence of racial discrimination. How could Nisei become part of America if European Americans continued to uphold barriers based on race? Rather than viewing the schools as sacred sites of democracy *or* instruments of the capitalist state bent on social control, the case of Japanese Americans suggests that they contained a more complex reality in which both elements were evident. Nisei schooling, moreover, is particularly instructive about the politics of race in education. An overview of the progressive educational environment will provide background for the examination of Japanese American school settings.

Policy makers and professionals have been vested with so much power, for ill or for good, that they have obscured the perspectives of immigrant populations that, oddly enough, rarely have been taken into consideration. Accordingly, this chapter argues that our understanding of Nisei schooling makes little sense without asking how Japanese Americans interpreted their own education. The experiences of these "marked" young women and men exposed the contradictions between the ideal and the reality of what an American education offered its citizenry. As Eileen Tamura's study has shown, real differences existed between those who sought to "Americanize" students and the ways that those students viewed and appropriated their education.[4] Incorporation of Japanese American perspectives enables a fuller and more complex picture of schooling to emerge. Too often, Nikkei have been portrayed as one-dimensional figures—exemplary pupils slavishly devoted to their studies. In fact, many grew disillusioned with their schooling. Prejudice blocked their entry into desired jobs and careers and prompted some thoughtful Nisei to assess the value of an American education. What emerges from life histories, newspaper articles, and other scattered sources are strategies that Japanese Americans employed to negotiate their schooling. Parents, for one, redefined the parameters and meaning of a Nisei education through Japanese-language schools to include the culture and language of their homeland. Language schools offered Issei a measure of control in shaping the overall content of their children's instruction and initially served families who intended to return to Japan. In addition, those settling in America saw language skills and the socialization process of the Japanese schools as important means of maintaining ethnic ties and of equipping Nisei to operate more effectively within the immigrant community.

For the second generation, education—both in Japanese-language and American schools—provided one of the few alternatives to an otherwise limited future. Although Nisei comprised only 3 percent of California's school population in 1930, approximately 35 percent of that number lived in Los Angeles county.[5] By 1940, attendance figures showed that a higher percentage of Nisei across age groups were enrolled in school than the overall population (see table 3). For many immigrant parents and their children, an education represented an investment laced with hope. Public schools provided access to training and careers that could lead to economic mobility and financial security. Unlike Japan, education in the United States was not reserved for the wealthy. As an icon of American democracy, the schools were a symbol of opportunity, even if Kazuo Kawai and others began to realize that the symbol masked a reality quite different from the rhetoric. Nisei increasingly discovered that school merely delayed entry into jobs that required no formal training. Some students turned to the notion of "being" as a bridge between the United States and Japan as a means of carving out a niche for themselves. In theory, Nisei were uniquely qualified to work within an international context in which they could draw on both their ancestry and their citizenship. Those who

Table 3. Nisei School Attendance, Ages 5–24, California and Washington, 1940

Age (years)	Nisei Population	Percentage of Japanese Americans in School	Percentage of Total Population in School
5–6	2,902	60.3	56.2
7–15	20,281	98.4	97.4
16–17	6,882	93.2	85.1
18–19	7,099	57.0	41.2
20	3,310	28.0	19.6
21–24	10,293	13.5	8.1

Source: Dorothy S. Thomas, Charles Kikuchi, and James Sakoda, *The Salvage* (Berkeley: University of California Press, 1952), 610.

Note: The data did not distinguish school attendance by state. The respective Nisei population figures for 1940 by state are: 60,148 (California), 8,882 (Washington). See Department of Commerce, Bureau of the Census, *Sixteenth Census of the United States: 1940,* vol. 2 (Washington, D.C.: Government Printing Office, 1943), pt. 1:516, pt. 7:304.

ventured overseas, however, often met with disappointment. Nevertheless, the idea of Japan provided a generation in search of opportunities another source of hope.

For his part, Kazuo Kawai, despite his discussions with the unnamed porter, decided to pursue an education and a career as a college professor. At the same time, Kawai knew the odds did not favor him: "In view of the vocational situation of the Japanese in America, I am not sure how I will come out. In the end, I may have to seek out my college-despising friend and beg for a job at his fruit-stand."[6]

Putting "Progress" into Education

Japanese Americans like Kazuo Kawai presented a challenge to progressive educators who faced swelling school rosters created by the large influx of immigrants to the United States in the late nineteenth and the early twentieth centuries. Migrants filled the need for labor and fueled America's economic ascendancy, but these groups also represented a "threat." Foreign masses might dissolve the ethos of republicanism and of middle-class, Protestant values that many Americans saw as the core of their national culture. Many adherents of progressive education also sought to address the seeming loss of moral order and social meaning manifested in alarming signs of disintegration such as corruption in politics, the growing gulf between the rich and poor, and problems embedded in rapid urbanization.[7]

Schools, of course, had long been identified with personal improvement and social progress and became the hope of those who viewed them as centers of reform and socialization. As Lawrence Cremin's classic study has noted, there was a steadfast belief that educators would contribute to the democratization of American society. New findings in psychology and the social sciences would enable experts to tailor instruction to the needs of an incredibly diverse student population. The conviction that education could solve social inequalities took on mythic proportions, drawing on an ideal already ingrained in the national psyche. The caveat was that progressive education seemed to take as many forms as there were adherents.[8] In her study of American education, Paula Fass has commented: "Schools were to be at once instruments of remedial socialization and primary agents of culture; they were to connect the democratic potential of an enormously diverse population to the unities of ancient citizenship; they were to educate for future success but be attentive to present needs. These fissures were not contradictions but the essence of progressive school ideology, and they

connected that ideology to the paradox of American society in the twentieth century."[9]

In the 1920s and 1930s, perhaps no state embraced progressive education, contradictions and all, more than California. The move to reform
began in the aftermath of World War I, when the Golden State experienced
continued population growth and urbanization. Within education, Americanization marked one of the ways that educators sought to make the
schools a central strategy in the shaping of society. Restructuring took place
in which superintendents and "experts" gained greater control of school
boards and districts. In part, reform meant making a conscious effort to
take education out of the corrupt hands of politicians and to entrust the
process to efficient and objective professionals.[10] The foundations of the
progressive agenda set in the post–World War I era continued to fare well
in the following decades, despite the Depression. According to Irving Hendrick, only during a brief period during 1932–33 did financial constraints
dominate the California educational landscape. Schools had often been
called on in times of crisis to work for the public welfare; and with educators busy retooling the schools, reform took on even greater significance.
The inability of politicians to ameliorate a depressed economy became
associated with the "old" education that progressives intended to overhaul.
Schools of moderate and large size experienced a boom of sorts with an
expanded curriculum, the growth of extracurricular and club activities, and
greater attention to the guidance of pupils.[11]

The expanded role of the schools also included the issue of how to deal
with a student population marked by tremendous diversity and largely
immigrant and racial ethnic in nature. In her monograph on Los Angeles
schools, Judith Raftery documents how part of the response to immigrants
drew the schools into the role of social service institutions. The establishment of penny-lunch programs, childcare centers, afterschool programs,
and kindergartens helped blunt the effects of poverty among immigrants
and aimed to ease their transition to life in the United States.[12] In addition, progressive education advocates often expressed confidence in their
abilities to customize education—efficiently and scientifically—so that the
schools could respond precisely to the needs of newer groups. The rising
tide of reform would elevate all segments of the student body and enable
education to accomplish its goal as the nurturing cradle of society. Translating rhetoric into viable programs proved to be more difficult because
of the complexity of the task and because of the mixed motives of progressive educators themselves. As a result, a reform impulse could go hand
in hand with nativist efforts to engineer the social environment.[13]

Americanization, California Style

As Nisei entered public schools, they encountered teachers and administrators who worked to facilitate their assimilation into American society.
Americanization efforts received a boost from World War I and became
part of the push to unify the nation in light of perils associated with the
war. Programs were designed to assimilate immigrants who had arrived
in unprecedented numbers. The movement included many groups and
activities, providing a rhetorical framework for those who worked with
immigrants. Some general characteristics of Americanization included a
staunch support for democracy, representative government, law and order, capitalism, general health (diet, hygiene, and sanitation), and command
of the English language. Public schools were a key component of Americanization, the aim of which was to transform immigrants into patriotic,
loyal, and intelligent citizens of the Republic. In his classic study *The
Movement to Americanize the Immigrant,* Edward Hartmann noted: "The
movement to Americanize the immigrant offered a program which would
solve the problem of the immigrant with the least disruption to the economic and political life of the nation; a program which would not result
in the loss of an exceedingly valuable labor supply to America."[14] The task
did not fall to any single institution, but the public schools played an integral role in the work with immigrants. Since their inception in the nineteenth century, California schools had been called on to assimilate a diverse mix of students. The creation of the California State Commission of
Immigration and Housing (CSCIH) in 1913 continued those efforts into
the twentieth century. Americanization accompanied the rise of the progressives to power, and the CSCIH was empowered to work with schools.
By 1920, the CSCIH had implemented citizenship and English classes,
home education for women, enforcement of truancy laws, migratory labor camp classes, and curricular development.[15] Though the CSCIH out-
lasted the demise of Americanization efforts in other parts of the country,
it too shut down by the end of the 1920s as immigration quotas, budget-
ary problems, and conflicts with other agencies worked against its survival. Part of the problem stemmed from differing notions of Americanization. Simon Lubin, a key leader in the CSCIH, envisioned Americanization
as a process of mutual exchange. Other powerful figures—like Stanford's
Ellwood Cubberley—pressed for a program of conformity to Anglo-Sax-
on ideals that viewed immigrant ancestries as having little to offer American society. Lubin eventually lost political backing, and the CSCIH suffered with him; but, during its tenure, the commission had been given

considerable power to do its work. Even though formal Americanization efforts had faded by the 1930s, the work continued in the schools through teachers and administrators who still saw the need for it.[16]

Professional journals of education in California during the 1920s and 1930s published items on a wide range of issues related to Americanization. Articles discussed home teachers, health, and sanitation as well as "success" stories of those who modeled the goals of Americanization.[17] Although much of the literature did not directly address Japanese Americans, items did appear that commented on the Nisei and on issues of race.[18] For example, Gertrude Allison published her teaching unit for third and fourth graders about Japan and Japanese Americans. The lesson encouraged comparisons of life experiences and asked students to think about the different types of people who lived in Los Angeles. Along with the standard interests in food, clothing, art, and dance, the unit asked students to think about why the Japanese may have immigrated to the United States.[19] Lucile Regan profiled the Japanese American students who lived in the fishing community of Terminal Island in San Pedro Bay and praised her students as displaying a great eagerness to learn. The second generation did well in school and often won the esteem of their peers and teachers— showing the possibilities of Americanization at work. Regan even noted that the Japanese American Citizen's League, a Nisei civic organization, took up the responsibility of encouraging other Japanese Americans to fulfill their duties as U.S. citizens. Her report commented that successful social assimilation of the Nisei foundered because of racism.[20]

The "Problem" of Race

While the objectives and methods of Americanization varied, most advocates, like Lucile Regan, recognized that race prejudice constituted a real problem. Researchers, drawing on their studies, redirected some of the blame from Nikkei to European Americans, who through their prejudices retarded the process of assimilation. The findings, of course, hardly surprised most Nisei, whose life experiences were so often characterized by the distinction of race. Ironically, social scientific studies suggested that the Nikkei themselves bore a great responsibility for their plight. Professor Edward Strong of Stanford expressed a sentiment that many others echoed when he criticized the second generation for too easily complaining about discrimination. According to Strong, every immigrant group in America had faced resistance and lack of acceptance. Rather than bemoaning their situation as somehow unique, Nisei should instead realize that their future rested largely in their own hands.[21] In a 1928 article, sociologist Emory Bogardus of the University of Southern California placed the onus of the problem on the second generation, claiming that groups should be aware of the traits arousing race prejudice and make the appropriate changes to overcome them.[22] Throughout his long and prolific career, Bogardus served as an "expert" on race relations and devoted his energies to the study of the diverse population that marked the greater Los Angeles area. A product of the influential school of sociology at the University of Chicago, Bogardus (Ph.D., 1911) followed in the footsteps of his mentor, Robert E. Park, who understood race relations in cyclical terms. Park's theory of race relations involved four stages: initial *contact* followed by *competition* that led to *conflict;* but, over time, conflict would give way to *assimilation.* Given this framework, Bogardus conceived of racism as an acquired trait, and one that could be controlled.[23]

Studies of Japanese Americans by graduate students at the University of Southern California and Stanford, however, pointed to European Americans as creating barriers for the assimilation of Japanese Americans. This subtle but important shift in thinking came as researchers noted that discrimination did not diminish with time. The second generation, who showed real signs of assimilation in dress, language, and other measures, met with much of the animosity that had been directed at their parents. In her study of Los Angeles's Little Tokyo, Gretchen Tuthill noted the irony of those who criticized Japanese Americans for being un-American and yet did their very best to shut down efforts by the Nikkei to participate as full members of society. Like many others, Tuthill believed that education could help eliminate race prejudice, but she also recognized the frustration of Nisei who quipped: "You know as well as I do that a Japanese, although well educated, has never an equal opportunity with an American no matter how uneducated that American may be."[24] In 1934, Ruth Fowler's research on Japanese Americans in Santa Clara concluded that race prejudice ran much deeper than met the eye. Ten years had passed since the immigration quotas that had blocked further arrivals from Japan, but the anti-Japanese sentiment that fueled such legislation lay just below the surface. From her fieldwork, Fowler discovered that at the mere mention of Nikkei, negative comments began to flow. Although Fowler still expressed hope that assimilation would take place, she envisioned it being a much slower process than first anticipated.[25]

Saikichi Chijiwa of Stanford seriously doubted whether Nisei would ever really be accepted by American society. Based on a study of Palo Alto and Menlo Park, Chijiwa noted how Japanese Americans paid the price for

Japan's actions, especially after the Manchurian Incident of 1931, which ignited Sino-Japanese tensions. Public sympathy for China in the United States meant that Nikkei had to deal with undifferentiated resentment toward Japan. Given these conditions, Chijiwa questioned the wisdom of Nisei taking any course of action that might weaken ties to the racial-ethnic community. Model citizenship and success in education, as it was becoming more evident, could not erase the racial differences that set Japanese Americans apart.[26]

By 1940, even an assimilation stalwart like Emory Bogardus had devised a separate second-generation race relations cycle based on his work with Japanese Americans. Using the idea of social distance, Bogardus monitored the relations between immigrants and their children. Early in life, the generations remained close, and parents and the ethnic community nurtured the Nisei. During the teenage years, however, the adolescents distanced themselves from their parents, reflecting the influence of public schools and access to the larger culture and society. Later in the second generation's teens, the barriers created by racial difference solidified, causing an inward turn by Nisei and by fellow Americans. Without abandoning assimilation, Bogardus alluded to the formation and development of a Nisei subculture—in many ways separate and separated from the larger society.[27] The persistence of racism dampened social scientific claims for assimilation.

Surveying the Scene

The work of Emory Bogardus and others on Japanese Americans had earlier ties to the 1920s, when Robert Park and others embarked on the Survey of Race Relations (1924–27). Directed by Park and funded primarily by the Institute of Social and Religious Research in New York City, the survey investigated the economic, religious, educational, civic, biological, and social conditions among racial-ethnic residents along the West Coast and Canada. Park assembled a team of researchers and institutions along the coast that formed local branches of the survey. Although a lack of funding curtailed the publication of a multivolume study and limited fieldwork in northern Mexico and Hawaii, in three years, the survey had generated 600 documents, totaling some 5,500 typewritten pages.[28] The core of the survey consisted of life histories that documented the experiences of individuals. Drawing on the pioneering work of colleague and sociologist W. I. Thomas, Park viewed the life histories as important records of firsthand experiences that allowed "a lively, intimate and authentic picture of the relations of the immigrant races and the native population." Park noted that, like the priest's confession, life histories should be "sudden, bitter and complete."[29]

Researchers were given a loose set of guidelines that aimed to elicit attitudes and opinions; the goal was to let subjects speak for themselves. The mixture of autobiography and oral history provided by Japanese Americans like Kazuo Kawai who participated in the survey represents a rich set of historical sources. These documents provide access to Nisei perspectives and the methodology employed by the researchers.[30] Though author of the race relations cycle, Robert Park recognized that race prejudice persisted against the "Oriental," relating their experience to that of the "Negro." Both groups, unlike European immigrants, could not lay aside their "racial uniform." Given this distinction, "Orientals" and "Negroes," as well as the rest of society, exhibited an intensified racial consciousness.[31] In the case of Asians on the West Coast, Park suggested that the interaction of races involved far more than simple economics:

> If human relations could be reduced to the simple and rational term of popular economics, life would be much less complicated and very much less interesting than it actually is. But economic relations are always more or less involved with stubborn and incalculable factors of human nature. Furthermore, the plain, practical interests of the economic man, theoretically so permanent and calculable, are always complicated with sentiments that change in what seem quite irrational ways, and in ways that are quite beyond our control. It is, on the whole, in the region of sentiments rather than of the interests, it seems to me, that the problem of race relations in the Pacific mainly lies.[32]

Japanese Americans were well acquainted with both the sentiments and the economics of race. "UZ," a first-generation immigrant whose life history is part of the Survey of Race Relations, conveyed his discouragement at having endured the hardships of migration and the struggle to work himself through school only to be turned away, with other Japanese American graduates, from jobs related to his degree in chemistry. Instead, the college graduate worked as a hired hand on a farm and then as a clerk in a Japanese grocery store. With no prospects of any immediate change, "UZ" considered returning to Japan. The opportunities for Nisei were worse: "When, however, I consider some of the American-born Japanese, I fear they will have a more difficult time—they will be considered Japanese almost to the same extent that I am, except that they speak better English."[33]

L. Toyama, a Nisei from southern California, confirmed "UZ"'s concerns as he related the instances of insult and injury experienced due to racial-

ethnic background: "In going through high school and college, I can't recall how many times I was cast aside just because I am a Japanese. I was
barred from parties, dances, swimming pools, etc. for the same reason
previously given. Truly America is for Americans and all other races are
not given its [*sic*] chance. Pretty soon, these other races might be rejected
from the supposed-to-be land of the free and the home of the brave and
what would then happen? Nothing but war." Toyama's use of the term
"American" underscored the power to define, since "American" was made
synonymous with those of European ancestry at the expense of "other"
Americans (read racial-ethnic). Despite the lack of commentary on the
internal dynamics of language, Toyama clearly understood the general
principle at work: "Americans are the narrowest-minded people in the
world. They think only about and for themselves and exclude all others
. . . a model to be avoided by all others."[34]

Race prejudice, coupled with the difficulties in finding meaningful work,
cast suspicion on the market value of an education. Wilfred Horiuchi's
newspaper column in the *Shin Sekai* (New World) voiced the doubt in the
minds of many people: Does a college education pay? A senior at the University of California at Los Angeles, Horiuchi had been told by his older
brother not to put too much stock in his degree. Not only did higher education not pay in terms of employment, but it actually made the realities
of life after graduation more painful because of the raised expectations that
schooling fostered. Horiuchi knew too many graduates who "loafed" because they viewed the jobs available as beneath them. Others, finding themselves in frustrating lines of work, alienated themselves from their peers
through superior attitudes. Women who went to college supposedly put
on "airs," looked down on their parents, spurned work, and usually ended up as old maids. The journalist painted an unkind portrait and stated
that the best thing one could do with the degree was to lock it up in a trunk
and forget that he or she ever attended college.[35] Another reporter, Tad
Uyeno, described the bittersweet feelings that many graduates donning caps
and gowns must have experienced during the ceremony that was supposed
to celebrate a new beginning: "As every commencement exercise rolls
around, educated speakers, scholars, men who claim to know nearly everything on the face of the earth, give advice to the young graduates and
picture them a brilliant future and possibilities for these graduates to emerge
forth as great men and women. Of the thousands that graduate only a mere
handful will occupy that position. The others must remain in oblivion."[36]

Despite the predictions that Japanese Americans would assimilate into
American life, racial barriers in California showed little sign of waning

during the interwar years. Educators could do little to change the attitudes of those who discriminated against Nisei. Regardless of their training or achievements, the second generation, time and again, met with closed doors.

Negotiating the Times

In spite of the difficult circumstances that they faced, Japanese Americans were not passive receptors but instead sought to make their education work for them. Nikkei, through their actions and their words, illustrated the portion of the equation that has often been omitted in educational history—namely, the students and their families. Appreciative of access to public education, parents sent their children to school and hoped that an education would lead to a stable and productive life in the United States. Accordingly, most immigrants expected the second generation to study hard, even if they had difficulty in actually guiding students through their lessons. Issei encouraged students to concentrate in "practical" areas like business and professions that would give them better odds of finding work.

Along with American schooling, however, many parents also believed that a complete education included Japanese-language school.[37] By their very existence, the language schools raised issues about Americanization and the socialization of Nisei. Unsure about permanent residency in the United States, the Issei originally set up the academies to provide supplementary education for their children. In California, forty schools operated in 1920. But as the Nisei increased, so did the schools, and in 1930, the number of schools had mushroomed to 248; by 1940, twenty more had been added. In the 1930s, Edward Strong estimated that approximately 69 percent of the second generation had attended the language schools. Most programs operated for an hour or so immediately following public school instruction on the weekdays and often offered class for a few hours on Saturday morning. Although most Nisei did not gain a firm grasp of the language, they strengthened ethnic ties.[38]

The Japanese-language schools came under criticism from those outside the ethnic community, especially as nativism and postwar zeal for Americanization cast a suspicious shadow on anything that might be labeled un-American. Legislative and social pressures did not force centers to close but did affect their operations, making them much more conscious of outside perceptions. Research on Japanese Americans at the time invariably addressed the issue of language instruction; overwhelmingly, the investigators did not see it as harmful or threatening to assimilation. The schools were seen as necessary for a stable home since many Issei, advanced in years, did not speak English well. Rather than promoting a separatist attitude, language instruction was depicted as aiding the quality of Japanese American home life.[39] Whether or not the schools fostered Americanization, they did, according to Chotoku Toyama of Columbia University, serve many of the needs of the ethnic community. Especially after the passage of exclusion in 1924, some Issei reconsidered their decision to stay in a country that denied the Japanese the right to enter as immigrants. If families returned to Japan, then the Nisei needed language skills to have any chance of success. Even for those who saw the United States as their home, Japanese language proved necessary for work within the ethnic community, the most probable place of employment. The language schools also served as centers of socialization, places where Nisei could form friendships and where parents built community networks through sponsored clubs and lectures.[40]

Many Japanese Americans presented the language schools as compatible with and complementary to Americanization. Textbooks and teachers encouraged the Nisei to be good Americans and become fully conversant with life in the United States. Michiji Ishikawa's research, however, presented a more nuanced understanding. Even before anti-Japanese sentiments reached a fever pitch, Nikkei differed about the role of the language academies. The Japanese consulate thought of the schools as part of the larger Americanization effort. In contrast, Japanese associations, geared to immigrant concerns, viewed the schools in more nationalistic terms. Ishikawa pointed out that, after 1924, greater consensus developed among all parties that the Nisei needed to learn the ways of the home country to avoid further racial humiliation. A recent study has concluded that the support of Americanization must be seen in the context of heavy anti-Japanese sentiment and activity that plagued the Nikkei throughout the prewar years but especially in the years prior to exclusion. The pro-Americanization rhetoric of Issei leaders reflected strategy as much as it did support of American lifestyles and perspectives.[41] Parents had a voice in the socialization of their children and used community resources toward those ends. As much a rite of passage as the public schools, the language schools provided an important shared experience for thousands of Nisei and reinforced generational ties. Language teachers may have sincerely believed in some form of Americanization such as good citizenship, but they clearly stressed that the second generation were Americans of *Japanese* ancestry. Given the racial climate, Nisei, even in their youth, needed little reminder.

Before their lessons in Japanese language and culture, the second generation went to English-language schools that represented the primary form of contact with society outside the home and ethnic community. Although students may not have always been conscious of the events unfolding before them, they had started a journey that by its very nature forced issues of identity and socialization to the fore. English-language usage and academic achievement did not entail the shedding of one culture and the adoption of another but a process marked by negotiation. That negotiation took place in the classroom, through activities, and on the athletic fields. At Roosevelt High School in Los Angeles, for instance, students took courses with others in traditional subjects like English, math, and history. Japanese Americans also served on student government councils and played on a wide range of teams, including football and basketball. At the same time, many Nisei joined the Japanese Club and helped sponsor activities that both excluded and included those not of Japanese ancestry.

Sources such as orations and essays by educators and second-generation students offer some ideas about education and Nisei life. Published in 1932 under the guidance of Paul Hirohata, a representative of the *Japan Times,* a volume entitled *Orations and Essays by the Japanese Second Generation of America* emphasized peace and international friendship in light of the summer Olympic games that had recently been held in Los Angeles. Most of the essays were written by high school students in California who spoke loyally of America and enthusiastically supported better understanding between peoples and nations. And yet, even within a volume intended to accentuate the positive, there were indications that all was not well. In the foreword, State Superintendent of Education Vierling Kersey referred to anti-Japanese sentiment and stressed the need to dispel fear and distrust. Although Kersey, like many others, pointed to ignorance as the culprit, the activity against Japanese in California had a long history that included organizations dedicated to fanning the flames of racial tension. Students could do much to alleviate the problem by working together to foster an environment in which people could appreciate each other's backgrounds.[42]

In his essay, Goro Murata, a student at Montebello High School in Los Angeles, wrote about the issue of hierarchy and social stratification in American society. Drawing on his study of U.S. history, Murata discovered that the nation had been founded on the principle of freedom from hierarchy—in opposition to monarchy. He suggested that "the laying of the basic social order that was uniquely American . . . was to be founded not upon men's distinctions, but on their common properties and instincts." Nothing characterized the American experience more than the frontier. Citing the historian Frederick Jackson Turner, Murata suggested that the

proud legacy of the frontier that had fueled American democracy continued to hold out possibilities of new understanding and shared humanity.
It is not difficult to imagine that Murata wanted to extend the frontier
analogy to Nikkei pioneers who had left their homes to settle in the American West. The notion of equality, then, not only applied to the past but
included the present as well.[43]

In assessing that present, Kay Sugahara, president of the Los Angles
chapter of the Japanese American Citizens' League, noted that economic
disturbances and cultural clashes had caused misunderstanding and unrest in the daily lives of Japanese Americans. As a blend of Asia and America, the second generation could bring their particular background to bear
on the problems that lay ahead. Sugahara expressed confidence in his fellow Nisei "trail-blazers."[44] Perhaps Sugahara referred to those like Haruko Fujita of Arcadia, California, who urged her readers to bring people
together, specifically the people of Japan and the United States. Fujita, like
many of the other contributors, viewed American-born Japanese as bridges
of understanding, since they uniquely embodied both the East and the
West.[45] The second generation could take what they had learned at home
and school to promote better relations at local, national, and international levels. The idea of a bridge, first introduced by Issei, had also been used
by a variety of groups in reference to Japanese Americans. Some Nisei
tailored the bridge metaphor to negotiate issues of identity and to balance
the demands of Americanization and the expectations of their parents and
the ethnic community.

Although Nisei as bridges of understanding primarily addressed political issues such as Japanese exclusion and international relations between
the United States and Japan, education and schooling also represented an
important aspect of the term.[46] In attending the public schools, the second
generation experienced firsthand the institution that socialized and trained
children for life in the United States. Nisei prepared themselves for their
roles as interpreters of America to Japan but also to their parents and the
ethnic community. Vierling Kersey congratulated graduates in 1937 on
their achievements in school and specifically lauded the bicultural heritage
of the Nikkei as a valuable asset for local communities.[47] At the same time,
Japanese-language schools aimed to keep up the other end through exposure to the mother tongue and culture. The language schools commonly
sponsored essay contests with the bridge of understanding as the theme—
so much so that it seemed that the contests were held for the purpose of
promoting the idea.[48] In the mid-1920s, Issei began to sponsor study tours
(*kengakudan*) to enable students to make trips to Japan that represented

their first time overseas. Immigrant newspapers often printed letters and stories describing the experiences of students abroad.[49]

For the second generation, the idea of linking Japan and the United States in practical terms spoke more to their concerns as Japanese in America than it did to international relations. The bridge concept moved beyond the mere status of interpreter and required the Nisei to be contributors to American life and to take up the responsibilities of U.S. citizenship. San Francisco attorney Saburo Kido, an influential second-generation leader, argued that only American-born Nisei loyal to the United States could serve as effective ambassadors. In an age in which the two countries vied for power in the Pacific, Kido argued that Nisei should be bridges with a clear sense of loyalty to America.[50] The issue of allegiance suggested that Japanese Americans felt the pressures of Americanization through the schools and from anti-Japanese activity. At the same time, the bridge metaphor allowed Nisei to maintain connections to persons and things Japanese, since they also had to deal with the expectations of their parents and the racial-ethnic community. In reality, very few of the second generation could have served as true bridges, since they lacked adequate knowledge of Japanese language, history, and culture. Nevertheless, the ties to Japan mattered particularly because the Issei could not acquire U.S. citizenship, and this fact served as a constant reminder of the vulnerability of the Nikkei in America. The second generation also worked for good relations between Japan and the United States, realizing that Japanese Americans often bore the brunt of American hostility toward Japan. The Japanese takeover of Manchuria and the Sino-Japanese War of 1937 acted as powerful confirmations of the ripple effect of events in Asia on the Nikkei in America. As World War II approached and relations worsened in the 1930s, many Nisei found it increasingly difficult to uphold the notion of the cultural bridge. Up to that point, however, the concept of a bridge of understanding, in the best sense of the word, enabled Japanese Americans to honor the various strands of their own experience.[51]

Regardless of how Nisei negotiated their time in school, as they moved toward graduation, students faced the issue of what lay ahead. Perhaps more than any other issue, employment went directly to the value and purpose of an American education. If schools provided the ticket to advancement in the United States, the Nisei discovered that their degrees did not count for much in the marketplace. Shut out largely from work outside the Japanese American community, graduates also faced tough times within an ethnic economy that strained to take in the growing second generation. Many helped with family-owned businesses, while others worked in agriculture-related jobs or in domestic service. Isamu Nodera calculated that 70 percent of the employable Nisei in the city (ages sixteen to twenty-five) in 1930 and 1935 worked in retail or wholesale produce markets. The other 30 percent worked in sixteen other types of businesses such as cleaning and laundry, nurseries, and gardening. In 1940, only 5 percent of Los Angeles Nisei worked for white Americans and, according to John Modell, did so within "Japanese" areas such as agriculture. The Reverend Kojiro Onoura's 1938 study of 161 Japanese American graduates of the University of California during the period 1925–35 found that only 25 percent held jobs indicative of their training and education. The rest of the graduates either worked for family businesses or had "blind alley" work: jobs requiring no special training and with no future. A poll taken by the *Rafu Shimpo* (Los Angeles Japanese Daily News) in June 1937 revealed that 70 percent of the men (800 surveys returned) wanted white-collar jobs such as bookkeeping, engineering, and architecture; commercial art, teaching, and nursing proved popular for the women.[52]

Given the occupational outlook, some Nisei thought that their future might be on the other side of the Pacific in Japan. According to one study, about 2,000 American-born Japanese went to Japan in the mid-1930s, with approximately 80 percent going to study the language.[53] Investing the time and money in going overseas seemed worthwhile, since many Issei and Nisei felt that Japanese-language skills could make the second generation far more employable—at home or abroad. Journalist Bill Hosokawa's own experience might have encouraged the second generation to pursue their education. A Seattle native, Hosokawa earned his bachelor's degree in journalism from the University of Washington in 1937 and then headed to Asia to write for the *Singapore Herald,* an English-language paper with ties to the Japanese government. In 1940, he had moved to the *Shanghai Times,* touring Korea, Manchuria, and North China. Making his way home just before Pearl Harbor, Hosokawa had managed to find work overseas.[54]

While some people found jobs abroad, most Nisei did not possess the language skills to make Japan a viable option. Even for those who could steer around the issue of language, cultural difference often made the stay abroad difficult. Alice Sumida, a 1931 graduate of Roosevelt High School in Los Angeles, wrote that while her time in Japan had not been bad, she really missed home. She had been taking part in a summer exchange program that sent American educators to Japan, and her role had been to report on the problems of the Nikkei in America. Although she had adjusted to life in Japan, Sumida still did not feel very comfortable and looked forward to heading back to Los Angeles.[55] Another student noted that, year after year,

A Nisei woman at a fruit and vegetable stand. (Security Pacific Collection/Los Angeles Public Library)

Nisei ventured to Japan and on their return spoke glowingly of their time abroad. Nevertheless, visiting a country and earning a living there were two very different matters. Echoing Sumida's sentiments, the student noted that it was difficult for the second generation to truly look beyond the United States, since it remained their birthplace and cradle of experience.[56]

Miya Sannomiya's experience further suggested that Japan did not hold much promise for Nisei. A Hawaiian-born Nisei, Sannomiya ventured to Japan as part of the 1926 summer study tour sponsored by the San Francisco–based newspaper, the *Nichibei Shimbun* (Japanese American News). After completing her studies at the University of California at Berkeley, and after a short stint as a reporter for the *Nichibei*, Sannomiya returned to Japan in 1933 to learn about its people and culture to better serve as a bridge of understanding. Initially working for the YWCA, in 1934 she moved on to the Society for International Cultural Relations. This organization, in effect sponsored by the Japanese government, disseminated information about Japan in European languages and acted as a public relations office to the Western world.[57] Sannomiya's decision to work in Japan stemmed in part from her encounters with American racism. As a young woman, Sannomiya had left her family in California and gone to Alabama, where she received a scholarship to attend a private, Christian school. She not only witnessed the effects of a segregated South but discovered that she too would bear the brunt of race prejudice through the "condescending kindness" shown to her by classmates and teachers. In an especially powerful episode, Sannomiya, sharing the scholastic spotlight with a classmate, suffered the humiliation of witnessing the presiding Methodist bishop laud her white classmate for not letting "the Jap girl" claim sole possession of the award. Disillusioned about race relations and the virtue of religion, Sannomiya packed her bags and headed back to California.[58]

During the course of her employment in Japan, Sannomiya also described a particularly unfortunate episode that revealed a great deal to her about the status of the Nisei in Japan:

> Sometime during 1936–37 our Society held a round table discussion for leaders of organisations connected with the care and education of the young Niseis studying in Japan. There were about 14–15 people representing various Buddhist groups, private schools, YWCA, YMCA, Japanese language school for foreigners, etc. For some reason I had been asked to sit in at the discussions and to take notes. No one there, except one prominent Christian woman educator, knew I was a Nisei. The whole discussion failed because not one constructive idea was taken up seriously. The participants spent the whole afternoon in derisive laughter and critical remarks about the "outlandish ways of these Niseis," their "horrible, low class, boorish, country style Japanese speech,". . . . They all nodded solemnly as one speaker said, "The Nisei are children of low class, peasant emigrants, so what could we expect of them?" In other words, they were saying that the Niseis were hopeless cases and they wanted to have nothing to do with them.[59]

While the United States presented certain difficulties, Japan clearly did not represent the solution to Nisei problems. The very fact that they looked overseas, however, spoke to the limited options that existed at home. Despite the bleak outlook, some Nisei kept hope alive and acted as if sheer will power would unlock doors. Hiroshi Yamashita, a student at Oakland High School, addressed the issue of vocation and the second generation for an oratorical contest sponsored by the Japanese American alumni of the University of California at Berkeley. Placing first, Yamashita's speech had been reprinted by the *Nichibei Shimbun* in April 1930. The high school student challenged racist claims that Nisei lacked the physical or mental capabilities or education to succeed in America. He claimed instead that race prejudice blocked access to jobs. Yamashita placed the condition of Nisei in a broader context, stating that Japanese Americans suffered from the historic discriminatory treatment aimed at racial-ethnic peoples, including American Indians and "Negroes." The white boss might have been a person of "high noble character and personality, but he will give as his refusal, 'My colleagues will not tolerate working with a Jap.'" Although he could not offer much of a solution, Yamashita vigorously challenged his readers to keep fighting.[60]

Reminding themselves about freedom and fairness, many within the ranks of the second generation upheld a vision of America that offered them the best chance to participate more fully in it. School may not have led to success, but it equipped the second generation with the skills and qualifications that might someday enable them to move into jobs and careers of their choosing. In any event, getting an education remained one of the few avenues open to many American-born Japanese, and it bought them a little time before they would have to confront what lay at the end of the educational journey.

Dreams Deferred

In her post–World War II study, Alice Shikamura stated that, as for so many Americans, education lined the dreams of the second generation: "the goal of all American youth to achieve the greatest economic and social successes in life through higher education and training [lay] behind the vocational aspirations of the Nisei college student. The Nisei are in a position where they are attempting to make a group advancement from the lower socioeconomic status of the first generation Japanese to a higher one achieved through professional and 'white-collar' jobs." According to some observers, the Nisei did not get the proper vocational guidance, but Shikamura noted that even expert advice could do little to mitigate the race prejudice that accounted for much of the woes of the American-born Japanese.[61]

Since his cross-country trek in 1925, Kazuo Kawai continued his schooling, specializing in Asian history and, in particular, East-West relations. After completing his undergraduate course of study at Stanford, Kawai stayed on at his alma mater, entering the graduate school and eventually earning his Ph.D. in 1939. In the winter of 1932, Kawai joined the faculty at the University of California at Los Angeles, as an instructor of Oriental geography and history. In 1937, with the start of another season of commencement exercises, Kawai must have thought about that train ride years earlier as he prepared his message to Nisei graduates. Kawai warned grade school and college graduates alike not to place too much faith in their diplomas. Times continued to be difficult for American-born Japanese, and the future remained a sober topic. Many of those who had been the brightest students would find themselves in less than satisfactory jobs. Nevertheless, well-spent time in school and exposure to a wide array of ideas could help the second generation navigate a course between "cynicism and gullibility."[62]

That course proved difficult to manage in the interwar years, since an appreciable shift in the occupational outlook for Nisei would not take place until after 1945. In the postwar period, opportunities for the second generation slowly opened up, and the investment in education finally started to pay some dividends. Until then, however, Japanese Americans had to endure years of frustration, and, in response to their circumstances, many students channeled their energies into laying the foundations of a Nisei subculture that included Buddhist temples and Christian churches.

KEEPING THE FAITH

If the public schools represented the main form of contact with the rest of American society, racial-ethnic temples and churches drew Nisei into spaces firmly rooted within Japanese America. From the early days of migration, religious institutions helped those who arrived in the United States and provided invaluable social services, community networks, and places of meaning. By 1924, when migration from Japan to the United States had effectively ceased, Buddhist and Christian groups had established a major presence within Japanese American communities in California.[1] In the years that followed, as Nisei came of age and families took fuller shape, clerics and lay leaders faced the challenge of serving two generations housed under one roof. The overview of the growth and development of Christianity and Buddhism among the Nikkei that is presented in this chapter documents how religion formed a vital part of an emergent Nisei subculture. Temples and churches provided an important framework that enabled Nisei to interpret and to negotiate what it meant to be second-generation Japanese Americans. Through a constellation of religious organizations, conferences, and publications, young men and women found ways to make sense of their bicultural status and to counter the racism that permeated their everyday world. Rather than fostering wholesale assimilation into American life, religion allowed many Nisei Buddhists and Christians to carve out a distinctive niche within immigrant and native contexts that actually reinforced generational and racial-ethnic ties.

Temple- and church-sponsored activities directly addressed the concerns of the second generation, highlighting religious traditions that encompassed all of life. Through a host of Nisei organizations, adherents found ample outlets to spend time with one another, to develop leadership skills, and to network with one another in local communities and also on state and national levels. Conferences and publications became a hallmark for both groups and provided valuable opportunities to discuss and exchange ideas about the particular issues that confronted them. Thought-provoking speakers and editorials challenged Buddhists and Christians to make sense of the times and their place in them. Under the aegis of religion, Japanese Americans found in these institutions a place in which they belonged as full-fledged members. Differences existed between the two traditions; but, more often than not, emerging religious sensibilities revolved around common generational and racial concerns. Both Buddhists and Christians felt each other's presence as they organized similar kinds of groups and activities, even if largely operating independently of one another. On occasion, bazaars and celebrations brought the two religions together. Takako Fuchigami, a member of the Marysville Young Women's Buddhist Association (YWBA), stressed the importance of making connections between Buddhism and Christianity, since both represented an important part of the Japanese American experience. She stated in a 1934 article that religious differences did not dissolve the ties that bound Japanese Americans to one another: "We cannot change our hair, skin, or eyes, therefore it is a grave mistake if we think we can be real Americans in every respect. We must carry on the excellent peculiarities of our race." Fuchigami recognized that, despite their differences, Nisei Buddhists and Christians shared much by virtue of their status as second-generation Japanese Americans.[2]

Paying attention to religion not only highlights one aspect of the subculture that Nisei built in California during the 1920s and 1930s but also suggests the importance of religion as a factor in America's past. Despite the noted connections between immigration, ethnicity, and religion, the case of Japanese Americans provides an alternative vantage point from which to view the terrain of American religion.[3] Nikkei experiences underscore the incredible diversity that has characterized religion and society in the United States from the very beginning and reminds us that belief and practice have always emanated from the confluence of many cultures, peoples, and places.[4] In particular, an examination of Japanese American Buddhism and Christianity underscores the relationship between religion *and* race and challenges the notion that religion has been the means by which immigrants have found eventual acceptance and access to American society and culture. Roman Catholics and Jews certainly faced their share of resistance; but over time, according to sociologist Will Herberg, they joined the mainstream once occupied solely by Protestants. This fundamental sea change in sensibilities reflected the role of religion in creating a triple melting pot.[5] Adding Japanese American Buddhists to that group, however, would have seriously undermined the force of Herberg's argument. Well outside the pale of a Judeo-Christian framework, Buddhists by their very presence may in fact have helped usher in the change that Herberg noted. Part of the American religious scene since the nineteenth century, Japanese American Buddhists discovered that the passage of time did little to remove the widespread suspicion that they could never really become part of the fabric of American life. Doubly marginalized by virtue of race and religion, Buddhists were cast as the "Other," masking how they were very much a part of their larger social-cultural contexts. For Japanese American Protestants, a shared faith with the dominant religious tradition of the nation was not enough to bridge the gap created by race. Although the prevailing assumption is that racial-ethnic Christians are more assimilated than their non-Christian counterparts, the fact remains that individuals and communities, including Japanese American Protestants, consciously forged religious identities in opposition to the discrimination that they experienced. Separate racial-ethnic churches, programs, and governing bodies, moreover, suggest the complex and contested nature of Protestant Christianity in America.

Along with issues of race, the religion of Japanese Americans in California takes us to the American West and revisits a region typically noted for its perceived absence of religion. Although its physical grandeur has elicited allusions to the supernatural, the West for most European Americans remains a place of cattle drives, gunfights, and brothels. Churches may appear in films and novels, but rarely are they more than window dressing—a vestige of civilization in an otherwise morally barren landscape. Popular culture, of course, is not the most reliable of guides; yet these persistent images illustrate the adaptability and staying power of the vision given voice by historian Frederick Jackson Turner in 1893. Despite the "new" Western history, the region continues to be a site vested with responsibility for the forging of the American character, made possible by the availability of "free land" and an encounter with the wilderness.[6] It is worth noting, however, that neither Turner nor his critics have said much about religion. Apart from passing references to the Mormons of Utah, the work of scholars in American history has tended to follow Hollywood's lead.[7] The ability to view the West as virgin territory, religious or otherwise, becomes considerably more difficult when one considers that the religions of Native Americans, Spaniards, and Mexicans had infused the area now referred to as the American West long before the arrival of the first Protestant European Americans. The eventual encounters that would take place—as well as the continued migration of people over the years—have only added to the complex layering of religion in the West. As a part of this palimpsest, Japanese Americans provide a point of entry into a region whose religious complexity and verve deserve as much if not more scholarly attention than has been centered in New England.

As much as Nikkei Buddhists and Christians help us to reconsider the racial and regional aspects of American history, the primary lens that religion supplies is insight into how men and women have interpreted, ordered, and constructed their own worlds. In his study of Asian Indians and Pakistanis, Raymond Brady Williams has suggested that immigrants are often more religious than they were in their countries of origin. Religion tends to counter the fragmentation that individuals and families undergo and in the United States is a means of developing a distinct identity. In the face of epistemological crisis, religion provides a crucial narrative structure that calls on a known world, even as that world necessarily changes and adapts to new environmental forces. Williams speculates that America's religiousness may stem from the central role that immigration has played in the peopling of the United States.[8] The narrative role of religion underscores the human need for story; and, at a fundamental level, we discover who we are through the stories that we are given and that we in turn shape by our interaction with them. In locating the self with the sacred, religious narrative touches on our deepest myths, hopes, and fears and represents a pivotal opening into the lives of Japanese Americans.

Pure Land in America

Like many others who migrated to these shores, those who ventured from agricultural regions in southwestern Japan to Hawaii and the mainland brought their dreams, belongings, and worldviews.[9] The majority of Issei came from Jodo Shinsu (True Pure Land) Buddhist backgrounds.[10] Temples and affiliated religious organizations addressed the needs of Japanese Americans, providing invaluable social services, promoting ethnic solidarity, and serving as places of meaning and faith. In an often hostile land, Buddhism offered acceptance as well as sanctuary to its members and represented the development and growth of ethnoreligious communities in California.[11]

Although Jodo Shinsu ("Shin") Buddhism traveled with the first immigrants to America, official missionary work, sanctioned by headquarters in Kyoto, did not begin until the end of the nineteenth century. Clerics received word from immigrant returnees like Nisaburo Hirano about the need for a Buddhist presence. In 1891, when Hirano disembarked in San Francisco, he struggled (as did many other Japanese) simply to survive. The services of the Methodist mission eased that transition and, although grateful for its aid, he declined the offer to become baptized as a Christian. A devout Buddhist, Hirano saw the need for English skills but not for a change in faith. On his return to Japan five years later, he met with two priests, requesting that they go before their superiors on the behalf of Buddhists in North America.[12] A scouting trip to California sponsored by Shin Buddhists in the summer of 1898 confirmed Hirano's observations. Protestant missionaries had set up shop among the Japanese immigrants; their mission efforts included a range of services such as housing, job placement, and English-language classes. Buddhist activity, in contrast, consisted of occasional informal meetings run by lay leaders. Before returning to Japan, the visiting priests worked with immigrants to establish the Young Men's Buddhist Association (YMBA) in 1898. The YMBA served the needs of the largely immigrant male population and represented the initial seeds of mission work.[13]

A year later, a pair of priests, Shuye Sonoda and Kakuryo Nishijima, landed in San Francisco. The 13 September 1899 issue of the *San Francisco Chronicle* featured a photo of Sonoda and Nishijima in full clerical garb, poised to begin their work. Priests had little difficulty in drawing people, as many Japanese Americans looked to the Buddhist faith for important rites of passage such as marriage and funerals. The ritual of remembering the deceased, known as *obon,* became a popular annual summer festival that often drew members from the entire Nikkei community, including those from other religious traditions.[14] In the years before the war, Jodo Shinshu Buddhism in the United States remained overwhelmingly Japanese American. A 1944 anthropological study indicated that Nikkei accounted for 55,000 of the 56,000 Buddhists in the United States.[15] Stanford professor Edward Strong's survey in the early 1930s found that 78 percent of the Issei claimed Buddhism; only 18 percent had taken up the Christian faith. In a more comprehensive if problematic survey taken by the War Relocation Authority (WRA) in 1942, 68 percent of all immigrant internees reported a Buddhist affiliation compared to 21.9 percent Christian. The figures for the Nisei showed gains for Christianity, but Buddhism still accounted for a greater percentage of the second generation: 48.7 percent Buddhist and 35 percent Christian.[16]

By the time Kosei Ogura, a priest and a graduate student in sociology at the University of Southern California, completed his thesis in 1932, the North American Buddhist Mission (NABM) had prospered. The humble work of two missionary priests and a dedicated lay leadership resulted in thirty-five temples in the United States and Canada.[17] Clerics ministered to some 30,000 Japanese Americans. Kyoto maintained its lifeline to the work in North American through the selection of the bishop and the training of priests. In thirty years, approximately 170 priests had been sent to the United States to serve an average of nearly five years each.[18] While important ties to Japan remained, North American Buddhism showed signs of vitality and independence. Ogura boasted that temples had raised approximately $300,000, an entire annual operational budget, without any outside support. In fact, funds had been sent from the United States and Canada to benefit work in Japan.[19] Vigor extended beyond finances to a laity that sought to direct the growth of an ancient religion to new soil. The founding of the temple at Sacramento illustrated that Shin Buddhism in America would be a variation of the original.

A Japanese American Buddhism

Lay leaders in Sacramento legally incorporated their temple with the state of California in June 1901 but vested power in a board of trustees and *not* in the priest, effectively eliminating clerical control over temple life. In Japan, the priest and his family usually owned an individual temple. Tradition dictated that the priesthood pass from one generation to the next and with it, a sense of ownership. Trustees also broke new ground by setting priests' salaries and controlling finances. Strange new ideas surfaced, owing to new contexts, such as paid membership.[20] Although males claimed official lay leadership positions, women also exerted their influence in temple life through Buddhist Women's Associations (or Fujinkai) that had been founded in 1900. At the core of religious activity in most temples, Fujinkai enabled women to develop networks and a sense of community. Their collective labor translated into service that included preparation of refreshments and food and organization of temple bazaars. The role of lay women, however, extended well beyond the kitchen as they performed important social services for the immigrant community as well as raising critical funds for temple operations. Priests and male lay leaders alike quickly found out that alienating the Fujinkai spelled real trouble. Women comprised the majority of adherents and often served as the glue that held the programs and activities of the temples together.[21] For women and men, the creation of important and powerful positions for lay leaders became a badge of prestige. Because avenues for community involvement had been severely restricted by the decision to migrate to the United States, immigrants looked to temple life to fulfill social opportunities that would have been more plentiful in their homeland.

Buddhists in America found themselves living in a society in which Christians wielded both religious and cultural power. Protestant missionaries often viewed followers of Buddha as heathens in need of conversion. The long history of anti-Japanese activity that resulted in exclusion in 1924 left Buddhists especially wary of public perceptions and misconceptions. Repeatedly, religion had been used against Nikkei as a sign of their incompatibility. As a strategy of survival, Buddhists, as had other religious groups, made adjustments to soften their differences from Protestant Christianity. Leaders recoded much of the terminology and outward practices—temples were called "churches," priests became "reverends." Architecture also reflected Buddhism's new surroundings as most congregations opted for rather plain, nontraditional buildings instead of the typical styles found in Japan. Inside, pews and lecterns gave the aura of a Christian church.[22] An individualized, less regularized format that characterized Shin Buddhism in the homeland gave way to a communal, scheduled worship on Sundays. Attending a morning adult service, one would typically find a format that included: meditation, reading or chanting of Buddhist scripture, a sermon, *gathas* (songs), the burning of incense, and announcements. Sunday school programs for children, the Young Men's and Women's Buddhist Associations, and Boy Scouts contributed to what sociologist Isao Horinouchi has called the "Protestantization" of American Buddhism.[23]

Casting religious adaptation in Protestant terms, however, is misleading because it implies change that compromises the integrity of Buddhism. Few adherents would have mistaken what took place at the temple as anything but Buddhism. As with any transition, some may have disliked altered terms and forms, but a distinctively Japanese American Buddhism emerged. On entering the church on Sunday morning, for instance, one might stumble over many pairs of shoes outside the sanctuary. One would find not only shoeless worshipers inside but also pews pushed against the walls with people sitting on the floor. Apart from the specific circumstances in the United States, Buddhism in general—and the Jodo Shinshu school in particular—exhibited a marked flexibility. As it made its way throughout Asia, Buddhism had a long history of being deeply affected by its surrounding cultures.[24] In explaining the adaptability of Buddhism, scholar Hajime Nakamura noted that "the doctrine of Buddha is not a system of philosophy in the Western sense but is rather a path. A buddha is simply one who has walked this path and can report to others what he has found. His standpoint is practical."[25] Jodo Shinshu itself emerged as a variant of Japanese Buddhism, in which Shinran (1173–1263) adapted the teachings of his master, Honen (1133–1212). During his training, Honen realized the impossibility of attaining enlightenment through precepts, meditation, and knowledge. Instead, the path to the Pure Land rested in the graciousness of the Amida-Buddha. Shinran, like Honen, stressed belief over a system of works but went further to claim that religious practice did not so much lead to the Pure Land as acknowledge what the Amida had already done for adherents. In the religious communities connected to Shinran, distinctions between the clergy and laity held less sway. In fact, Shinran broke with tradition by getting married and having a family. Given the Protestant bias of the United States, notions within Buddhism akin to "salvation" and "grace" as well as an emphasis on the laity lent themselves well to religious life in the United States.[26]

In relating to the changes and transitions within Buddhism among Japanese Americans, officials at the headquarters in Kyoto realized that the rules of the old country did not always apply abroad. Minutes from the 1927 annual conference indicated that the Nikkei "seem now to be reconciled in the making of permanent homes in America," and, in light of this, "the priest should help them to realize the American idea of 'Home Sweet Home' with the Lord Buddha as universal parent." New contexts required a harmonization of Buddhist ideals with those of the host culture. Instructions to clerics included commentary on the education of children:

> For their child to be a good American citizen, parents must secure a birth certificate from the proper authority, in the first place; secondly, must send their children to public school regularly; thirdly, they must be taught to take an interest in various movements of Americanism. Every Buddhist minister must know this and see to it that the parents are not amiss in their conduct in this regard. In your dealings with children, particularly in your official capacity as teacher, you must not forget that you are speaking to American citizens of Japanese parentage. Do your utmost to make yourselves familiar with American ideals. Get a right understanding of true Americanism. This is essential to the work of a Buddhist minister.[27]

The charge to missionary priests by leaders in Japan acknowledged the contexts into which Buddhism entered in the United States and also reflected a commitment to minister to Japanese Americans. A Buddhism that mixed traditional elements with newer modifications emerged, offering space and meaning to its adherents, whose decision to sink roots in America and to raise families meant facing hardships and prejudice.

Issei realized that they needed to stake their claim for a future in America with their children. The arrival of picture brides during the first two decades of the twentieth century enabled families to form and initiated the birth of a new generation. Lay and clerical leaders who worked to establish Buddhism in America naturally wanted to pass on their religious tradition.[28]

Bussei Era

Under the aegis of temple life, the second generation gathered to worship and to share life's journey—religious and otherwise. Sunday school and Japanese-language schools served as initial sites of contact with the faith. As they grew older, Nisei Buddhists (also known as Bussei) joined a variety of young people's groups. Through organizations, conferences, and publications, Japanese Americans created their own spaces within Buddhism. The YWBA and the YMBA became the primary vehicles for drawing the Nisei. At the turn of the century, the YMBA consisted of young immigrant men. But by the 1920s and 1930s, the YMBA and the YWBA became Nisei organizations under the guidance of the Reverend Herbert Tansai Terakawa. Separate groups eventually united under the banner of the joint YMWBA and later as the Young Buddhist Association (YBA).[29]

Born and trained in Japan, Terakawa had come to Hawaii in 1917 to serve a church in Hilo; in 1921, he moved to Stockton, California, where he entered Pacific College (University of the Pacific), completing his bachelor's degree in 1924. He then continued his studies at Stanford University. Terakawa's passion for learning fostered excellent English-language skills, a rarity for priests of his generation. A desire and vision to work with young people also set Terakawa apart from his peers. In January 1926, Terakawa presided over a gathering of YMBA representatives from northern and southern California and formed the YMBA League of North America, representing a step in the consolidation of Bussei organizations. On tour in the United States at the time of the meeting, Deputy Sonyu Otani, representing the Lord Abbott of Jodo Shinshu Buddhism in Japan, met with and encouraged Terakawa and other leaders of the newly formed league.[30]

The Young Women's Buddhist Association began in July of the following year at a conference at White's Point in San Pedro, California. During an earlier tour in 1925, Deputy Otani had expressed his hopes of seeing an organization of young women started in the United States and contributed fifty dollars toward that end. Bussei women had already created informal networks as teachers, lay leaders, and volunteers and were the backbone of temple schooling and education. Local meetings among teach-

Young Men's Buddhist Association delegates to the Pan Pacific Conference in Honolulu, Hawaii, July 1930. Rev. Herbert Terakawa is seated in the middle of the first row. (Buddhist Churches of America Archives, San Francisco)

ers expanded in 1924 when women and priests throughout California met at the church in Watsonville. The success of that event prompted more meetings in which leaders met to exchange ideas about educational programming and religious life. Eventually, the North American Federation of the YWBA League formalized the annual gatherings. Fifty-two representatives from the northern, coastal, central, and southern regions met during the summer of 1927.[31]

The formation of the leagues for young men and women started a tradition of conferences that became significant gathering places for Nisei Buddhists. Regional and statewide conferences drew hundreds of participants and enabled Nisei from different parts of the state to meet, develop friendships, and discuss not only their religious faith but also a host of other issues. Some went in search of romance and found it. Others anticipated programs and activities that provided relief from the routine of school and work. The meetings also enabled Nisei from varied backgrounds to socialize. For some residing in rural areas, the meetings represented a chance to see the larger world, including cities like San Francisco or Los Angeles.[32] A Nisei delegate heading to the seventh annual meeting of the YMBA in the spring of 1932 might have traveled by car with fellow Buddhists to the temple in Stockton. Standing in line to register, delegates craned their necks, looking for relatives and friends. Name tags attached and programs in hand, men and women attended an opening service/ceremony and spent the day in a whirlwind of meetings, panels, and roundtable discussions. Official business ended at 5:30 in the afternoon, and hungry participants enjoyed a Chinese banquet dinner, featuring the culinary innovation of chop suey. An oratorical contest generally followed the meal. The second day consisted of more services and meetings, including the election of the next year's leaders. Delegates eagerly anticipated the evening social that capped the two-day affair.[33]

Fred Nitta of the Watsonville Buddhist Church, legendary in Young Buddhist circles for his lifetime support of these groups, got his start at Stockton; he recalled: "As this was my first participation in the state-wide conference where over 1000 devoted young Buddhists of my own age assembled, the spiritual impact upon me was tremendous. I received great inspiration by direct contact with the leaders. . . . The friendly atmosphere created by the fellow young Buddhists from other cities made me feel at home. . . . It really surprised me to see so many capable boys and girls who believe[d] in the same Amida-Buddha as I [did] in the conference."[34] Others must have shared Nitta's sentiments as the group continued to grow; by the end of 1941, paid membership surpassed 4,000.[35] In addition to the social benefits, conferences fostered leadership skills. Host chapters coordinated and oversaw publicity, registration, programming, housing, meals, and budget. An impressive array of subcommittees handled the bulk of the work with minimal supervision. Given the large numbers of Nisei who attended these events, the planning and preparation required considerable effort. Bussei also learned about public relations and about skills needed to bargain for services from local merchants. Equally demanding was the work required of leaders who had to balance the egos of local leaders and clerics, whose status in the community demanded recognition.[36]

Crafting Worldviews

Conferences and temple life not only occupied the energies of the second generation but also allowed them to craft ways of seeing their world and their place in it. Religious faith helped other Bussei cope with the harsh realities of marginalization they encountered. Buddhism influenced the construction and negotiation of Japanese American identities. Like so many other children of immigrants, Nisei spoke about the challenges of living in two worlds and their plight of being a generation "in-between." Masao Kubose, an undergraduate at the University of California at Berkeley, and a leader among Bussei, interpreted the situation not so much as a liability but rather as an opportunity. The "Pacific Era" was dawning, a moment in history in which the rise of the United States and Japan marked a shift in influence from the declining civilization of Europe to the Pacific Rim. A new culture, blending the best of the East and the West, would emerge and set the agenda for world affairs. Although the Pacific Era encompassed much more than events on campus, Kubose made the connection between the unfolding epoch and the opening ceremonies for a new Buddhist student organization.[37]

Kubose's optimism no doubt was buoyed on a crisp September afternoon in 1932, when students, faculty, and administrators gathered at the International House to welcome the Buddhist group on campus. In addressing those present, University president Robert G. Sproul pointed to the inauguration as a sign of the times: "It is a proper place and proper time to have an organization such as yours, because we are facing a new Pacific Era in which the civilization of the East and West must melt together and because our institution is an intellectual center and located on the Pacific Coast." With an official Bussei presence on campus, students could learn about Buddhism, pursue spiritual enlightenment, and harmonize the two great civilizations of Japan and the United States. Kubose, who later entered the priesthood, believed that Nisei had an important role to play in international affairs as cultural bridges between the two leading countries of the Pacific Era. More importantly, Bussei were positioned to make a special contribution because they literally embodied the material riches of the West coupled with the spiritual depth of the East. The Pacific Era appeared to offer a solution to the dilemmas of the second generation.[38]

The idea that the vexations of identity could be the means of improving international relations appealed to Nisei who pondered such matters. For Kubose, the prominence of Buddhists helped secure their place in the United States by introducing the value of their faith to American society. Bussei labored to expand religious mind-sets beyond a strictly Judeo-Christian framework. Hopes for a new epoch, however, went largely unfulfilled. Nisei could do little to halt deteriorating relations between the United States and Japan during the 1930s. Competing imperial visions heavily infused notions of a Pacific Era for elites on both sides of the ocean and eventually culminated in war. More than anything else, Bussei at Berkeley entertained an international perspective in response to the limited opportunities at home. In looking to Asia, Nisei also realized that, despite being raised and educated in the United States, they continued to be defined in foreign terms. It is telling that, given the American birth of the members of the new campus group, the inauguration took place at the International House.

The tenuous nature of Japanese American identity was not lost on Manabu Fukuda. In 1934, as a contributor to the Buddhist journal *Bhratri*, Fukuda painted a bleak picture. By definition, a Nisei was "not an American nor [was] he a Japanese" but an unhappy and depressed person without a country. Unlike Kubose, this writer placed little trust in international relations or nation-states. In looking for answers, however, Fukuda suggested that Japanese Americans could find acceptance in the "Land of Buddha." Fukuda remained vague about what it meant to be a citizen of Buddha, but he implied that status in this country was far better than the other options available to his readers. Buddhism held no magical cures for the woes of Nisei, but it did represent a religious tradition accustomed to life's dilemmas.[39]

Bussei who turned to their faith responded in part to a social context in which their status as the Other severely limited life chances. Overt job discrimination translated into extremely restricted opportunities for meaningful work. A depressed economy made matters worse. Restrictive covenants made it difficult for the few who did secure good jobs to buy homes. Despite the odds, many Issei pushed their children to pursue the American dream. The road to success lay through the schools, and Japanese Americans earned top grades and college degrees from prestigious universities in many fields but to little or no avail. Hard work, playing by the rules, and investment in education guaranteed nothing. Many met with disappointment and frustration, even as desire and ambition remained unabated. One student counseled peers to keep matters in perspective: "The Bussei must remember that no amount of money or fame can win him happiness unless he has filled a natural niche in civilization. He must strive to better himself continuously to benefit both he and society. . . . It is good and well to enlarge our scope of learning through the high schools and universities, but religion must not be of secondary significance. . . . moral training is necessary to enable man to live at peace with himself."[40]

While Bussei encouraged each other not to lose sight of religion in the quest for material security or educational achievement, Takeo Yamanaka of West Los Angeles reminded others that Buddhist faith in particular could sustain the second generation. Yamanaka recognized that missionaries and Japanese American Christians could give the impression that being Protestant somehow made one more fit for life in the United States: "I once heard a person say, that only a real Christian, can be a true American. If that were so, then we Busseis couldn't be true Americans, could we? But is it true? Just because I don't happen to be a Christian, can you say that I am not a true American? We may be referred to the Constitution of the United States, and find written there, the guarantee that an American citizen, may worship whatever religion he chooses." By invoking the U.S. Constitution, Yamanaka called on his rights to exercise freedom of religion. As an American, he had indeed learned his lessons well. Prudence may have dictated that Buddhists be sensitive to their surroundings, but he wanted to dispel the notion that Christians possessed a greater claim to American identity. In fact, Yamanaka urged the spread of the faith since it so ably served Japanese Americans and any others who became Buddhists. Accordingly, Bussei could state without hesitation that "a real Buddhist, can be, a true American!"[41] In the process of constructing worldviews, many Buddhists realized that ignorance and misconceptions often cast their faith in an unfavorable light. The religious currents of the day, moreover, clearly favored Nisei counterparts who professed a Christian faith. Despite this, Bussei believed that their tradition offered meaning and purpose.

Although religion at times divided Nikkei communities, Christians and Buddhists shared not only a common ancestry but also an existence in which racial concerns often overshadowed other important distinctions. It is not surprising, then, that Buddhist-sponsored conferences and publications acted as forums for social and cultural issues that women and men saw as part of their identities as Bussei and as second-generation Japanese Americans. In the years before World War II, the Buddhist organization at the University of California produced a semiannual journal, the *Berkeley Bussei*. Its editors informed readers that they would find articles "dealing with not only Buddhism, but for the Niseis in general" and explained the rationale for their more inclusive approach:

> Another major endeavor of this issue will be to interpret for you the nature of the dilemma facing the Nisei and the possible solution of these problems, as viewed by contemporary Nisei thinkers and writers . . . since the Busseis are a substantial element within the minority called the Niseis, it is more than natural that the concern of the second generation Japanese in the United States should be considered of primary importance to us, and that any defining of their problems would be of material benefit to all of us as Niseis.[42]

Writers most frequently tackled issues of identity, expressing frustration over the second-class status of the Nisei in the United States. In seeking full recognition as Americans, the second generation wanted access to opportunities and a chance to enjoy a quality of life befitting citizens. Instead, the imprint of racial discrimination marred the experiences of men and women who simply desired that their racial-ethnic status not be held against them. Again and again, voices cried out for fair play and the opportunity to compete on equal terms. More than adolescent musings, the emphasis on identity spoke directly to the quality of life that these Americans could hope for in their native land.

While Nisei could not always control life circumstances, Florence Funakoshi urged the readers of *Sangha,* a Buddhist magazine, to be forceful and clear about who they were, especially in contexts that could perpetuate damaging stereotypes. Funakoshi sketched out a hypothetical but familiar scenario to illustrate her point: a young Nikkei in Los Angeles, gazing out of a streetcar at the end of a day, felt the nudge of an elbow. Turning his head, John Nisei discovered an elderly woman sitting next to him who inquired: "I beg your pardon, sir, are you a Japanese or a Chinese?" John answered: "Neither, m'am, I am an AMERICAN!" To dispel misconceptions, public education extended beyond the classroom and into the streets. Funakoshi added: "whether we be farmers, fruit-stand workers, students, or the envious holders of a white collar job . . . however large or small our contacts may be, like the boy on the streetcar, we must make them realize, 'We, too are Americans.'"[43] Historian Eileen Tamura has shown that the stress on American identity had much more to do with issues of access than with notions of wholesale assimilation.[44] Rather than becoming something they were not (European Americans), many members of the second generation claimed their status as Americans as a means of opening doors shut on the basis of their being "Japanese." "Americanizers" and casual observers alike mistakenly viewed outward signs of acculturation like English-language ability and interest in popular culture as a blanket attempt to shed one culture for another.[45] Kiyo Nogami, for one, doubted whether such shedding was even possible given the racial divisions in American society. Nogami, an Alameda Bussei, nevertheless knew that racial politics and power relations mattered: "In a sense, the old saying— 'In Rome, live as the Romans do', is applicable."[46] References to Rome and empire may indeed have captured the feelings of Nikkei in America who held the status of citizen but remained on the fringes of society.

According to George Muramoto of the San Francisco YMBA, Nisei needed to underscore the "peculiar" position that they occupied in the United States. In effect, Muramoto suggested that Nisei opt for a balanced identity in which constituent elements complemented instead of canceled each other out: "Together with our loyalty to America . . . we must not forget the true identity of ourselves. . . . Our value to the American public as American Citizens rests wholly in the ever present consciousness that we are Japanese. . . . Assimilation does not necessarily mean that we must lose our racial integrity." Muramoto saw racial consciousness as a key to the future of Japanese America. By affirming who they were and using their particularity to improve relations at home and abroad, the second generation could make a contribution to society in ways that affirmed their heritage.[47] While Muramoto recommended an integrated identity, James Sakoda, a student at the University of California at Berkeley, commented on the downside of forgetting one's roots. Classmate Dick Kobayashi's recurring dream/nightmare was the subject of Sakoda's paper for an abnormal psychology class as well as an article directed to his Nisei readership. As Kobayashi drifted off to sleep, he saw himself as a hermit crab that frantically moved its arms but could not get off the ocean floor. Worn out from the futile attempts to move, Kobayashi gave up; at that point, a large fish appeared with "frightful eyes and a big mouth. . . . I think the fish is going to gobble me up, and I scream. I wake up and find myself sweating down my back."[48] Dick Kobayashi may not have appreciated being on display, but Sakoda apparently felt no qualms in subjecting his classmate to analysis. Sakoda recalled that Kobayashi had been quite popular among his European-American friends, even living with them in a college housing cooperative. He did not associate with other Nisei and had expressed contempt for "those damn Japs, huddling together like cattles [*sic*]." Using his psychoanalytic skills, Sakoda suggested that the big fish represented white Americans. Kobayashi tried to imitate them but could not, since he was a crab and carried on his back his Japanese American heritage and identity. The crab that apparently had been able to swim to some degree at an earlier point could now no longer move. This immobility fit nicely with the fact that, after graduation, Kobayashi could not find work because of his racial background. He drifted from job to job as a domestic: "He must have clung desperately to the thought that America wouldn't let him down and that he wouldn't depend on the Japs, but his present job was offered by one of his father's friends. His few friends now were mostly Japanese."[49] Whether this event actually took place is not clear, although no reference was made to the account as fictional. While Sakoda's interpretation of Kobayashi's life certainly said as much as (or perhaps more) than the dream itself, it is clear that the reading sent a message stressing the importance of remembering one's racial-ethnic identity.

For all their efforts to negotiate the complexities of being Japanese American, Bussei ran into difficulties as tensions mounted between the United States and Japan during the 1930s. An unwillingness by most Americans to distinguish between Japan and Japanese Americans placed an extraordinary burden on Nisei as the two nations headed down a collision course. Among Nikkei themselves, Bussei felt the considerable added pressure of being religious outsiders. Japanese American Christians, on the other hand, had access to resources and support networks as part of larger Protestant denominations. As U.S.-Japanese relations soured, Buddhism came under increasing attack and suspicion for its connection to things Japanese. The efforts by Buddhist leaders over the years to explain and to educate the larger public about things religious and racial had fallen largely on deaf ears. Aware of the threatening clouds on the horizon, members of the YBA repeated their loyalty to the United States in a public statement during the summer of 1941: "Today we find ourselves in a difficult role of trying to strengthen the foundation of our religion," declared YBA president Manabu Fukuda, "and at the same time make our Occidental friends realize that the spirit of Buddhism shall in no way conflict with the ideals of the American Democracy and the American way of living." In an effort to dispel suspicion, leaders of the YBA encouraged its members to do their part as patriotic Americans.[50]

As war approached, loyalty and identity emerged as unavoidable issues within Japanese American Buddhism. As ethnic institutions, however, temples had never been limited strictly to religious concerns. Buddhism played a role in the lives of the Nikkei that went far beyond the numbers registered on membership roles or in statistical percentages. Conferences, journals, and campus groups helped Bussei to filter the ambiguities of being Japanese American through the lens of their religious tradition. Shared journeys included a common ancestry, immigrant parents, and the harsh realities of prejudice and racial discrimination. Bussei gravitated toward temple life because it helped them to negotiate their times and to construct their identities as Japanese Americans. Although religion did not supply easy answers, Buddhist belief did give the second generation a meaningful way of seeing the world and their place in it.

Protestant Foundations

Protestant beginnings among the Japanese in California, like Buddhism, centered around social services for newly arrived immigrants. Unlike Buddhists, however, Issei Christians moved within the religious contexts of American Protestant home missions, even as the first generation labored to establish their own churches. The ties to missionaries gave Issei access to a cultural capital that Buddhist counterparts did not enjoy but also entailed operating within a paternalistic institutional setting that dated to the very founding of the immigrant community. Japanese who ventured to the United States discovered Protestant missions that offered English-language classes, lodging, job information, and referrals. Early converts like Kanichi Miyama and Kumataro Nonaka had come to America in 1875 and had been baptized by the Reverend Otis Gibson of the Chinese Methodist Episcopal Mission. Living and meeting in the dark and damp basement of the Chinese mission, student laborers gathered by candlelight for Bible study; when the candles went out, they slept in hastily constructed bunks that replicated the steerage accommodations Issei had endured across the Pacific. From those humble beginnings, Miyama, Nonaka, and other Christians founded in October 1877 the Gospel Society, an important group for the Japanese that later spawned similar organizations across several Protestant denominations.[51]

In turn, Gospel Societies led to the formation of churches beginning with the First Japanese Presbyterian Church of San Francisco, organized on 16 May 1885. By 1919, the United Church of Christ claimed twelve congregations located in Japanese American communities ranging from the Bay Area to San Diego. The northern branch of the Methodist Episcopal Church had fifteen Japanese churches by the time of exclusion in 1924 and, by 1940, added another eight churches to reach a total of twenty-three. Thirteen Presbyterian and eight American Baptist congregations had been established throughout the state at the time of Pearl Harbor. Donald Fujiyoshi's study of Los Angeles in 1942 listed forty-six churches in ten southern California counties. Protestant groups such as the YM/WCA and the Salvation Army also worked among the Japanese.[52]

While linked to denominational structures, immigrant churches were Japanese American organizations with a high degree of ownership by their members and were deeply rooted within the larger racial-ethnic community. According to Y. Caspar Horikoshi of the Wesley United Methodist Church in San Jose, "the Japanese Christian churches were not established as a separate institution. They were born out of the struggles of Japanese communities, as they faced many problems. The history of the Christian churches parallels the history of the Japanese people in this country."[53] A recent historical study of the Christian churches in Sacramento has suggested that the churches sought to be free from mission funding as soon as possible. Given the strains of immigrant life, not all of the churches managed to gain full control over their budgets, but financial independence

remained the goal. Management and leadership of the churches fell largely to Japanese Americans because of culture and language—two factors
that reinforced racial-ethnic foundations. Interestingly, attempts after the
war to integrate the churches with other local congregations failed, even
though language posed a lesser issue. The identification of the churches
as Japanese American continued over the years.[54] According to Ryo Yoshida's research, some immigrants initially may have been attracted to Christianity as a means of gaining acceptance in the United States. Missionaries in Japan had painted a picture of America as a Christian nation in which
the "brotherhood of man" reigned supreme. Those who arrived on these
shores, however, often found a different America. Discrimination and social division actually promoted autonomy and expressions of faith that
heightened a sense of race and ancestry. Based on their experiences in the
United States and given the ties to their homeland, many Issei Christians,
like other immigrants, saw their nationalism toward Japan as quite compatible with their faith.[55]

The strong identification of immigrant churches as Japanese American
institutions could complicate denominational relationships and efforts
toward self-determination. Underscoring issues of power, Issei, denied
naturalization rights and marginalized in other ways, relied on a missionary "defense" to represent their concerns. Unfortunately, immigrants discovered that, beyond issues of immigration and exclusion, most Protestant patrons did little to critique the exploitation of Japanese labor or to
challenge seriously the daily realities of racial discrimination. Moreover,
many missionaries continued to defend the United States as a Christian
nation whose manifest destiny included global supremacy.[56] Deference paid
to missionaries by Japanese American Christians reflected their understanding of their relationship to Christ in hierarchical terms: as servants to a
master. In that regard, missionaries often took on the role of devoted "parents" who cared for their "children." In their study of Asian American
churches, Michael Angevine and Ryo Yoshida have suggested that Japanese American Christians in the early 1900s struggled to develop their own
sense of identity but did so within the confines of a paternalistic nineteenth-
century American Protestantism. The difficulty that Japanese American
Christians had in separating their own efforts toward agency from their
loyalties to missionaries could create situations that pitted one impulse
against the other. In 1914, for instance, the formation of the San Francisco
Japanese Church of Christ, a merger of the Congregational and Presbyterian churches, signaled an important step in Issei efforts to create an independent Japanese American denomination. At a special session meeting on

17 November 1914, discussion centered on separating the work of the Japanese YMCA from the Church of Christ—a move to loosen missionary ties. The entire body, with the exception of Presbyterian missionary Ernest A. Sturge, voted in favor of the measure. On recognizing Sturge's objections (the YMCA came under his care), the session reversed itself, leaving the connection between the church and the YMCA intact.[57]

Nevertheless, Japanese American Protestants continued to press for their own agenda within and across denominations, and the formation of federations of immigrant congregations represented an important development. In 1910, Nikkei leaders founded the Northern California Japanese Christian Church Federation (NCJCCF) "to keep up the morale of the community due to incidents of racial prejudice and persecution in business, school and work." The federation represented a move to address concerns that went beyond the boundaries of denominations and that recognized the common bonds of faith as well as Japanese American identity. The NCJCCF sponsored speakers, coordinated events and relationships between churches, and also explicitly included in its mission the education of the Nisei. The northern California segment of the Young People's Christian Conference (YPCC) found staunch support from the NCJCCF.[58] Churches in southern California also joined forces. Sixteen parishes in the greater Los Angeles area formed the Southern California Church Federation, Japanese American, in 1910, the same year as their northern counterparts. The federation's programs included a successful Christian summer school on Terminal Island that ran from 1932 until the outbreak of World War II. The churches believed strongly in serving the racial-ethnic community, and the southern California group organized a credit union, social center, and an orphanage.[59] In addition to federations that crossed denominational lines, Japanese American churches within the same denomination formed coalitions. The Japanese Presbyterian Conference (JPC), still operative today, created a lasting and important form of identification for Nikkei Presbyterians. Congregations often felt much more connected to and invested in the JPC than to their denomination.[60]

Nisei Structures

In laboring to build Japanese American churches, Issei leaders ministered to the needs of two generations. Nisei were the future of the churches, and immigrants encouraged their children to take part in the life of the congregation. The second generation inherited from their parents a desire to practice a brand of Christianity that spoke to their specific needs as a racial-

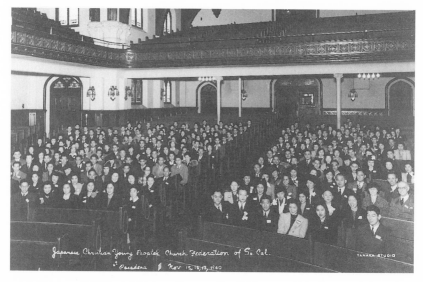

The Japanese Christian Young People's Church Federation of Southern California, Pasadena, California, November 1940. (Shades of L.A. Collection/Los Angeles Public Library)

ethnic group and as a generation. Toward that end, American-born Japanese from three San Francisco churches—First Reformed, Pine Methodist, and Japanese Church of Christ—gathered on the evening of 14 May 1933 to hold an English-language service run entirely by Nisei. The event illustrated the needs of the younger generation that were not being met by immigrant contexts of worship. The issue of language and socialization required Issei and Nisei to reconsider existing arrangements. The Young People's Union Church (YPUC) came as a response to those circumstances and emphasized ministry to and by the second generation. Koji Murata, who four years later would become the first ordained Nisei elder at the Church of Christ, and his colleagues Tad Fujita and Dave Tatsuno played active roles in the YPUC. Like many of those who joined them for fellowship and services, Murata, Fujita, and Tatsuno served as key leaders in the morning Sunday school programs at their respective churches. As night fell over the city, Nisei made their way to the parlor of the Sturge Memorial Building on Post Street for evening worship and fellowship. In effect, the Young People's Union Church served as a Nisei church. In addition to formal services, the YPUC put together popular artistic productions that raised funds and increased the visibility of second-generation Christians in church networks and in San Francisco's Japantown. The *Nichibei Shim-bun* (Japanese American News) reported that approximately thirty Nisei comprised the initial nucleus for the YPUC. Although an outbreak of infantile paralysis (poliomyelitis) suspended services for a stretch in the summer of 1934, the group apparently continued to meet in the years that followed.[61] To the south, in Los Angeles, the Centenary Methodist Church sponsored programs and activities geared to the second generation and in 1937 had the resources to hire the Reverend Lester Suzuki and his wife, Seda.[62] Nisei themselves, the Suzukis brought understanding, stability, and fostered growth. That the second generation operated like a church within a church was reflected even in the changes within the church newsletter, the *Japanese Methodist Episcopal Church Weekly News*. Until 1935, only the Japanese language appeared in the weekly publication; but then the first traces of the English language emerged in a small portion of a page dedicated to Nisei news and announcements. By March 1937, English had taken over about one page of the two-page layout, occasionally exceeding the space devoted to Japanese. Starting in January 1939, the Nisei published their own newsletter, *The Methodist Voice,* on two full legal-sized pages.[63]

The growth and dynamism of second-generation ministry depended heavily on the dedication and maturation of clerical and lay leaders who no doubt took some cues from their elders. The Suzukis, who received only thirty dollars per month, did not see their salary increase during their entire tenure of service from 1937 until the time of forced removal in 1942. In fact, a closer reading of the newsletters indicates that the salary did not always get paid. The treasurer's report for the month ending 31 March 1938 recorded that only $14.50 of the associate pastor's salary had been paid for March.[64] Occasional annual fiscal reports seemed to indicate that expenses had been met, but it must have taken creative bookkeeping and a credit line to make ends meet for the pastor and his family. Lester and Seda Suzuki recalled that those were indeed lean days. "We felt sorry, at times, not so much for ourselves, but because we didn't have much to give to our girls," Seda Suzuki said, "but most of the time, we didn't think about it too much. I guess we just expected that it was supposed to be that way."[65]

In addition to the work of local churches, a national religious organization called the Japanese Student Christian Association in North America (JSCA) had also begun to address the needs of the second generation. Although founded in 1924 to target students from Japan in the United States, the JSCA recognized an affinity between those from Japan and Japanese Americans not only in terms of ancestry but because other Americans often confused the two groups. The organization's publications and activities created a forum and framework that proved important in assessing the situation of the Nisei. Based in New York City, the JSCA grew out of the Student Volunteer Movement and was affiliated with the Friendly Relations Committee of the YMCA. Founded by the well-known church leader John R. Mott, the committee promoted the development of Christian character among foreign students. The JSCA shared office space with the committee at 347 Madison Avenue in New York City and had three major goals: "(1) to unite all Japanese, especially Christian, students and to cultivate an organized effort; (2) to promote growth of Christian character and fellowship among its members and to spread the Christian way of life among Japanese students in America; (3) to stimulate capacity for service and render needed services for the general welfare of Japanese students in America." The JSCA organized chapters on many college campuses throughout the country and also in Canada.[66] Students enjoyed a range of services, including assistance in travel, lodging, mail service, employment searches, and counseling. Members could also borrow materials from a circulating library, and good writers might even earn some extra spending money through an essay contest.[67]

Publications connected students to one another and provided an outlet for leadership and members to share news and voice their concerns. The *Japanese Student Bulletin* served as the main source of information, beginning its run with the founding of the group until funding problems shut it down in 1940.[68] Circulation figures in 1932 topped 3,000 despite periodic changes in publication formats and frequency.[69] In its coverage, the *Bulletin* clearly indicated a concern for and inclusion of the Nisei. American-born Japanese contributed articles, held offices, and found institutional support from the JSCA. In fact, Hideo Hashimoto, then a Nisei at the Union Theological Seminary in New York, became the president of the organization during the 1938–39 academic year. Hashimoto recalled his initial ambivalence toward his election: "In due time I was nominated, elected, and served as President of the Japanese Student Christian Association (JSCA). . . . Being a native born American, I hesitated to take the position or even to belong to the organization." Toru Matsumoto, the general secretary, was also a Union graduate; he convinced his classmate to accept the post. Perhaps to sweeten the offer, Matsumoto arranged to have Hashimoto, an active participant in the world ecumenical movement, attend a major conference in Amsterdam, the Netherlands.[70]

The JSCA welcomed Nisei involvement and viewed the second generation as an important part of its constituency despite the differences between second-generation and international students. The linking of Japanese and Japanese American students reflected a larger reality in which the fate of the immigrant community often rose and fell with events overseas. A JSCA editorial in December 1926 claimed the allegiance of and responsibility for the Nisei: "the problems of the second generation Japanese on the Pacific Coast are becoming more acute every year and the JSCA, having many second generation in its membership, can do worthy service toward their solution by devoting a special section of the national movement for this important work." A year later, the JSCA had established a field secretary and office in Los Angeles to work specifically with the Nisei. The goals of the field office were to strengthen the overall work of the JSCA on the Pacific Coast, establish a vocational bureau, conduct research, and produce a magazine, the *JSCA Pacific Coast Echoes,* for the second generation.[71]

Roy Akagi, the leading figure within the JSCA during his time as general secretary (1924–29), kept the Nisei on the organization's agenda. Born in Japan, Akagi had immigrated to the United States as a teenager with his family, attending Alameda High School in San Francisco's Bay Area.[72] As a student of history, Akagi earned an array of degrees and awards at the most prestigious universities in America: the University of California at Berkeley (B.A.); the University of Chicago (M.A.); Harvard University (fellowship); and the University of Pennsylvania (Ph.D.). Akagi often lectured about the Japanese in America and about the second-generation situation as he traveled throughout the country as the representative of the JSCA. His vision not only included the establishment of a West Coast branch; Akagi also took a leave as general secretary to personally oversee the creation of the office in Los Angeles.[73] Several years earlier, during the winter vacations of 1924 and 1925, Akagi met with students in Asilomar, California, to discuss the second-generation "problem." The JSCA named Ruby Hirose of the University of Washington, Francis Hayashi and Kazuo Kawai of Stanford University, George Kaneko of the California Institute of Technology, and Frank Nakamura of Occidental College to work with Akagi toward the publication of a pamphlet. In June 1926, the JSCA began distributing a thirty-nine-page booklet, *The Second Generation Problem,* that presented the dilemma facing the Nisei: "Much has been talked about and a great deal of ink has been spilled over this question, but little is yet accomplished, or being accomplished, in providing practical plans. . . . What follows is . . . an attempt to present some definite plans and suggestions to meet their needs, especially from the point of view of the second generation themselves." In the simplest terms, the Nisei faced the "problem" of maladjustment, in which they found only qualified acceptance within both the immigrant ethnic community and in the larger American society. As men and women without a country, where did they belong?[74]

Although the authors did not ultimately answer the vexing questions, they did offer an early explication of the issues—significant in terms of its recognition and attempt to deal comprehensively with the "problem." Some blame lay with the United States, which had barred further immigration, denied naturalization rights, blocked land ownership, and even sought to strip the Nisei of their citizenship. America had been anything but a hospitable place for Japanese; as *The Second Generation Problem* argues, "America is thus forcing the race question, no matter what the explanation may be on her part. . . ." The issue of race, moreover, distinguished the plight of the Nisei from other second-generation groups that had struggled in adjusting to life in America. The committee clearly recognized that fellow Americans would continue to see the Nisei as Japanese because of skin color and other physical features.[75] In laying out its key principles, or "points of view," the committee included that being of Japanese ancestry "both outward and inward" should be a source of pride and be fully integrated into the fabric of their American citizenship. And yet, as Americans, the Nisei needed to cast their lot with the United States and to fight for respect and acceptance as Americans in the fullest sense. In keeping with the JSCA vision, the group also argued for a broader perspective that would include national and international dimensions. As a generation, the Nisei needed to find their own solutions since, "heretofore, the first generation [has] . . . tried to force their interests and ideas and conclusions over the second generation."[76]

Nevertheless, American-born Japanese needed to realize that their future in America was intimately tied to the Issei; as such, the two generations had to work together. Dinners, fellowship opportunities, home education, questionnaires, and literature/publicity could all be employed to improve relations. Churches in particular allowed the Issei and the Nisei to meet on common ground. Any viable solutions to the "problem" had to take into account the place that the Nisei would occupy within the immigrant context. In the same way, education, personal contacts, interracial groups, and knowing about Japanese culture could help build positive ties to other Americans. In essence, the pamphlet stressed the familiar role of a bridge. Because of the limits they faced in belonging to either group, the second generation as bridges not only contributed to better relations between the two, but also benefited in finding their place in America—namely, in the middle, as conduits of culture and understanding.[77]

In addressing issues such as vocation, education, and religion, Akagi and the committee thoughtfully offered the second generation advice and strategies for navigating the tricky waters of the future. Not surprisingly, jobs and careers always ranked high among the concerns, and the committee recommended an employment bureau to help place students following graduation. An education geared toward agriculture and to trades applicable to the ethnic community made sense during tough economic times exacerbated by race prejudice. Raising funding for student scholarships and endowing chairs in Japanese studies at American colleges offered ways in which Nisei could take greater control of their education. Part of that education included physical activity, and organizations like the YWCA and YMCA provided healthy environments that in turn fostered connections with other "Y's."[78] In the area of values and principles for living, the pamphlet raised the issue of religion as a means to offset the "materialistic tendency of the day, [and] the pioneers of tomorrow should experience spiritual awakening and revaluation of life." The study highlighted the role of junior or English-language congregations and young people's societies. Church socials, retreats, conferences, and even music provided ways that the churches could connect with the second generation.

Given the origins of the organization, it is not surprising that the JSCA included religion. In its presentation, however, the committee spoke to issues that affected all Nisei rather than simply Christians. Religious faith might provide insight and meaning, but it did not erase the issues that touched the lives of Nisei, regardless of their religious persuasion. In this way, the pamphlet and the JSCA served the larger concerns of the Japanese in America, whether they happened to be Buddhist or Christian, foreign- or American-born. That flexibility and sensitivity opened up an avenue for the Nisei to take part in the work of a group that committed itself to their betterment. The ideas presented in the pamphlet represented a thoughtful assessment of the social context of Nisei and also anticipated much of the discussion that would surface during the 1930s, when more of the second generation came of age.

As the JSCA got underway in New York City in the mid-1920s, another group drew Nisei Christians throughout California under the banner of the Young People's Christian Conference (YPCC). With direct ties to immigrant churches, the YPCC influenced its members primarily through local and regional conferences and experienced its peak years during the late 1930s and the early 1940s. The YPCC concentrated its work almost exclusively on the Nisei, and its meetings enabled the second generation to meet and discuss issues that they faced together as Japanese Americans and as Christians. The origins of the YPCC in many ways were linked to the life of Tokyo-born pastor the Reverend Suzunosuke Kato. After completing theological studies at Butler University in Indianapolis, Kato settled in Berkeley, California, as the pastor of the Japanese Christian Church (Disciples of Christ) in 1923. Kato began his ministry at age thirty; as a relatively young minister, he directed much of his concern and energy to the second generation. On 30 September 1925, he launched the Fellowship Circle, a ministry for college students who attended the University of California at Berkeley. Less than a month later, on 24–25 October, the Fellowship Circle's first conference took place at the Japanese Methodist Episcopal Church in San Francisco. The registration brochure invited delegates from all parts of the state over the age of fifteen to participate.[79] Unfortunately, the Reverend Kato did not live long enough to see the growth and success of the YPCC. He succumbed to tuberculosis on 28 August 1926 in Los Angeles, where he had gone for the warmer and drier climate. More than 500 students mourned his loss at the memorial held for him at the University Christian Church in Berkeley. In memory of Kato, Nikkei Christians started a scholarship fund in 1929 to help support Japanese American students entering the ministry. More than the scholarship, though, Kato's legacy lived on through the YPCC, which not only spread throughout California and the West Coast but continued during the war and enjoyed a strong postwar history among younger Nisei and older Sansei.[80]

A key contribution of the YPCC came through its development of leadership skills as Nisei worked together to host conferences, and—unlike Issei organizations—two women held the highest office for the first five years of the conference. Margaret Tann served as chair in 1925 and 1926; Sumile Morishita guided the YPCC for the years 1927–29. After finishing her B.A. at the University of California (1927), Morishita matriculated at the Pacific School of Religion, obtaining an M.A. in religion (1929) and a Bachelor of Divinity degree (1930). Freshly minted degrees in hand, Morishita accepted the post of director of the young people's division of the Methodist Episcopal Church in northern California. She spoke extensively at churches and at conferences and continued as an active leader in the area until she set sail for Japan in the fall of 1934, where she went to teach and serve.[81] The organization aimed to raise Christian leaders who could then strengthen their local churches. Tad Fujita and Dave Tatsuno recalled that organizing the conferences took a great deal of effort and gave those in charge a chance to hone their administrative and organizational skills and to become leaders who could serve the broader Japanese American community.[82] Because of the size and location of the events, Nisei needed to handle arrangements outside Japanese America, since most delegates stayed in private homes, including those of European Americans. Intergenerational relations could also be delicate, and leaders needed to exercise diplomacy in choosing which merchants to patronize and deciding how local clergy and active laity might participate.

Aside from the leaders, the delegates attended interregional and local gatherings and, in so doing, accomplished another goal of the group: to unite spiritual forces. In short, the YPCC wanted to bring second-generation believers together so that their interaction could foster the spread of "deeper Christ-like living." Grace Kaneya, who attended the 1938 northern California meeting, stated: "Faith is a necessity in our everyday Christian living. For with faith, we, as Christians, are able to face the huge obstacles of our chaotic life with an optimistic attitude. It gives us the strength, the power, and the hope in the face of un-Christian forces at work in the world today." Kaneya alluded to Hitler, Mussolini, and the events taking place in Europe that boded ill for the future. Faith did not simply mean personal salvation; it also enabled Nisei to filter their daily challenges through their beliefs. On the other side of the world—but much closer to home—Bill Hata's editorial in the conference compendium addressed the Sino-Japanese War. Hata recognized the growing inability of peoples and nations in resolving conflicts peacefully and called on his fellow Nisei to spread the gospel: "We, as the rising generation, can do much toward the establishment of peace among the nations of the world. We must spread our convictions of Christianity through channels of service under the banner of the cross."[83]

As the 1930s drew to a close, racial tensions at home, in Asia, and in Europe weighed on the minds of Nisei who sought to make sense of their world in light of their commitments to Christianity. At the 1939 YPCC gathering, the delegates participated in a symposium. The program guide listed several themes that had been discussed and debated. Under the heading of civic issues, conveners asked: What should the Christian attitude be toward citizenship? Is patriotism to one's country a really great quality? Is the Japanese American Citizens' League really necessary? Desirable? In the same way, conferees raised thoughtful and revealing questions about race. Moderators pushed the audience to ask whether race should and/or did make a material difference in their attitudes toward people and whether racial antagonism operated as an inherent element of human nature. In responding to the reality of race prejudice in their lives, the conferees talked strategy—how to defend oneself, whether there should be retaliation, and how much good, realistically, was education in diffusing racial discrimination. Interestingly, the organizers of the session asked the delegates to turn the question of race on themselves. What attitudes did they hold, and should their experience on the receiving end of discrimination act as a deterrent toward exhibiting the same behavior toward others?[84]

Unfortunately, the conference program did not list the answers, but the questions indicated something of the thought processes at work. The Sino-Japanese War, citizenship and loyalty, and race prejudice represented important concerns for American-born Japanese; and, in that respect, it is understandable that these subjects came up when Nisei Christians sat together at conference tables. As they came of age, the second generation faced a troubled world at home and abroad, and their connections to these events and realities surely prompted many more questions than answers. Michael Yoshii has suggested that the YPCC reflected the development of a "vocational consciousness" in which this generation sought to assess their place in history and link this to a sense of Christian vocation.[85]

Deciphering their times did not prove to be an easy task, and many Nisei found in the Christian churches a place to gather with other second-generation men and women who shared much in common, including a basic worldview derived from Protestant Christianity. American-born Japanese undoubtedly associated and joined groups like the Young People's Union Church or the JSCA for other reasons, but the meetings offered an opportunity for people to come together as Japanese Americans. That fact touched almost everything about the process, from standing in line to register to the evening socials that concluded many conferences. Though neither completely nor in every way, the churches reinforced a sense of racial-ethnic identity that undermined any simple notion of assimilation to American society. Nisei had few doubts about their adherence to a Christianity rooted in Japanese America. True equality did not conform to their experience on Sunday morning or any other day of the week. Most Nisei, however, probably spent little time thinking of such matters. They had too much to do among themselves. In those quiet moments, though, some of the more reflective among the second generation must have thought that full fellowship and acceptance should be part of worshiping the same God.

Common Ground

How second-generation Buddhist and Protestants negotiated their times provides insights into the issues of immigration, race/ethnicity, and religion. The stories of Nisei contribute to a more nuanced understanding of the migration process, working against monolithic portrayals that conceal the differences that existed within immigrant groups and between generations. Japanese Americans, moreover, remind us that some immigrants, by virtue of race, chose from a fundamentally different set of ethnic options that left them a marked people. Despite its dynamic and constructed nature, race nevertheless proved to be an enduring element of difference. That difference extended even to those who stood under the umbrella of shared faith, thus complicating religious affiliation in America. While Bussei were obvious outsiders, Nisei Christians only peripherally benefited from the power and currency of Protestantism within American culture and society.

In serving Japanese American communities, temples and churches played a role in the lives of Nikkei that went far beyond the numbers registered on membership roles or in statistical percentages. Religious institutions offered a form of community to Issei and Nisei alike. Even in their youth, the second generation encountered the harsh realities of being racial-ethnic minorities, and some viewed their experiences through the lens of their faith. Others found in their religion a space to socialize, make friends, and wrestle with the issues of the day. Despite their differences, Buddhists and Christians shared common ground in being second-generation Japanese Americans, and both groups contributed to a vibrant Nisei subculture that emerged during the interwar years.

MAKING THE HEADLINES

With another three o'clock deadline unmercifully approaching, Togo Tanaka, the English-language editor of the *Rafu Shimpo* (Los Angeles Japanese Daily News), stepped out of his cubbyhole and took a breather from the hot and cramped pressroom. If still quite warm, the sidewalk outside offered a break from the noise. From his vantage point in Little Tokyo, Tanaka surveyed the scene that often appeared in the pages of the paper—a Japanese American community in motion. Keeping up with the Nikkei of southern California during the late 1930s challenged the staff of the *Rafu Shimpo* on a daily basis.[1] Many Nisei who read the rumpled newspapers lying on the coffee table quickly scanned the pages for English-language text. Familiar notices appeared for upcoming events at Buddhist temples and Christian churches. Announcements heralded the academic accomplishments of students. The papers chronicled a Nisei subculture in full bloom, one that uniquely spoke to their situation.

Throughout the years prior to World War II, coverage of racial issues pervaded the English-language sections of the Japanese immigrant press. The newspapers reflected as well as influenced the process by which the Nisei defined themselves as individuals and as a generation. Tanaka recognized that as these men and women came of age, they would have to grapple with what it meant to be Americans of Japanese ancestry. In examining newspapers from this period, at least three general themes emerge. First of all, in their presentation of race prejudice, many journalists advocated a "racial responsibility" in which the burden of change rested largely on the shoulders of the Nisei. Initiative and hard work would pave the way toward greater acceptance. Given this stance of responsibility, it is not surprising that the institutional aspects of racism received little attention. A second area highlighted the dynamics of race in personal relationships—

namely, dating and marriage. In this sphere, the papers issued a call for "racial solidarity." Tuned in to pressures from within the ethnic community and from society at large, the press advised its readers to stay within Japanese America. Celebratory wedding announcements of Nisei couples and stories of interracial misfortune spoke to the virtues of honoring racial-ethnic ties. The third theme moved from the personal to the international as those in the pressrooms encountered the racial politics set into motion by the outbreak of the Sino-Japanese War in 1937. The English-language staffs chartered a course between Issei support of Japan and general American sympathy for China. Largely skirting the issue of the war itself, most Nisei journalists focused on what they viewed as misleading pro-Chinese propaganda and cast Japanese Americans as suffering from "racial victimization."

The themes of racial responsibility, racial solidarity, and racial victimization are admittedly selective, but they offer insights into how the newspapers responded to the racially subordinate position of Nisei in America.[2] The press's coverage, moreover, documents the highly contextual nature of "race" in the lives of Japanese Americans. An effort is made to counter the tendency to view race in undifferentiated terms that mask as well as mystify the role that race has played in American history. Instead, the emphasis is on understanding how racial politics translated into specific historical settings. As the work of journalists suggests, incidents of race prejudice, for instance, elicited quite different responses from the second generation than did the role of race in dating and marriage relationships. International events tied to Japan's imperialistic designs, moreover, strained intergenerational relations and those between Nikkei and their fellow Americans. Within each of the three themes, individual experiences of Nisei varied considerably. Second-generation Japanese Americans in California maturing during the interwar years consciously embraced and had imposed on them distinctive racial markers. The ethnic press provides glimpses of how Nisei negotiated these various sets of relations and contexts.

As part of the ethnic press in the United States, Japanese American newspapers represent an invaluable documentary source that provides the reader with a wide-ranging overview of the life of a given community. As Sally Miller has pointed out, the ethnic press expressed a group's values, heritage, and changing sense of identity. The newspapers also served an educational function for immigrants, helping them to adjust to a new life as well as socializing them within the socioeconomic contexts of their time. The years before World War II, as with much of the ethnic press, constituted the heyday for Japanese American newspapers.[3] The press wielded considerable influence because of the tightly knit, highly organized nature of the Japanese American community.[4] During this golden era, second-generation readers scoured pages for information about Nisei sports leagues and the hundreds of Nisei clubs and organizations. Editorials, columns, and feature stories relayed both opinion and fact concerning international, national, and local events of interest. Aspiring poets and writers, often members of Nisei literary groups, found an outlet for their work.[5] Leading newspapers like San Francisco's *Nichibei Shimbun* (Japanese American News), its local archrival, the *Shin Sekai* (later the *Shin Sekai Asahi*), and the Los Angeles–based *Rafu Shimpo* and *Doho* (For Equality, Peace, and Democracy) not only chronicled local news but connected readers throughout California and the West Coast.[6] One Seattle paper, the *Japanese American Courier,* published a weekly edition strictly for a Nisei reading audience.[7] Together, these publications comprised a network of news and information specifically geared toward the second generation.[8]

The emergence of the Nisei press paralleled the growth of the second generation and the years between the world wars that marked an important period of transition for Japanese America. The second generation wrestled with issues of identity as a generation and as a racial-ethnic group and also laid the foundations of a Nisei culture. Within this process, the Japanese American newspapers played an important role in the lives of Nikkei as sources of information and as shapers of public opinion.

The Rise of English-Language Sections

Early attempts to include the English language in Japanese American newspapers dated as far back as 1905, but not until 1925 did a regular English section appear in the *Nichibei Shimbun.*[9] The editor and publisher of the *Nichibei,* Issei leader Kyutaro Abiko, recognized the need to incorporate the Nisei more fully into the life of Japanese America. The paper sponsored study tours for the second generation to visit Japan in 1925 and 1926. Abiko and his wife, Yonako, felt that the American-born Japanese needed to have some understanding of Japan to serve effectively as a bridge of understanding between the two countries. Letters written by the Nisei describing their experiences in Japan comprised the beginnings of the paper's English section.[10] Following the *Nichibei*'s lead, the *Rafu Shimpo* in February 1926 began issuing a portion of the paper in English. An editorial announced the new feature as a paper "for the Nisei by the Nisei."[11] According to Togo Tanaka, publisher H. T. Komai took this pledge seriously and heartily supported the English section by attaching very few

Nichibei Shimbun (Japanese American News) typesetters at work, San Francisco, California, 1928. (Gift of the Yasuo William Abiko Family, Japanese American National Museum [92.127.9])

strictures to its publication.[12] The *Shin Sekai* started its English edition in September 1929 after an unsuccessful attempt in January of the same year. The opening editorial stressed the urgent need for an English section for its Nisei readership, and the paper referred to itself as the "Daily Friend, Counseler [*sic*] and Servant" of the Nisei. English editor Iwao Kawakami oversaw the modest three columns of text that featured editorials and local news.[13]

The *Doho* in Los Angeles reserved one page of its semimonthly publication for the second generation, and in June of 1938, the first English type appeared next to the Japanese. Representing an unabashedly pro-labor, progressive voice within the Japanese American community of Los Angeles, the staff of the *Doho* chastised other papers for their unwillingness to represent the views of the ordinary Japanese American. During its relatively short run, the *Doho*, with its socialist leanings, focused on issues of unionization, the work of Nisei Young Democrats, and the effects of the Sino-Japanese war.[14] The *Japanese American Courier* launched its publication on 1 January 1928 and stood in contrast to the others in publishing four pages of exclusively English text on a weekly basis. Independent of support from a Japanese-language daily, the *Courier* endured financial hardship throughout its publishing history. Yet it managed to publish continually from 1928 until April 1942, when the incarceration of Japanese Americans forced it (and most of the other Japanese American papers) to shut down its operation. Without question, James and Misao Sakamoto formed the heart and soul of the *Courier*, and James's influence more than any other gave shape to the paper's all-American content and message. Despite its limited circulation, the paper remained connected to the network of West Coast Nisei who pondered the future of the second generation by means of newsprint.[15]

It is difficult to determine how many Nisei actually read the papers. Circulation figures do not indicate readership by generation, and, in most cases, the Nisei presumably read papers subscribed to by their parents. As the largest daily before the war, the *Nichibei* published two editions in the 1920s (San Francisco and Los Angeles) with a combined circulation of over 25,000.[16] By 1930, the *Nichibei*'s press run in San Francisco totaled 16,000; its Los Angeles operations soon shut down due to a 1931 strike.[17] From 1931 until the war, the paper's circulation hovered between 10,000 and 15,000; 1941 figures are listed at 9,400.[18] In 1930, the *Shin Sekai* circulated 13,500 copies; throughout the prewar period, the paper usually trailed the *Nichibei* slightly. The statistics from 1940 show that the *Shin Sekai Asahi* edged out its rival by some 900 issues. The readership of the *Rafu Shimpo* remained steady from the mid-1920s until the war, with circulation totals of approximately 8,000. Given the strictly Nisei orientation of the *Courier*, it perhaps is less surprising that its circulation figures in 1940 only amounted to 1,300.[19]

The appearance of English sections in the established Japanese dailies aptly symbolized the dependence of Nisei on the immigrant generation. Issei publishers underwrote expenses as American-born Japanese could not muster the financial resources to publish a daily newspaper. Making space for the Nisei represented an investment in the future of Japanese America and in potential subscribers.[20] The papers kept the generations together and reinforced racial-ethnic ties, but those writing in English enjoyed a wide leeway. Minimal collaboration took place between the two language staffs as linguistic differences and the rigors of publishing a daily paper combined to secure a measure of editorial freedom for the Nisei.[21] Little detailed information exists about the English-language staffs. The frequent turnover of reporters and editors reflected the low wages as well as the transitional nature of the trade. Both women and men held top positions, although a clear gender bias favored men. Many reporters had some college background. All five papers surveyed published in major urban settings, and coverage generally favored urban news. Regional correspondents contributed news about rural and semirural areas, but city staffers made the editorial decisions.

At the *Rafu Shimpo,* a board of editorial counselors comprised of community leaders helped the staff think through methods of reporting the news. In July 1941, Togo Tanaka reported the events of a lively board meeting held at the Alexandria Hotel. Spirited debate surrounded the publication of Japanese American brushes with the law that appeared in a column entitled the "Police Blotter." Joseph Shinoda, owner of the San Lorenzo Nursery and a successful business leader, commented: "It gets me down to open up the paper at dinner time and read that Hiroshi so and so has been arrested in some red light house and caught in the act and hauled with some prostitute to the jail. . . . For pete's sake, can't we keep such tripe out of our home newspaper." Others disagreed, arguing that running such news would act as a deterrent against delinquent behavior. Some of the advisers wondered whether the "Police Blotter" might hurt subscriptions. After several rounds of discussion, the board suggested that the paper run editorials in Japanese for parents to let them know that antisocial behavior jeopardized the entire ethnic community. On their way home from the meeting, publisher H. T. Komai advised Tanaka on the use of such meetings: "they're good for getting community sentiment, but when there is disagreement, the staff just better go ahead and use its common sense."[22]

The items that appeared in the newspapers reflected the diverse experiences of the second generation, who saw themselves in the pages of the press. The images contained therein represented an effort to inform, interpret, and shape opinion.

Racial Responsibility

In covering the news, journalists wrote about a generation enmeshed in a highly racialized society. American citizenship spared Nisei the ordeal experienced by their parents, who had been denied naturalization and land ownership. Other forms of racism, however, affected them and were made manifest in antimiscegenation laws, restrictive housing covenants, unequal employment opportunity, and discriminatory policies in access to public facilities like city swimming pools. In the decades before the war, racism often operated in broad daylight. The second generation responded to such realities by creating a world of its own. Organizations numbered in the hundreds during the 1930s; and, by any standard, the Nisei did not suffer from a lack of activities or clubs from which to choose. Yet the plethora of community choices for Japanese Americans underscored a poverty of alternatives outside Japantowns and Little Tokyos. Nisei sports leagues, Japanese American YMCAs and YWCAs, and ethnic church youth activities usually did not highlight racial issues, but their very existence underscored the restrictions of race.

Overall, the press promoted an ideology of racial responsibility that encouraged Nisei to respond to racism by embracing life in America as loyal, hardworking citizens who would "prove" their worth. Many contributors conveyed an unwarranted optimism and, in essence, offered a sense of hope and agency within a difficult racial climate. Nisei had come up against the ugliness of race prejudice enough to know that erasing its legacy would be an uphill climb. Although discussions of race could border on naïveté, more often than not, writers advocated a strategy for survival. Signs of shortsightedness often reflected relative youth and limited perspectives—one a function of age, the other a sample of racism's effect on the imagination.

If Nisei had any chance of breaking the grip of race prejudice, they needed to establish relationships outside of the ethnic community. Masao Satow, secretary of the Los Angeles Japanese YMCA, argued that racial discrimination stemmed largely from ignorance. Like all other difficult areas of human interaction, he maintained, "the racial problem . . . must be approached upon the basis of one personality upon another." Writing in the *Courier*'s 1934 New Year's edition, he urged readers to make a resolution: "If each one of us during this coming year were to go out of our way to make one or two meaningful contacts with Americans on the basis of sympathetic understanding and mutual appreciation, we could accomplish much toward hastening the day when we American citizens of Japanese ancestry shall be duly recognized as such." Satow boldly stated that the future and "our very life" depended on whether the Nisei could make themselves known to their fellow Americans. Greater visibility meant taking risks and displaying a willingness to endure unpleasant situations and the potential scorn of other Nisei who might not look kindly on reaching to those outside Japanese America. Still, "someone must be willing to go out into the wilderness that others may enter the promised land."[23] Publisher James Sakamoto shared Satow's outlook and felt that the Nisei needed to foster an educational exchange through which others could come to appreciate Japanese Americans. In weaving themselves into the fabric of American life, the second generation would see the specter of racial discrimination disappear as it had for earlier immigrant groups. The partially blind former boxer who managed to keep his newspaper afloat during the Depression knew something about putting up a fight. Curiously, however, in not taking into account the plight of other racial-ethnic minorities, Sakamoto underestimated the opponent.[24]

Regardless of the odds, attorney, newspaper columnist, and second-generation leader Saburo Kido latched on to individual effort and ability as two of the main keys that would unlock closed doors.[25] The philosophy of the Hawaiian-born Kido may very well have come from his own experience. He moved to San Francisco at the age of nineteen to attend law school at the Hastings College of Law, where he received his degree in 1926. After graduation, he established a law practice in the city and served as a founding member and key leader of the Japanese American Citizens' League (JACL). Kido also found an outlet for his interest in Nisei affairs by contributing a regular column ("Timely Topics") in the English section of the *Shin Sekai*. Fluent in both Japanese and English, Kido maintained good relationships with Issei community leaders as well as white American civic leaders in San Francisco.[26] Kido's emphasis on the merits of individual effort and achievement revealed a self-proclaimed conservative political orientation.

He looked askance at collective efforts of change represented in unionization and especially warned readers of the Congress of Industrial Organizations (CIO). If the CIO had its way, Kido argued, "we may look forward to every business being regulated under the dictatorship of the labor unions."[27] Unions undermined Issei employers, and pressure might very well cause Japanese American–owned businesses and farms to buckle, leaving both generations at the mercy of a highly racialized workforce.[28] Such an argument sounded logical; but, according to columnist John Kitahara of the *Doho*, when "the protection of Japanese industry means only the protection of the interests of the Japanese owners and very little protection for the workers, we begin to wonder if it isn't a clever scheme to dupe the workers." The workers were largely responsible for the success of Japanese American fruit stands; and, as such, workers deserved decent wages and work schedules. Kitahara deplored the "squeezing" of workers for the sake of the owners' greed. Nisei laborers needed to unite with other workers: "Everywhere trade unions are growing to protect the workers from savage attacks upon their rights. And it is no exception with the Nisei."[29]

In facing the issue of race prejudice, many commentators tended to portray racism in the United States as an anomaly, a misconception to be dispelled or the work of a few misguided agitators rather than a pervasive societal phenomenon. Unsavory individuals, usually unnamed, fomented racial tensions as a pretense to further their particular agendas. Politicians, for example, found racial scapegoating as a way to win votes by drawing on people's frustrations and fears.[30] Japanese Americans were assured that the manipulation of race, while disturbing, did not represent the sentiments of the majority of Americans. By being model citizens, the second generation could appeal to the egalitarian sensibilities embedded in American society.

Nisei efforts to win over fellow Americans even included a politics of deference toward former *Sacramento Bee* publisher Valentine Stuart McClatchy, who had made a career out of anti-Japanese activity. Not satisfied with the passage of the 1924 Immigration Act, McClatchy devoted his energies to the California Joint Immigration Committee (CJIC), which became the successor to the Japanese Exclusion League once the "victory" of exclusion had been achieved in 1924. The reconstituted organization enjoyed the backing of the Native Sons of the Golden West, the California Federation of Labor, the American Legion, and the Grange. Under McClatchy's leadership, the CJIC carried on the crusade against the Japanese in America.[31] The committee became a stubborn thorn in the side of Nikkei. McClatchy used his resources and influence to fight attempts by Japan and Japanese Americans to repeal exclusion. The CJIC also targeted Nisei and actively supported plans to revoke their citizenship, reviving the earlier efforts of James Phelan and others. In May 1937, McClatchy seized some headlines when he declared: "The Tokyo government is conducting an extensive campaign throughout Japan to induce some 50,000 American-born Japanese who have returned to the land of their fathers to return to the United States." McClatchy supported proposed congressional legislation to strip Japanese Americans of citizenship and block the reentry of those who could not satisfactorily justify why they had been outside the United States for more than a year. Had the bill been successful, it would have created major problems for those who had gone to Japan primarily to study Japanese language and culture.[32]

Togo Tanaka considered McClatchy to be a critic rather than a cheap politician "whose sincerity is less open to doubt" despite his consistent record of anti-Japanese activity: "Who is to deny that the motives inspiring the McClatchy brand of so-called 'anti-alienism' do not arise out of virtuous consideration for the welfare of the nation. The disagreement between the nisei [*sic*] . . . and McClatchy . . . may be traced to a disagreement over the fundamental issue of HOW the interests of Americanism may best be served." The editorial claimed that McClatchy was familiar with Japanese Americans and that such knowledge somehow made his agitation more legitimate.[33] In fact, after McClatchy's death in May 1938, the *Rafu Shimpo* paid measured tribute to him, reminding readers that McClatchy had counted leaders like Kyutaro Abiko and Saburo Kido among his personal friends. The article absolved the newspaper magnate of intentional wrongdoing, although his policies contributed to a stamp of inferiority being placed on the Japanese in America. The story added: "Despite an unfailing, critical watchfulness over activities of the immigrant Japanese and their native-born second generation offspring, McClatchy was never an anti-Japanese protagonist in the sense of a jingoist. He was an intelligent, analytical observer with remarkable foresight and steadfast opinions. . . . As a highly respected critic of the second generation Japanese, McClatchy invariably claimed to have the interests of Pacific amity and friendship at heart."[34] Unfortunately, the story minimized the fact that McClatchy and his organization, however legitimately, had administered a powerful campaign of anti–Japanese American activity.[35]

The kid-glove treatment of McClatchy indicated a reluctance to delve into the broader implications and contexts in which racial discrimination operated. Accordingly, legal barriers erected by white Americans to perpetuate the racial divide rarely made the headlines. The theme of racism seemed to be taken as a given of the Nisei experience that required a response—but in ways that did not tease out issues of power that framed the very way one conceptualized race relations. Tellingly, in almost every case, the press used the term "American" to refer solely to white Americans, adding racial and/or ethnic qualifiers to denote other groups, including themselves. In fighting for equal status and recognition, writers employed language that excluded and divided along racial lines and privileged European Americans as normative. In de-emphasizing the institutional aspects of racism, moreover, the papers did not do justice to the complexity, virulence, and protean nature of race prejudice.[36]

At the same time, the newspapers stressed that Nisei needed to view themselves as agents of change. In that respect, racial responsibility carried with it the virtue of Japanese American agency. Even overly optimistic assessments of the racial climate urged American-born Japanese to work overtime in creating a better place for themselves. Journalists forcefully reminded readers that sitting on the sidelines and waiting for things to change would guarantee nothing but the continued exclusion of Nisei from full participation in American life. The papers, by and large, advocated a strategy that reflected the racially subordinate position of the Nikkei in America.[37]

Racial Solidarity

In challenging Nisei to make friendships with "Americans," Masao Satow did not specify whether that included dating and marriage. Almost certainly, he would have exempted such cases because of the legal restrictions and social stigma attached to interracial relationships. Antimiscegenation laws in California dating back to the 1880s had been periodically updated and revised to bar unions between people of color and whites. The "threat" to Anglo women posed by the influx of Japanese immigrants prompted legislators in 1905 to expand section 60 of the California Civil Code to make marriages between whites and "Mongolians" unlawful.[38] In addition to legal codes, Nisei also received clear messages from their parents and the Japanese American community to stay within racial-ethnic bounds.

Aware of both the internal and external pressures on the second generation, the newspapers clearly encouraged "racial solidarity" in interpersonal relationships. The press coverage suggested that in matters of the heart, Japanese Americans would be best off with one another. Because American-born Japanese came of age in the 1930s and 1940s, it is not surprising that the papers addressed this concern. The median age of Nisei at the outbreak of World War II was only seventeen, but approximately 20 percent of the second generation did marry before the war.[39] Nisei and their parents no doubt thought quite a bit about dating and marriage, especially when they considered the future. As the second generation would increasingly discover, interpersonal relationships uncovered values and expectations within families and the ethnic community.[40] Pressure from all sides pushed Nisei toward other Japanese Americans for romance and long-term relationships.[41] Marriage announcements frequently appeared in the papers and acted as a positive reinforcement. The wedding of Henry Takahashi and Barbara Yamamoto, prominent Nisei in San Francisco, merited a full-length article. Over 500 guests attended the gala affair in June 1930. The *Nichibei Shimbun* story detailed the wedding colors (green and white), the floral arrangements, and the types of dresses worn by the bridesmaids. The Takahashi-Yamamoto wedding represented the Nisei elite. Both the bride and the groom had graduated from the University of California at Berkeley. Takahashi, an optometrist, enjoyed professional status and also served as president of the San Francisco chapter of the Japanese American Citizens'

League. Yamamoto graduated with a degree in nursing and had been a leader of the Japanese American Women Students Club at Berkeley.[42]

In writing about dating and marriage, journalists also touched on gender-role expectations. In general, the majority of gender-specific items in the papers dealt with women. Columns on fashion, cooking, and homemaking appealed to female readers, providing women with opportunities to enter the newspaper world—albeit in circumscribed roles. The English-language press did not shut women out; indeed, some served as editors and reporters, though in smaller numbers compared to the men.[43] Men, moreover, generally wrote the unrestricted columns that offered broad commentary on Nisei life, and in these spaces, they discussed the place of women. The mixing of women's roles with dating and marriage issues revealed the gender biases not only of those who wrote the pieces but perhaps also illustrated ethnic community expectations of women as keepers of the culture.[44] Columnist Tad Uyeno of the *Nichibei Shimbun* complained that the Issei unfairly condemned the second generation for a host of reasons, and the most serious complaints had been reserved for Nisei women: "The lopsided critics say that the girls don't know how to cook and they haven't any manners. Moreover the critics say all that the girls know how to do is to have a good time. The American Japanese men are urged by the critics to go to Japan to find their own wives. It doesn't seem right to let their criticisms go unchallenged. I am going to rebel against the idea of seeking brides in far away Japan. There's no sense in the suggestion." Although linked by heritage, Nisei did not have much else in common with the Japanese in Japan. In Uyeno's opinion, differences in environment, customs, and general outlook spelled trouble for second-generation men who sought marriage partners overseas. For reasons of compatibility, Nisei-Nisei couples had the best chances of success, and Uyeno declared: "I believe that the girls raised in this country will make excellent wives for American Japanese men."[45]

Iwao Kawakami apparently did not share in Uyeno's positive appraisal; in a 1930 editorial, he chided Nisei women for not marrying early and labeled them "old maids." The English-language editor of the *Shin Sekai* pinned the hesitation of women in their early twenties to unrealistic desires on their part to be taken care of. Kawakami reminded readers that marriage still represented one of the best "careers" available to women; and, if need be, he would resort to name-calling to straighten out wayward women. Difficult economic times meant modest lifestyles for most Nisei, and Kawakami hoped that more and more women might adopt the fol-

lowing attitude: " 'It does not matter that my young husband is not rich
or influential now, but I'll stick by him and we'll work together, even if it
may mean hardships in the first few years of our marriage.' "[46]

Over the next two weeks, letters to the editor indicated that Kawakami's editorial had sparked a lively debate in which both women and men
boldly stated their views on marriage and the opposite sex.[47] One woman
from Sacramento, identified as "Una Mujer del Secundo [sic] Generacion,"
scolded Kawakami: "How can you be so imbecilic to blame us—the second generation young women—for not marrying as soon as we get into
our twenties?" She stated that only a few Nisei men warranted serious
consideration:

> Real good ones are scarce—and the rest of them are surely a sorry lot for any
> respectable second generation woman to consider. . . . The "rest of them" are
> not making enough to support themselves—let alone two people! You say that,
> "A second generation should work together with her husband." Oh yes—
> that's all well and good in the first few months of marriage, but if babies start
> coming—what then? Do you expect her to keep working? I suppose you'll
> try to edge in here with something about "birth control." You men would—
> if you can't support children either!

Una Mujer viewed herself as old-fashioned since she felt the woman's first
priority should be to establish the home. In that respect, she did not agree
with a "fifty-fifty" conception of marriage. She questioned any man who
would ask his wife to work, take care of the home, and also have children.
Una Mujer, unmarried but "practically engaged" to a very nice young Nisei
man, did not appreciate questions from other Nikkei about why she still
had not married. Nevertheless, she braved unkind references to "old maids"
because, she wrote, "I am quite willing to wait a few years more and do
what I can to make our marriage a success from the start." She signed her
letter "Your severest critic" and, for good measure, added a warning: "I'll
kick plenty, even when I'm married, if one of you 'lordly men' start 'razz-
ing' us second generation women."[48]

A few days later, a male reader from the Fresno area, "Un Joven," responded to the charges of Una Mujer. He started with a history lesson that
reminded Una Mujer that Issei couples like her parents had "worked side
by side on that hot strawberry patch to buy you a bottle of milk. And you—
ashamed to work for your husband!" Decent second-generation women,
according to Un Joven, would be willing to work for several years to help
their husbands get on their feet. "Any sane man," he declared, "can see
that the future of the second generation is not very bright." The letter al-

luded to the limitations that Nisei faced in a highly color-conscious society in the throes of an economic depression. Una Mujer had obviously struck a nerve in her characterization of Nisei men, and Un Joven minced no words in his reply: "You're the kind of girl who brings criticisms from the first generation. I am not wishing you bad luck, but your marriage, if you ever get married, is sure to land in the divorce court. I can almost picture you. You're the type that plays all day or attends the matinee while your darling husband is out in the fields picking pears in the blistering sun." Un Joven had given up on Nisei women, even though he considered himself an eminently eligible bachelor—six feet tall, handsome, college graduate, and a dynamic personality in possession of a roadster and plenty of money. "I am not going to give the spineless second generation girls the great opportunity of marrying me. I am going to the land of the Cherry Blossoms to pick a nice sweet maiden for my life companion."[49]

The letters from Una Mujer and Un Joven, along with Kawakami's editorial, testified to the mix of expectations, aspirations, and tensions associated with marriage, family, and career. Everyone involved in the exchange assumed marriage as normative and expressed ideas about gender roles for men as well as women. Even if Un Joven had no financial worries, his comments suggested that many Nisei men would have had a difficult time supporting a family on one income. Neither Un Joven nor Kawakami indicated that men did not strive or desire to "take care of their wives," but few could, and the harsh words, in part, seemed to underscore frustration over the lack of opportunity. Un Joven also detected a lack of appreciation in Una Mujer's letter that he felt would not be there from women who lived in Japan. At least some Issei had conveyed thoughts similar to those of Un Joven; and, in the heat of the moment, he may have indeed felt that the grass was greener on the other side. At the same time, Una Mujer appeared to be responding to slanderous characterizations of Nisei women and to unfair charges of being "old maids" when she and other second-generation women willingly worked and waited to make marriage viable. Una Mujer's and Un Joven's conceptions of marriage did not vary much, even if their perceptions of one another did, suggesting how Nisei ideas of marriage reflected their experience of growing up in America. Kawakami described marriage as a "career" that Nisei women might enter, presumably alongside others; such a perspective would certainly have been quite foreign to the Issei. Similarly, the phenomenon of women staying at home or being "taken care of" did not mesh with the experiences of or possibilities for the vast majority of Nisei couples and spoke to middle-class values most likely borrowed from American culture. The very debate itself illustrated the fact that American-born Japanese struggled to make sense of how interpersonal relationships entered into their identities as Nisei and as men and women.

The attempt to influence attitudes about dating and marriage continued well beyond the *Shin Sekai* debate and often revolved around women's roles. James Sakoda wrote about Shizu, a Nisei woman who had gone to Tokyo and found work as a singer in a jazz band. Although she had not planned to stay permanently, Shizu ended up marrying a member of the band. Life after marriage had been difficult: she shared a squalid and cramped home with her newborn child, her husband, and in-laws. She discouraged women from coming to Japan and, by the time Sakoda met her, had herself given up hope of returning to the United States. "I don't see why," she said, "the Nisei girls aren't satisfied with a thirty-five dollar home, a baby and a milk-bottle on the porch every morning and a car. I'd be if I were they." Shizu's depiction of the life awaiting women as wives of fruitstand workers may not have seemed very glamorous, but in comparison with life in Japan, it seemed attractive.[50] The article sent a not-so-subtle message to Nisei women to appreciate building a life with Nisei men in America. Given the language handicaps and other cultural differences, it is doubtful that many Nisei women would have sought out Japanese partners. Sakoda's article reinforced the merits of Nisei marriage. At the same time, he sought to safeguard the self-image of males while lowering material expectations of what Nisei women might expect after marriage.

For all the anxiety over marriage, Mary Oyama saw no real cause for alarm. Most readers knew Oyama as "Deirdre," advice columnist for the *Shin Sekai Asahi*. From 1935 to 1941, Mary "Molly" Oyama, also a leading Nisei writer of the period, dispensed wisdom on a daily basis. Historian Valerie Matsumoto has shown that Deirdre supported women in their efforts to chart their own course, and the column itself gave Nisei women and men a chance to ask questions, voice opinions, and receive feedback.[51] Stepping outside her role as Deirdre, Oyama wrote an article under her own name in the *Nichibei Shimbun* on marriage. She claimed that unmarried women in their twenties, contrary to popular beliefs, posed no "problem": "Eventually, sooner or later, the enterprising young nisei [*sic*] women will marry whom they will, be it an American-born nisei, Japan-born young man or even an American. It is only a matter of time. Here in America where living standards are so high, it takes a longer time for a young nisei man to arrive at an age and status where he can adequately support a wife." Oyama stated that the psychological temperament of the woman dictated whom she should marry. A decidedly Japanese disposition meant that a Japanese-born man would be best; a Nisei man would better suit a more Americanized woman. "If she is ultra-Americanized," Oyama explained, "she may even marry an American.[52]

If Oyama's outlook soothed some of her colleagues' worries about Nisei marriage, then her comment on interracial relationships stirred up another hornet's nest. In fact, the openness exhibited in Oyama's article rarely found expression in the pages of Japanese American newspapers. The press encouraged racial solidarity because they knew that the second generation might venture outside Japanese America. The newspapers in part reflected the strong bias within the ethnic community toward endogamy. In his study of intermarriage, Paul Spickard has argued that the immigrant generation's distaste of interracial relationships carried much weight and also spoke to a strong sense of peoplehood. Many Issei believed in the racial superiority of the Japanese, and exogamy meant, among other things, shaming the family in the eyes of the larger Japanese American community.[53] Most parents had little real cause for alarm as the outmarriage rates remained low throughout the prewar period. Only 2.3 percent of the women and 3.1 percent of the men married non-Japanese Americans. Nisei figures represented an increase over Issei intermarriage but fell far short of the 30 percent rate for children of European immigrants. Historical circumstances may have had more to do with Nisei endogamy than natural inclinations, since most Nisei came of age at the time of mass incarceration in an artificially homogeneous environment.[54] Apart from Issei propensities and community pressures, Nisei also faced hostility from society at large in the form of antimiscegenation laws. California and many other western states aimed to prevent interracial marriages. Determined couples with resources could and did get around the barrier by getting married in states without such laws. Even couples legally wed, however, faced a social context that largely disapproved of mixed marriages.

Editors did their part in discouraging interracial relationships by running stories that told of the misfortunes of those who dared to cross racial lines. Wise readers would want to avoid the shame and tragedy that haunted those poor souls. The coverage depended on the interracial context, and the papers generally highlighted two types of relationships: Nisei–Filipino American and Nisei–European American.

Contact between Filipino immigrants and Japanese Americans took place mostly in farming communities in which the Filipinos worked as laborers on Nikkei-run farms. Eiichiro Azuma's study of the rural Japanese community of Walnut Grove noted an attitude among the Issei toward Filipinos as a "menace" to Japanese American women. Mixing with the "lazy blood" of Filipinos, Issei feared, would result in diluting their racial superiority. Azuma noted that, as a community, Walnut Grove took steps to safeguard against Filipino American advances by portraying farmworkers as subhuman. The lavish gifts, attention, and flattery of suave Filipino men supposedly masked their true intentions of violating Nisei women. Issei leaders strongly recommended that farmers minimize interethnic contact.[55]

Many Japanese Americans saw themselves above Filipinos on a racial hierarchy,[56] and newspaper stories strengthened such sentiment. In 1930, an unsigned editorial commented on the recent race riots against Filipinos in Watsonville. Filipinos had reportedly issued pamphlets in which they had made the outlandish statement: "We have as much right to American girls as Americans." No matter how badly Filipinos had been abused, according to the writer, Japanese Americans would never be so foolish as to make such a statement because the Japanese did not condone intermarriage: "Perhaps the whole trouble is due to the fact that the Filipinos do not bring women of their own kind from the Islands, but come here to work and just go crazy about marrying an American, Japanese or Chinese girl. Such cases are becoming quite common . . . for their own good, the Filipinos should give up such ideas and stick to marrying women of their own race, so that they may not face such horrors as race riots in the future again."[57] Writing in 1938, Saburo Kido devoted his column to the growing concern of Issei farmers over the question of interracial relationships between their daughters and Filipinos. Kido conceded that in cases of mutual love, little could be done. The danger, however, seemed "to lie in the fact that there are those [Filipinos] who act in a group to seduce young Nisei girls." From what he had heard, Kido reported that "intimidation is being practiced" and that "in extreme cases . . . lives of the family were threatened to bring young girls under their influence." Kido recommended that investigations be undertaken by the authorities before things got any worse.

Stories of what had happened several years earlier to Alice Kaneko fed the fears and prejudices of Japanese Americans. Kaneko's family farmed in the rural community of Newcastle in northern California, and the *Shin Sekai* reported on 12 January 1934 that Alice, twenty-three, lay in the hospital suffering from gunshot wounds. The article—whose headline read, "Girl Shot by Mad Filipino"—told of the harrowing events that had taken place the day before. An unnamed Filipino worker from the Kaneko farm had apparently proposed marriage to Alice, but her family never seriously

considered the offer. Instead, Kaneko had planned to marry Shizuo Haramoto of Sacramento. The article did not divulge whether some relationship existed between Kaneko and the unnamed Filipino, nor did it discuss
the circumstances surrounding the proposed marriage to Haramoto.[58] On
11 January, the day before the Kaneko-Haramoto wedding, the distraught
Filipino shouted that if he could not have Kaneko as his bride, then no one
else would. He then moved toward Alice Kaneko and fired, hitting her at
close range. Turning the gun on himself, the farmworker shot himself in
the head, dying instantly. Although Kaneko did not die at the scene of the
crime, she lay in critical condition at the hospital with little chance for recovery.[59] The Kaneko case graphically illustrated the disaster that interracial situations could cause for Japanese Americans. In the case of racially
charged news coverage involving Filipino Americans, stories and editorials drove home the point that the Nikkei had been wronged by an alleged-
ly lesser race.

The milder treatment of Nisei-white relations also took into account a
racial hierarchy—but one in which white Americans occupied the top rung
of the ladder. The stories lacked the sense of violation that characterized the
coverage of Filipino-Nisei situations. Opposition to interracial dating and
marriage remained but in understated tones of sadness and tragedy. Reports
highlighted the unfortunate underside of not remaining loyal to racial solidarity. "What would you do," asked reporter Kay Nishida, "should Cu-
pid play a trick on you?" The "trick" entailed falling in love with someone
other than a Japanese American. Speaking in general terms, Nishida predicted the demise of Nikkei racial exclusivity and attributed this process as
a natural part of migration. He pointed out that the Japanese outmarriage
rate in Samoa approached 90 percent because very few females from Japan
lived on the island. In the United States, Nishida noted that in areas not
hampered by antimiscegenation laws, some Japanese Americans had married outside the race. Marie Kunitomo of Denver, Colorado, for instance,
was the daughter of a prominent Japanese American physician who had
married an Irishwoman. Kunitomo's story, however, served as a negative
example of intermarriage.

In 1929, Kunitomo had been engaged to a "strongarmed fireman of the
Caucasian race" and looked forward to a large and festive wedding. Two
days before the nuptials, the groom disappeared; according to Nishida, he
had skipped town "because he did not want to marry one who was 'A
Daughter of Two Worlds.'" As gifts poured into the Kunitomo home, so
did grief and shame, engulfing the young bride-to-be. Police later found
Kunitomo dead inside of her father's car. A revolver lay at the side of

Kunitomo's slumped body. Layers of tragedy lined the story of Marie Kunitomo: a child of intermarriage took her own life in the failure of another proposed marriage between two races. The painful experience had deeply affected two generations. "All things considered," Nishida reflected, "a nisei's [sic] marriage with members of an alien race may prove hazardous, may entail suffering and humiliation and disappointments. The chances for happiness are so much more meager."[60]

Sam Kurihara's experience confirmed the odds against interracial relationships and stressed the senselessness of not staying within one's race. Kurihara, twenty-four, a Nisei farmer in the Dinuba area, had been dating Jennie Jean Salsan, nineteen, for over a year. Her father, A. C. Salsan, had warned Kurihara to stay away from his daughter, but Sam and Jennie Jean continued to meet. One day in mid-January 1938, Kurihara followed his ritual of discreetly parking his truck and making his way by foot to the Salsan house. This time, however, Mr. Salsan was waiting. As Kurihara neared the front door, Salsan approached him with a loaded shotgun. Kurihara fell backwards as the blast struck him in the abdomen. Jennie Jean, on hearing the gunshot, swallowed a prepared vial of poison, believing her lover to be dead. Rushed to the hospital, Kurihara lay in the emergency room, unaware that, in the adjoining room, doctors had pronounced Salsan dead on arrival.[61] Kurihara survived the shooting and decided not to press charges against the elder Salsan. The pain of lost love could not be mended through legal action. The article closed with a reminder: "A California Statute forbids the marriage between an Oriental and a Caucasian." The apparent moral of the story was that Kurihara and Salsan really had little hope for the future, even if Salsan's father had not intervened.

Whether through the misfortunes of ill-fated love or in stories celebrating Nisei-Nisei couples, the press stood for racial solidarity. Journalists recognized the subordinate position of Japanese Americans in the United States, which was most vividly reflected in antimiscegenation laws. At the same time, the ethnic community stressed endogamy as a means of preserving racial and cultural boundaries. The subject of dating and marriage also raised concerns about gender, most often expressed in the examination of women's roles. Discussions of what made a suitable partner uncovered the ways that marriage captured the hopes and fears about the future of Japanese Americans. In advocating racial solidarity, English-language sections of the immigrant press aligned themselves with prevailing mores against interracial relationships in the ethnic community and society at large.

Racial Victimization

While most editors of the English-language sections followed the party line in terms of personal relationships, they took a different tack under the pressures of an international event with special significance for the Nikkei. Although thousands of miles away, the outbreak of the Sino-Japanese War in July 1937 had a tremendous effect on both Japanese and Chinese in the United States. The respective immigrant communities rallied support for their home countries. Many Issei collected funds, prepared care packages, and held gatherings, all to support the cause of Japan in China. Likewise, the Japanese-language dailies consistently took a pro-Japanese stance in their coverage of the events.[62]

In contrast to the Issei, the Nisei faced a difficult situation that pitted their ancestry against their citizenship. America's support for China, as well as worsening U.S.-Japanese relations, placed the second generation in a precarious position. In its characteristic frankness, the *Doho* blasted the militarists in Japan for wreaking havoc in Asia and implicated Issei who supported Japan's cause. The pro-democratic, antifascist stance of the *Doho* reporters no doubt rankled those like newspaper editor Sei Fujii of the *Kashu Mainichi* (Japan-California Daily) whose ardent support of Japan was just one of many reasons for the *Doho*'s criticism of the Issei leader. The position taken by the staff of the *Doho* on the Sino-Japanese question illustrated a growing divide between generations and, ironically, placed the *Doho* in the company of the Japanese American Citizens' League, whose hyper-Americanism and conservative politics frequently drew the ire of the paper's writers.[63] Apart from the *Doho*, however, most of the second-generation press, after early support for the Japanese, deflected attention away from the conflict itself and focused on the "racial victimization" of the Japanese in America.[64] Journalists presented the Nikkei as victims of misinformation and "propaganda" spread by China, Chinese Americans, and their American allies.[65] Ironically, the pro-Chinese forces also claimed victimization at the hands of a brutal and imperialistic Japan. Vying for status as victims signified the racial subordination of both groups.[66]

Editorials accused the Chinese of fabricating their own victimization to gain the sympathy and support of Americans. Kazuo Kawai, history professor at UCLA and former English editor of the *Nichibei Shimbun,* pointed out that popular authors such as Lin Yutang (*My People*) and Pearl S. Buck (*The Good Earth*) served as persuasive apologists for China's cause. According to Kawai, Japanese America also needed able interpreters to offer the American public a more balanced perspective on the war.[67] Despite its charges against pro-Chinese "propaganda," the Nisei press did not hesitate to promote propaganda of its own and generated coverage designed to gain sympathy for Japanese Americans. The 22 October 1937 issue of the *Nichibei Shimbun* reported that a seven-year-old Japanese American girl had been pelted with stones by Chinese American youths as she walked to her parents' store in San Francisco's Chinatown. The story evoked images of a defenseless girl being attacked by a group of angry, rock-throwing Chinese Americans. The incident also brought into question the character of Chinese American children, who had gained citywide attention by picketing Japanese-owned stores located in Chinatown.

Violence had also spread to Sacramento, where Susie Yamigawa, a young Nisei woman, had been shot by a Chinese American while selling tickets at a Japanese-owned movie theater. Her assailant, Lum Dong, told police: "I had a terrible dream about the Sino-Japanese war in the Orient. I rushed outside and I saw a Japanese girl—so I shoot." Dong apparently tried to commit suicide but instead shot himself twice in the leg. Yamigawa suffered from chest wounds and a pierced lung but survived. When asked about the incident, she replied: "I never saw him before in my life." The article ended with a note implying that Dong lived in an alley and had been a drug abuser.[68] In both cases, the papers sent a clear message. The Nisei suffered violence for a war they had no part in and because of their racial-ethnic background. Stories of victimization provided an opportunity for the press to make a causal link between antisocial behavior and pro-Chinese propaganda. In early October 1937, fists flew between Chinese and Japanese American youths at Central Junior High School in Los Angeles. According to Togo Tanaka, sixty-five American-born Chinese and thirty-five Nisei fought in the school yard, located near the Los Angeles Civic Center. At the end of the altercation, several boys from both sides required hospital attention. To make matters worse, this brawl represented the second skirmish in two days.[69] From reporter Larry Tajiri's vantage point, two main factors stood out in trying to explain the incident: "One is the inflammatory U.S. press, which today has united in bitter denunciation of Japan's war with China. The other, and perhaps the most directly connected with the shaping of the opinions of the impressionable schoolboys, is the attitude of many U.S. teachers who, it has been reliably reported, have given biased accounts of the situation in China to their classes."[70] Individuals and newspapers like the *Los Angeles Times* had the right to their opinions, but Tajiri decried the fact that so many had not presented both sides of the issue. Japan, along with the Nisei, had been condemned without a hearing.

In an attempt to offer the other side of the story, the *Nichibei Shimbun* and the *Shin Sekai Asahi* enlisted the aid of the Nisei by announcing an essay contest in December 1937. Usually fierce rivals, the two leading Japanese American papers of San Francisco joined forces, indicating the level of concern generated by the war. Contestants needed to answer one simple, but loaded, question: "How can I as a Nisei Justify Japan's Case in China?" The sponsors presumed, of course, that Japan's case could be justified and that Nisei might appeal to the American public, providing a corrective to widespread sympathy for China. The contest announcement solicited essays from across the nation and, as an added incentive, offered fifteen cash prizes.[71] The *Nichibei* printed the winning essays in the 14 March 1938 issue. In the general category, first prize and thirty dollars went to Daisy Kuwano of Denver, Colorado. The well-crafted essay made the point that Japan had entered China to protect its interests, the right and prerogative of any sovereign nation. Drawing an analogy to the United States' policy in the Philippines, Kuwano argued that "this conflict has been forced upon her [Japan] by the immediate need of protecting her nationals and investments and . . . [the] far-reaching need to insure her own existence as a nation." Kimi Ogawa of Brooklyn, New York, took top honors in the high school category and, while echoing some of Kuwano's arguments, spent most her essay describing the negative effects of the war. Ogawa's own experience at school illustrated the dilemmas of the second generation: "I do become speechless when girls in the gymnasium show me their socks, remarking, 'Look I'm boycotting Japanese goods, so I can't wear silk stockings.'" Many Nisei like Ogawa expressed feelings of guilt by association. The essay ended by asking other Nisei to join together to support Japan for the sake of their parents.

As cosponsors of the event, the Japanese Association and the Japanese Chamber of Commerce of San Francisco used their dollars and influence to promote a pro-Japanese position. They left little to chance, as executives from Japanese corporations acted as the judges of the competition. The judges, furthermore, may have chosen two women from areas outside of major Japanese American settlements to give the contest more of an all-American feel. Feeling under siege, those who backed Japan sought to enlist the help of American citizens of Japanese ancestry.[72] The essay contest illustrated the pressures Issei could exert on the next generation and, in turn, the obligations the Nisei felt toward their parents. Moreover, the events in Asia swept up all of Japanese America, and their fate rested less on citizenship than on a common ancestry.[73] Therefore, the English-language press tried to cast a softer light on the nationalistic stance of many of the Issei. One article stated that the first generation kept "Japanese ways" because they had been shut out of American life through a barrage of legislation that denied them access to citizenship, land, and other basic rights. Despite all this, the editorial noted that the Issei had invested their lives in the United States and, as with so many other immigrants, viewed America as home for themselves and their children.[74]

The Nisei press also tried to show how the Nikkei in America had been bearing the brunt of the hostility that should have been directed overseas. Immigrants in America had no say in Japanese foreign policy and yet suffered the consequences of it. As Kay Sugahara of Los Angeles observed: "Conditions are being made ripe for blatant jingoism of the super-super-patriotic type, which feeds on the excrement of persecution, to rear its ugly head. Circumstances are making it such that the burden of proof of loyalty will rest upon the accused, rather than the proof of disloyalty on the accuser."[75]

The Sino-Japanese War dealt a heavy blow to U.S.-Japanese relations already hurt earlier in the decade by the Manchurian Incident in 1931. The abrogation of the commercial trade treaty in 1940 and the freezing of Japanese assets in the United States in 1941 clearly signaled a path toward confrontation. The downward spiral that headed toward Pearl Harbor made it increasingly difficult for the press to chart a middle course and led to unqualified support for the United States.[76] Consequently, the gap widened between the two language staffs; and in the case of the *Rafu Shimpo,* the paper exhibited a dual character in which perspectives splintered along linguistic and generational lines.[77]

Journalists tried to circumvent the issue of war by focusing on the plight of the Japanese in America as victims of false and misleading propaganda. In that scenario, Asia mainly provided the backdrop for Nisei commentary on events taking place in the United States. Hopes of honoring both ancestral ties and American citizenship gradually faded as the conflict in Asia dragged on and as the rift between the United States and Japan widened.

War on the Horizon

The Sino-Japanese War consumed much of the energy of the Japanese American press as the 1930s drew to a close. The growing polarization in the coverage also signaled the tensions between the generations caught up in a political context not of their own choosing. The stakes grew higher for the racial and generational concerns of an ethnic community within a nation—and world—headed for war. While many observers anticipated bad times, even seasoned reporters could not have foreseen the circumstances leading to America's entry into the global conflict and how such events would affect Japanese Americans.

During the years before the war, the ethnic press did suggest ways that Nisei might negotiate their racial and generational identities within the confines of racial subordination. Journalists encouraged their readers toward a racial responsibility in which the second generation took charge of combating prejudice. Establishing greater contact with white Americans, one sign of being responsible, did not mean, however, that Nisei should enter into dating and marriage relationships with them. The newspapers urged Nisei to confine their romantic liaisons to other Japanese Americans and did not hesitate to illustrate what could happen if they crossed racial lines. In part, the press pushed for racial solidarity because it knew antimiscegenation laws prohibited marriage with white Americans. At the same time, endogamy meshed well with a deep racial and cultural pride among the Nikkei. Feelings of pride translated into superiority when the Nikkei encountered the possibility of Japanese-Filipino relationships. In discussing interpersonal issues, reporters also aired notions of gender-role expectations that focused largely on women and their place within the ethnic community.

News coverage also included international events, and journalists discovered how deeply the Sino-Japanese War of 1937 could influence the Japanese and the Chinese in America. The second generation faced a juggling act that included their ties to their parents, Japan, the United States, and interethnic relations with Chinese Americans. English-language sections hoped to dodge the issue of war by underscoring how Nikkei in America had been victimized by virtue of their ancestry. As the signs pointed to war, the Nisei press fully identified itself with America.

The treatment of racial issues by the English-language sections suggests some of the ways in which American-born Japanese sought to define themselves during the years preceding World War II. The second generation found its concerns over racial and generational identity centrally addressed by journalists who shared the fate of their readership. This process of definition, as with other children of immigrants, entailed reconciling the world of one's parents with the multiethnic and multiracial context of the United States. Unfortunately, Japanese Americans confronted forms of discrimination that in America had been reserved largely for people of color. Events following Pearl Harbor—leading to forced removal and mass incarceration—accentuated the historic treatment of Japanese Americans and shipwrecked any hopes that U.S. citizenship would safeguard the Nisei.

THE FIRESTORM OF WAR
AND INCARCERATION

Yoshiko Uchida remembered spending a quiet Sunday with her family after worshiping at the Japanese Independent Congregational Church of Oakland. She was glad that her father had not invited the usual score of church friends over for an afternoon meal. As lay leaders, Takashi Uchida and his wife, Keiko, had offered food and other forms of support to families and student-laborers who struggled to adjust to life in the United States. While the Uchidas ate their noodles, a news bulletin interrupted the program on the radio with an announcement that Pearl Harbor had been bombed. Takashi assured everyone that there must have been some mistake. The strange news did not make much of an impression on Yoshiko, whose thoughts were preoccupied by upcoming final exams at the University of California at Berkeley.[1]

Later that evening, however, Uchida felt an uneasy quiet in the house after returning from the library. She discovered to her dismay that her father, an employee of a Japanese corporation, had been arrested by the FBI, along with hundreds of other Japanese Americans: "Without Papa things just weren't the same, and none of us dared voice the fear that sat like a heavy black stone inside each of us. 'Let's leave the porch light on and the screen door unlatched,' Mama said hopefully. 'Maybe Papa will be back later tonight.' But the next morning the light was still burning, and we had no idea of his whereabouts." Yoshiko, her mother, and her older sister, Kay, located Takashi at a detention center in San Francisco. The joy of their reunion soon gave way to sorrow as Takashi told his family that he would be shipped out in a few days to a detention camp in Montana. As the visitation time drew to a close, a silence fell over the Uchida family: "none of us could speak for the ache in our hearts. My sister and I began to cry. And it was Mama who was the strong one. The three of us watched Papa go down the dark hallway with the guard and disappear around the corner. He was gone and we didn't know if we would ever see him again."[2]

Like so many Japanese Americans in December 1941, the Uchidas struggled to cope with chaos in the aftermath of Pearl Harbor. The downward spiral would continue as the U.S. government eventually incarcerated over 120,000 West Coast Japanese Americans during World War II. While Pearl Harbor and World War II served as the spark, the concentration camps represented the culmination of decades of race prejudice. By virtue of race and ancestry, Nikkei found themselves under armed guard and behind barbed wire—prisoners of war in their own country.

The story of the camps, once hidden from view, increasingly has come to define Japanese Americans within the history of the United States. Activists, journalists, and scholars in the late 1960s and those who labored for redress and reparations in the 1970s and 1980s did much to break long-held silences of survivors and government officials.[3] In addition, numerous oral history projects, films, scholarly studies, museum exhibits, and novels have documented the subject. The wide range of perspectives not only demonstrates the significance of this episode but also suggests the complex nature of historical memory in which individuals, communities, and institutions have vested the camps with meaning.[4] These varied stories have brought a depth of understanding to the wartime experiences of Nikkei.[5] Given the attention focused on the incarceration of Japanese Americans during World War II, this chapter is selective in its treatment of the war years. No attempt is made to offer a comprehensive account; nor is a detailed overview provided, since others have done this already.[6] Instead, the narrative continues to examine the issues of race and generation, extending the analysis from the years before the war into the camps. An argument is made that the foundations laid in the 1920s and 1930s continued to provide a critical framework for the second generation during the war. Because the camps symbolized an outgrowth of a legacy of prejudice, the organizations and structures that the Nisei built before Pearl Harbor represented vital if altered spaces in which they could process the events taking place. As they had for decades, Japanese Americans turned to one another and to the institutions that they had established. Longstanding racial subordination fostered a sense of ethnic solidarity and provided valuable experience in battling discrimination. While nothing could have prepared the Nikkei for incarceration, their history did serve them in their attempts to cope with the camps.

In emphasizing the experiences of Nisei and the role of their subculture, this chapter contributes to the social history of the concentration camps, and the narrative begins with a brief summary of the wartime experience. A discussion of the assembly centers follows, along with analysis of education and religion in the camps, providing a thematic link to earlier chapters.[7] Nikkei reconstructed important elements of the life they had known before the barbed wire compounds became their homes. Education and schooling offered one of the few ways that the second generation could invest in the future. From the perspectives of government administrators, schools could continue the program of Americanization that had marked progressive educational contexts in California during the 1920s and 1930s. In serving many needs, the schools carried different meanings for those associated with them. Students saw the contradiction between what they learned in class and their daily lives. Lessons on democracy, freedom, and equality stood in stark contrast to the guard towers and armed sentries that surrounded the makeshift classrooms. At the same time, ironically, camp schools created an opportunity for Nisei teachers to finally put their training to use. For older second-generation men and women, opportunities to attend colleges and universities in the Midwest and the East offered one of the early roads to the world outside.

Since the late nineteenth century, Buddhist temples and Christian churches had been cornerstones within Japanese American communities. During the days leading up to their removal, religious leaders helped others with the daily tasks of survival. In the assembly centers and the camps, temples and churches offered comfort and a source of meaning through a variety of religious activities. For many Nisei, religion, far from being an opiate, served as a venue in which the second generation critically explored the meaning of their plight. Documents associated with religious life in the camps suggest how Nisei Buddhists and Christians assessed their incarceration, offering social commentary and engaging in a form of resistance. Consistent with their witness, racial-ethnic temples and churches continued to serve their constituencies.

As Nisei struggled to make sense of their situation, nothing could prevent the violation they experienced as individuals, families, and communities. As historian Richard Drinnon has aptly suggested: "The most that can be said is that incarceration had unintended consequences and by-products, not all of which were negative."[8] For the Nikkei, the war confirmed a sense of racial-ethnic difference: how else could their imprisonment be explained? Being Japanese American determined one's fate far more than politics or professions of loyalty. Despite the tremendous diversity of experiences that marked the camps, the bonds of Japanese American identity, for better or worse, tied the Nikkei to one another.

Since That December Sunday

From 7 December 1941 to the spring of 1942, Nisei, like all Americans, experienced the uncertainty of a nation joining a global war; but, as reporter Larry Tajiri noted, they also stood apart: "We are Americans by every right, birth, education and belief, but our faces are those of the enemy."[9] The failure to distinguish between the people of Japan and Americans of Japanese ancestry during the 1930s meant that Issei and Nisei bore the brunt of American hostility toward Japan for its acts of imperial aggression in Asia. The declaration of war by the United States on Japan made matters considerably worse, adding to the decades of discrimination aimed at Japanese Americans. Within forty-eight hours of Pearl Harbor, FBI agents had taken into custody nearly 1,300 individuals who were guilty by association—Buddhist priests, Japanese-language schoolteachers, employees of Japanese firms, and anyone else perceived to be too Japanese. Nikkei were apprehended without charges, denied visitation, and were soon shipped off to detention centers. In the process, the government stripped Japanese American communities all along the West Coast of key Issei figures, creating a leadership vacuum that added to mounting confusion and anxiety.[10]

Over the next ten weeks, military and government officials would orchestrate the decision to incarcerate Japanese Americans along the West Coast, a strategy made possible by the signature of Executive Order 9066 on 19 February 1942 by President Franklin Roosevelt.[11] Under the thinly veiled argument of "military necessity," the order allowed for designated areas "from which any or all persons may be excluded as deemed necessary."[12] With a succession of Japanese victories in the Pacific, the tide of public sentiment had turned, and West Coast special interest groups called for the forced removal of Japanese Americans. Their treatment would be predicated on notions of racial difference, a policy also applied to the war in the Pacific.[13]

With the series of events that followed Pearl Harbor—including the loss of leadership, frozen assets, curfews, military and government rationale, and public opinion—Japanese Americans could do little to reverse the impending doom of mass incarceration. Nisei leaders of the Japanese American Citizens' League, moreover, stepped into the breach and spoke on behalf of the Nikkei community, pledging full cooperation with authorities. With no elected officials or popular cultural icons like Joe DiMaggio, Americans of Japanese ancestry lacked access to the positions of power that might have stopped the wheels of injustice. Despite such overwhelming odds, a few Nisei—such as Minoru Yasui of Hood River, Oregon, and Gordon Hirabayashi of Seattle—fought for their constitutional rights through test cases of resistance that would ultimately end up before the U.S. Supreme Court.[14]

By the end of February 1942, the U.S. Navy issued an order giving Nikkei residents of Terminal Island in San Pedro Bay forty-eight hours to vacate the island. Throughout the rest of the winter and spring, federal authorities laid the groundwork for mass incarceration: establishing military areas, restricting free travel, and meeting with state governors in the interior to ascertain which states would receive the imprisoned population. The notion of the mass incarceration of aliens and citizens alike, hardly conceivable several months earlier, would become a reality.

Phase One: Assembly Centers

During the spring of 1942, the military-run Wartime Civil Control Administration (WCCA) directed the operation of the assembly centers that acted as temporary quarters during the construction of permanent camps. Japanese Americans began serving their time close to home, awaiting transfer to interior sites that would be completed by early November 1942. Two locales—Manzanar, located in the Owens Valley in eastern California, and Poston, part of the Colorado River Indian reservation in Arizona—served as assembly centers and concentration camps. Most Japanese Americans lived in makeshift quarters, including actual horse stables at racetracks in Santa Anita and San Bruno, California.[15]

In his journal, Fred Hoshiyama, a University of California at Berkeley undergraduate whose education had been put on hold, recorded that the first wave of San Francisco's Bay Area Issei and Nisei entered Tanforan (San Bruno) at the end of April 1942. As a fieldworker for Berkeley sociologist Dorothy Swaine Thomas, Hoshiyama and other University of California students joined the Japanese [American] Evacuation and Resettlement Study (JERS) that Thomas directed. A massive documentary project, JERS gathered extensive data on Nikkei in the camps and, to a lesser extent, on their reentry into U.S. society.[16] At Tanforan, Hoshiyama noted that nearly 8,000 Nikkei lived on the 118-acre converted track, newly equipped with guard towers and armed military police on duty twenty-four hours a day. As Hoshiyama described his surroundings, he noted that on the western boundary ran El Camino Real, a major highway, on which "passing autoists would slow down and watch with curiosity, the assembled Japanese." On the northern side lay vacant lots; to the east sat railroad tracks and

Santa Anita Racetrack Assembly Center reception area, Santa Anita, California, April 1942. (Security Pacific Collection/Los Angeles Public Library)

streetcar lines that had for many years carried Nikkei residents between San Mateo and San Francisco. A residential section of San Bruno lay to the south.[17] Within the compound, hastily whitewashed horse stalls became "apartments" with smelly reminders of what had been there before. The more fortunate lived in one of the thirty-five barracks (20' × 100') subdivided into tiny apartments with no conveniences and even less privacy. The lack of preparation on the part of the WCCA matched the indecency of their treatment of Japanese Americans struggling to survive a veritable nightmare. Some of the administrators also lived in Tanforan and, quite fittingly, occupied the clubhouse.[18]

Tamie Tsuchiyama, another student on Thomas's staff, kept a journal during her stay at the Santa Anita racetrack in southern California. Over 18,000 people trudged their way to breakfast (6:30–7:30), lunch (11:30–12:30), and dinner (5:30–6:30) at the mess halls for unusually unappetizing fare devoid of the fresh vegetables and fruits that the Nikkei had made California famous for. Many in the centers attempted to make their surroundings more livable through the cultivation of plants and small gardens. Similarly, expressions of the soul surfaced in poetry and other artistic efforts by those held prisoner.[19]

Observers commented on the growing anger and disillusionment, especially among the American-born prisoners. According to Tsuchiyama, "most of the Nisei were extremely resentful of being 'shoved into jail.' They felt that the U.S. government had no right to 'imprison' its own citizens in 'concentration camps.'" The most bitter Nisei seemed to be those who had recently graduated from high school or had been in college when war broke out. Their crushed hopes weighed heavily on these Nisei. Older second-generation members tended to be more philosophical, having more experience with the virulence of race prejudice; but, as Tsuchiyama writes, "even these [the older] Nisei with a definite chip on their shoulder informed me that it had not occurred to them on Dec. 7 that war hysteria could be carried so far as to cause the wholesale removal of U.S. citizens of Japanese ancestry from the Pacific Coast."[20] In his visit to assembly centers at Pomona and Santa Anita, a well-known European-American muckraking journalist and historian found to his surprise that Nisei had not assumed leadership of the center council. Then a friend explained that the second generation felt disgusted by the entire process: "It's a helluva note to talk to us about democratic self-government, etc., when we can't even exercise our rights as American citizens."[21] As one historian has pointed out, nonparticipation in government charades constituted not only healthy cynicism but also represented a form of resistance.[22] In a foretaste of things to come in the concentration camps, resistance also took other forms, including an 800-person, sit-down strike at Santa Anita. Slated to work on camouflage netting, the strikers demanded that the center staff respond to the lack of food. Outright violence also erupted at Santa Anita when a large crowd of angry Japanese Americans protested the alleged confiscation of personal property by guards for their own use. One accused guard was badly beaten; in response, military police imposed martial law and tightened security.[23]

Nisei soon discovered that confinement went beyond physical incarceration; it also included the censorship of opinions. A group of experienced journalists from San Francisco's Bay Area formed the heart of the *Tanforan Totalizer*, the assembly center's newspaper, but soon ran into roadblocks of one kind or another. A Japanese American Citizens' League (JACL) leader questioned the liberal sympathies of the staff and did not hesitate to bring his concern to the attention of the center manager. Every issue had to pass muster with both administrative and army censors. Because no guidelines existed to give editors a sense of what could be printed, the staff remained at the mercy of the censors from the very first issue to the last. Moreover, the two censors did not always agree and created a mess of last-minute changes and headaches for both the writers and the production staff. Even the use of the mimeograph machine did not go unsupervised. The element of control underwent changes but always in the direction of more red tape. A journalist described the labyrinthine approval process that was in effect in July 1942:

> Here is how our copy goes now. I get data (say from the Finance Department) and write it up. Then it goes to McQueen (official Army censor) for his ok. Then it goes to Davis (center manager) for his ok. Then it goes to the head of the department for his ok. Then the dummy is set and it gets an ok, again from Davis. Then the stencil is cut and sent up to Davis again for his ok. Then it gets sent to the supply room and it sits on the desk of the chief until he gets around to giving it final approval and checks to see if it has Davis' signature on it.[24]

The administrative stranglehold made the staff realize that the paper had limited value. Charles Kikuchi, an indefatigable diarist and member of the JERS staff, also worked on the *Totalizer* and commented that after writers patted themselves on the back for producing the best of the assembly publications, they conceded that their conceit mattered little. In reality, "all of the papers were the same—all lousy because we could not print what was really going on and that it presented a false picture of things by only mimeographing the bright side of things."[25] The news—like so many other aspects of life—could not help but be affected by the context of imprisonment. Freedom of the press rang as hollow as other notions of democracy. The editor, Taro Katayama, grew increasingly frustrated with the restrictions placed on the newspaper. According to Kikuchi: "TK says that he doesn't give a damn about the paper because it is so limited and could not have any value as social documentation." Given the working conditions, Kikuchi suggested that the *Totalizer* might be seen more as a lifter of morale than as social documentation.[26]

Japanese Americans educators did their part to raise morale and help Nikkei make the transition to life behind barbed wire even as they, too, had to adjust to a new life. Schooling had been abruptly interrupted by the war; and although the stay at the assembly centers would be temporary, Nikkei took an active role in all phases of the educational program. Twenty teachers, all Nisei, served as volunteer faculty at the Tanforan High School; all had college degrees from the University of California, Stanford University, Mills College, and Fresno State College. As chair of the advisory council, the Reverend Taro Goto called on his contacts on the outside to secure badly needed school supplies. Ernest Takahashi oversaw much of the practical day-to-day details of running the schools and also dealt with personnel issues.[27] The schools at Tanforan had no official status; yet despite voluntary attendance, some 670 students had registered on 9 June 1942 at Tanforan. Classes started on 15 June and ran for thirteen weeks. Henry Tani, supervisor of the high school, commented: "The surprising aspect of the whole educational program of the high school is the spirit in which the curriculum is carried on. The students are most anxious to keep busy attending classes and learning what there is to learn. The teachers are experiencing a new field of endeavor and are really enjoying their teaching job."[28]

Nisei who had aspired to become teachers before the war knew that school districts simply did not hire Japanese Americans. In a strange twist of events, the war offered second-generation men and women a chance to venture into a field previously closed to them, albeit in an unofficial capacity. Nevertheless, teachers took their task seriously; at a faculty meeting at Tanforan, they identified three main objectives for the schools:

1. To give each child the maximum educational benefit of which he or she is capable.
2. To keep a record of teaching methods, subjects and results to build up a body of reference material to forward to the War Relocation Authority (WRA) Centers.
3. To develop a Parent-Teacher Association (PTA) in order to educate the parents as well as the children in the importance of proper schooling.[29]

In developing and implementing an educational program, Japanese Americans experienced a limited opportunity to guide the process of instruction. Consistent with efforts before the war to "Americanize" immigrant children, officials responsible for education saw the camps as a prime opportunity to assimilate Nisei. Professional educators from the Stanford School of Education carried on their legacy of working with Japanese American students and offered a model of "community education" that sidestepped the fact that imprisoned students hardly constituted a normal community. Faith in the ability to bring about positive change overrode the misgivings that educational technocrats had regarding the dangers of social control and coercion.[30]

Japanese Americans recognized the tensions that affected their schooling. "Besides the basic three R's," one Nisei observer noted, "the children are taught 'Americanization' which consists of saluting the flag and singing national hymns." Would education help keep faith in democracy alive at a time when those beliefs hit an all-time low? The heart of the educational dilemma lay in the emptiness of promoting democracy to Americans who had been convicted and condemned not for their actions but on the basis of ancestry.[31] Ultimately, the efforts of Japanese Americans not only reflected a belief in education but also a commitment to the racial-ethnic community, even in the most trying of times. All those involved understood the limitations facing them but continued to move forward because of the desire to provide schooling for students. The newly minted teachers experienced a small victory in securing grade promotions from school districts for just over half of its student population. As the Nikkei moved into the camps, their experience in assembly centers enabled them to continue their involvement with the educational process.

The initiative and energy of Japanese Americans involved in education also extended to those participating in religious life. Both Buddhists and Christians experienced a swell in attendance that suggested more free time, opportunities to get together with others, and a search for meaning during a period in which it could not easily be found. At Tanforan, a Buddhist priest recognized that not all who attended services did so for religious purposes; yet he stated: "As far as I am concerned I should like to see them come to church for other reasons, but if they come, we shall try to make them good Buddhists and good Americans."[32] Tamie Tsuchiyama noted that at Santa Anita, while many went to Buddhist services, others hesitated because of fear that they might become the target of investigations. Despite their constitutional right to freedom of religion, Nikkei Buddhists had already experienced a guilt by association in which things "Japanese" were suspect. Among others, Buddhist priests had been included as part of the prewar surveillance by the FBI and military intelligence; and in the wake of Pearl Harbor, many clerics had been arrested, leaving congregations without spiritual leaders in a time of crisis. "At the outbreak of war," Tsuchiyama observed, "numerous Buddhists began attending Christian churches for they naively felt that by embracing 'American' religion they might receive kindlier treatment at the hands of Whites."[33]

The harassment and discriminatory treatment that Buddhists experienced at the hands of the federal authorities did not seem to extend to interfaith relations, according to a report from Tanforan. Those in charge of activities attempted to include Buddhists and Protestants on the program. Among the religious groups themselves, Buddhists, Protestants, and Catholics worked together:

> The issei [sic] leaders seem to take a back seat in camp and since the nisei [sic]leaders are taking a leading role, there seem to be better relationships and less age-old barriers between religious groups. One reason may be attributed

to the fact there . . . is less competion [*sic*], if any, for any sort of financial support from the community which was not true in the home town situation. Here the leaders in both or three of the religious groups work side by side as in the Recreation Department for instance and so understanding is easier to achieve and cooperation more equal.[34]

Forced removal took religious groups out of their natural context, and since most of the basic, day-to-day needs were not an issue, clergy and church leaders could focus their time and energy on serving others.

Worship services became an integral part of life in the assembly centers and, later, in the camps. Catholics, a Protestant federation, Episcopalians, and the Holiness Association all conducted regular programs on Sundays, and Seventh-Day Adventists held their gatherings on Saturdays. With the exception of Roman Catholics, Issei (Japanese-language services) and Nisei (English-language services) met separately. In addition, many centers initiated a Young People's Fellowship on Sunday evenings for young adult members of the second generation. At Tanforan, thirteen Protestant denominations created a council of Nisei who planned services and other activities. In a spirit of fellowship and solidarity, the council decided to let each group take a turn leading in a fashion consistent with the denomination's particular faith tradition.[35]

If church and schooling occupied the energies of many Japanese Americans in the assembly centers, few could escape the cold fact of being prisoners of the U.S. government. "Ken Ishii"[36] and a fellow Nisei climbed to the very top of the Tanforan racetrack grandstands and looked out on familiar terrain:

> We could see the Bay in the distance and just beyond the barbed wire fences of Tanforan . . . [and] on the knoll above South San Francisco there is the imposing sign, "South San Francisco The Industrial City." How often I had seen that sign on my way to the University, and yet, from the grandstand seat, it seemed as though I were gazing on a strange landmark. We were both getting despondent. This wasn't good for us, and yet, here we could contrast two worlds it seemed—the old one from which we had come and this new fettered one, we couldn't help but feel we were suffering unjustly.

Ishii complained not about the poor food or the physical inconveniences— these came as part of wartime conditions. The real anguish lay in the distrust of friends and of a country to whom Ishii and other Nisei had been loyal. "By loyalty," Ishii explained, "we didn't mean overt acts of flag waving, but a silent faith and conviction that this was our country, our way of life, our beginning and ends." That anguish would grow as Japanese

Americans along the West Coast boarded trains with darkened windows that headed for War Relocation Authority (WRA) camps in the interior of the United States.[37]

Camp Life

The concentration camps that would become home to many Japanese Americans during the war years hardly proved to be an improvement over the assembly centers. Families crowded into stark, one-room "apartments" in hastily constructed tar-paper barracks that offered very little privacy. Standing in line for substandard food in dining halls did not boost morale, nor did the arrangement help families deal with an environment that fostered disintegration. Communal bathroom facilities, including toilets without stalls, added to the dehumanization of the Nikkei, as did severe dust storms, bouts with mosquitoes, and extreme weather. Along with the physical hardships came the considerable psychological challenges: the loss of homes, property, livelihood, freedom; the stress of captivity and the uncertainty of the future. As time wore on, Japanese Americans exhibited a range of responses to their circumstances. In late 1942, riots broke out in the camps at Poston and Manzanar, and protests also took other forms, including draft resistance at Heart Mountain, Wyoming. Some Nikkei channeled their energies into camp-based jobs that paid a mere pittance but filled time. Others tended to vegetable and flower gardens or expressed themselves through the fine arts.

As Japanese Americans endured the camps, the federal officials in charge viewed mass incarceration as an opportunity to assimilate this "problem" population into the rest of American society. As models of democracy, the camps would seek to eliminate doubts about the loyalty of Japanese Americans. Toward that end, efforts were made to bring camp life in line with the overall aim of molding and shaping Nikkei into ideal members of the nation. In February 1943, WRA officials, in conjunction with the U.S. Army, devised a disastrous application for leave clearance for persons eighteen years and older. Responses to a series of questions would determine whether one was eligible for early resettlement to unrestricted areas of the country or for military service. The JACL leadership had promoted the idea of a segregated Nisei fighting unit to prove the loyalty of Japanese Americans. The questionnaire was fatally flawed, as evidenced by the two most troubling inquiries. Question 27 asked Nisei men behind barbed wire and under armed guard whether they would be willing to serve in combat duty for the United States armed forces wherever ordered. Question 28, in asking Japanese Americans to forswear allegiance to the emperor of Japan, assumed that Nisei had indeed been loyal to Japan. For Issei, an affirmative answer would effectively render them stateless, since they were ineligible for U.S. citizenship. The confusion and anxiety surrounding the questionnaire created havoc in many families and resulted in qualified answers, no responses, and answers motivated by desires far more complex than a mere test of one's loyalty or disloyalty to the United States.[38] As a result of the application, "no-no" respondents were shipped to the Tule Lake camp in northern California that had been redesignated the camp for troublemakers.[39] Others were cleared for leave to continue their education and to take jobs in the midwestern and the eastern parts of the United States.[40] Nisei men from the mainland who volunteered for the U.S. armed forces served with distinction.

Those who served in the U.S. military represent the most celebrated dimension of the wartime experience of Japanese Americans. More than 20,000 Nisei answered the call, the majority of them being from Hawaii, where Japanese Americans were not subjected to mass incarceration. About 6,000 persons, largely bilingual in English and Japanese, were part of the Military Intelligence Service (MIS), the majority of whom were Nisei. After intensive training first in San Francisco and later at Forts Savage and Snelling in Minnesota, MIS troops were attached to various American units fighting in the Pacific. Nisei MIS, also known as "Yankee Samurai," deciphered captured Japanese documents, interrogated prisoners of war, and even slipped behind enemy lines. Although their story is not well known, the Japanese American MIS have been credited with saving American lives and shortening the duration of the war.[41]

By comparison, the saga of the segregated 100th Infantry Battalion and the 442d Regimental Combat Team of the U.S. Army has received much attention. The 100th traced its history to prewar Hawaii, where volunteers and draftees served in National Guard units. In June 1942, the Hawaii Provisional Infantry Battalion was sent to the mainland for further training and would eventually become activated as the 100th Infantry Battalion, a "separate" fighting unit of approximately 1,300 soldiers. After time at various sites, the 100th shipped out for North Africa in August 1943 and was assigned to the 133d Regiment of the 34th Division of the Fifth Army. The 100th met with fierce battles in Italy and, in January 1944, just after the Allied capture of Rome, Nisei from the 442d Regimental Combat Team arrived. The 100th had already earned its renown with some 900 casualties. The 100th became the first battalion of the 442d in June 1944.[42]

The history of the 442d dates to July 1942, when the army chief of staff

Nisei soldiers of the 4th Platoon, Company F, 2d Battalion, 442d Regimental Combat Team, 36th Division, Chambois Sector, France, October 1944. (U.S. Army Signal Corps photo, courtesy of Harold Harada, Japanese American National Museum [NRC.1997.94.1])

G-2 Section met to consider whether a small Japanese American military unit should be formed, since some 4,000 Nisei soldiers had been inducted by that time. Some of these soldiers were in training with the 100th, but many others had been relegated to noncombat duty. Assistant Secretary of War John J. McCloy helped push through the decision to form a new unit at the end of 1942. McCloy wanted to counter Japanese propaganda that Japanese Americans faced discrimination in the United States. In February 1943, President Roosevelt announced the formation of the 442d Regimental Combat Team. A call went out for volunteers, and over 10,000 Hawaiian Nisei responded, with over 2,600 accepted for induction. Mainland numbers were much smaller, with 1,256 volunteers and 800 accepted for induction. There were some tensions between Hawaiian Nisei and mainland Nisei during their training that were based largely in perceptions of the other. The Hawaiians viewed the mainlanders as reserved and arrogant; mainlanders saw the Hawaiians as loud, crass, and bullying. Relations improved over time, however, especially as they fought side by side. In March 1944, the 442d received its overseas orders and would eventually see heavy fighting in Italy and France. The 442d experienced 225 days of combat and was the most decorated unit for its size and length of service in U.S. military history, suffering over 700 killed. After the war, the 442d was received by President Truman at the White House, and the commander in chief told them: "You have fought not only the enemy but you fought prejudice—and you have won."[43] It is clear that the soldiers had battled not only for their country but also for Japanese Americans. For those Nisei from the mainland, most entered the army from the camps, knowing that they risked their lives to defend a country that continued to hold loved ones captive.

Lessons of a Wartime Education

Those who remained in the camps would also learn a lesson of survival of a different sort. For many Nisei, life in the camps entailed a continuation of their schooling. Students encountered New Deal bureaucrats who attempted to extend the progressive agenda of immigrant education that had been set before the war. In particular, the WRA viewed education as a primary means to an end: assimilation. Instead of being disturbed or even questioning the incongruity of teaching democratic ideals to an imprisoned student population, officials envisioned the camps as a golden opportunity. A cure could be administered to the social pathology of Japanese Americans that had required the U.S. government to segregate them as a "special" segment of the population.[44]

The very foundation of schooling in the camps suffered from false assumptions that guided the educational philosophy of those in supervisory roles. In the summer of 1942, Dr. Paul Hanna of the Stanford University School of Education and his team of researchers met with WRA officials. Hanna and associates advocated a community-based model of education in which Japanese Americans would have an active role in participating in their schooling:

> Briefly, a community school is one which bases its curriculum on the life of the community in which it is located. It becomes an institution of service in the community's development, as well as an institution for the development of the individual. . . . It also has a double effect on the life of the children and the youth since: (a) it contributes to an improved set of environmental conditions through which they will be better nurtured, and (b) as they participate in the attack on community problems through the school, they further their own best development.[45]

In theory, Hanna's vision seemed ideal; but in reality, it ran into major obstacles that undermined the notion of a community school. For one, those in charge of dispensing a democratic education had no intention of allowing Japanese Americans to have any substantive input with regard to their schooling.[46] Moreover, education became a form of indoctrination in which overtly patriotic responses from students drew high marks and praise. In his dissertation on the educational programs of the internment camps, Robert Mossman noted that students who toed the administrative line received disproportionate opportunities to express their opinions through public speeches and printed items. A definite system of rewards and achievement promoted WRA efforts to control the tone and direction of camp education.[47]

Perhaps the greatest oversight by professional educators remained the fact that the camps never came close to replicating stable communities. Riots, the stresses of daily survival, and the draft affected the lives of Japanese Americans who could hardly mistake their situation as normal. Anthropologist Lane Hirabayashi has questioned how students could be taught the democratic way of life in racially segregated schools run by the U.S. government under armed guard.[48] Government bureaucrats took it on themselves to decide the needs of Japanese Americans and, in the area of education, undermined any real commitment to community building by imposing their agenda of mainstreaming Nikkei students.[49]

As had been the case before the war, the best laid plans of professionals did not always materialize. The educational program, like every other dimension of camp life, suffered from the disorganization of creating instant "communities" in deserts and on swamplands. During the 1942–43 school year, the student-teacher ratio ran forty-eight to one for elementary and thirty-five to one for secondary instruction (compared to a national average of twenty-eight to one).[50] In addition to large classes, pupils and their teachers braved physical conditions that included intense heat, freezing cold, and blinding dust storms. Barracks and classrooms often lacked basic equipment like chairs and tables. Supplies and books proved scarce, and teachers faced an incredible challenge to assemble even the most basic forms of instruction. The hardships reflected the harried state of the camps. In time, some improvements did take place, but education throughout the war remained anything but ordinary.

At first glance, the curriculum appeared rather traditional as students took courses in subjects such as English, social studies, math, and home economics. Schools also sponsored sports leagues and offered students an opportunity to exercise their creative talents on the yearbook or the school newspaper. In every aspect of their education, however, Nisei encountered the message of Americanization. Many of the schools focused on the fundamentals of reading, writing, and arithmetic but did so in ways that stressed an appreciation of the English language and American democracy.[51] Teachers generally supported Americanization in camp education but did not always prove effective in promoting that agenda. Turnover rates remained high. Teachers opted for higher-paying, war-related jobs and for work under less trying circumstances. Many of the 600 white American teachers had never seen Japanese Americans before, and the lack of previous contact—as well as the disregard for the cultural particularity of the Nikkei—did not help matters. Carole Yumiba's study on the Arkansas camps revealed that establishing a rapport constituted one of the biggest problems between the teachers and students.[52] The Japanese Americans on staff, 50 certified teachers and 400 teacher's assistants, did help ease the educational exchange, but early resettlement, grueling work, and low pay took their toll. In addition, Nikkei teachers who had enjoyed greater latitude and autonomy in the assembly centers faced tighter controls under the WRA and subsequently felt less invested in the process.[53]

Nearly 30,000 Japanese American students came under the jurisdiction of the WRA during the war.[54] Most of the pupils went to classes eleven months out of the year, receiving some 180 days of instruction. A typical day at Jerome High School was comprised of six class periods that ran from 8:30 in the morning until around 4:00 in the afternoon. The elementary school schedule ended one-half hour earlier and alternated between class lessons and recesses.[55] Given their confinement, many Nisei went to school because it gave some structure to their dislocated lives, but the effects of confinement also spilled into the education of the second generation. Americans of Japanese ancestry experienced a drop in morale as uncertainty and despair characterized their future more than anything else. The results of a survey of graduates from Jerome High School indicated that many Nisei had given up their plans to go to college. Before the war, close to 50 percent of the students in the class of 1943 had intended to get a college education, but that figure had plummeted to 14 percent. Finances, family concerns, and other matters were certainly factors, but the war and the experience of being placed behind barbed wire also demoralized students.[56]

Schools had been sites in which Nisei had accessed American culture and society, and they had been told that as U.S. citizens, they too could claim their rightful place alongside fellow Americans. The current plight of the Nikkei left many students bitter. Paul Kusuda of Manzanar expressed his frustrations and reflections through numerous letters to Mrs. Afton Nance, his former teacher.[57] Born in Los Angeles in 1922, Kusuda had attended public schools in the city and had begun an electrical engineering program at Los Angeles City College before the war interrupted his studies. Kusuda wrote to Nance on 12 May 1942 to announce that he and his family had prepared to leave Los Angeles for Manzanar. "We leave this Saturday, May 16," Kusuda noted: "At last, I can find out for myself the existing conditions of camp life." Six days later, Kusuda sat in the camp library composing a letter to Nance detailing the trip and transition to Manzanar. He decried the work available to internees at the rate of 4.5 cents an hour. According to Kusuda, the government offered slave wages, and he sarcastically commented that with such prospects, the future loomed bright for the second generation. Another letter further expressed his state of mind: "Please bear with me because everything in which I formerly believed in has been shot to H. . . . From now on, I'm not going to trust anyone when it comes to governmental affairs. To think that I got fairly good grades in civics, American History, Political Science, etc., makes me laugh because I reall [*sic*] believed in all that I studied."[58]

Exercising his rights as a citizen, Kusuda wrote a pointed letter to Franklin Roosevelt, explaining to the chief executive the lessons that he had learned in school. He expressed his disappointment with the wholesale evacuation as well as the use of the term "Japs." Did not the term "Americans" also apply to the Nikkei? Kusuda continued:

In schools, everyone is taught that in the eyes of the law, all persons are considered innocent until proven to be guilty. But, why was it that *we* were branded as potential spies, *we* were singled out as threatening democracy, *we* were and are considered dangerous? That hurt! What cases of sabotage promoted by us can be said to justify the up-rooting of our hard-earned way of living? What can justify the fact that we Americans are not allowed to aid the war effort? What can justify the fact that many students are cut off from education without reason? Is that at all fair? Try as we may, the answers cannot be found to such questions.[59]

Kusuda found life in the camps to be anything but fair, and it angered him to see the preferential treatment accorded to European-American staff and visitors at Manzanar. For instance, WRA personnel received higher wages to compensate for the hardships of living in inhospitable surroundings. Observing a coexistence clearly defined by racial hierarchy, Kusuda questioned notions of equality. "Time and time again, I have argued that America is not a democracy for white people only," Kusuda told his former teacher. "Was I wrong? God help us all if I am or was because what a future is in store for everyone in a false democracy!"[60]

The bitterness and disappointment of Paul Kusuda's experience also affected many other Nisei whose notions of America faded under the harsh lights of the guard towers. Along with a decline in morale, some students also vented their frustrations by a lack of participation and through acts of resistance. Thomas James's study of education in the camps noted the rise of student activism during 1944. Mass walkouts of classes took place in Topaz, Utah, and students pressured the administration at Minidoka, Idaho, to protest the dismissal of a well-liked principal. After a teacher slapped a junior high student at Minidoka, students refused to return to class until an assembly of the entire school had been called during which the teacher apologized to the student.[61] Vandalism also broke out at some of the camp schools and left very visible reminders of dissatisfaction. In Tule Lake, California, which had become the official segregation center for "problem" internees after the summer of 1943, education reflected the condition of those who had been branded as disloyal and troublemakers. Acts of resistance prevented any classes from being held between the summer of 1943 and January 1944. After delays, a new high school opened in February 1944 but with only 68 percent of previous enrollments. Kibei Nisei and others took matters into their own hands and formed private schools that tried to replicate a Japanese curriculum and mode of schooling. The range of such responses illustrated that Nisei did have some say in the educational process.[62]

The actions or inaction of Japanese American students disturbed WRA administrators, who envisioned education as a key component of a planned and highly controlled camp environment. After unrest in several of the centers erupted in mass protest, the WRA worked with the National Japanese American Student Relocation Council (NJASRC), a college placement service, to get Nisei out of the camps and into environments more conducive to assimilation. Early resettlement of second-generation students who received leave clearance fit nicely with the objective of scattering Japanese Americans in the Midwest and East and weakening familial ties by separating Nisei from their parents.[63] The NJASRC evolved from the efforts of educators, religious leaders, and students on the West Coast concerned about the schooling of Japanese Americans. An informal group, the Student Relocation Council, first met in March 1942 in Berkeley, opening branch offices to coordinate efforts in California, Oregon, and Washington. A year later, a central headquarters had been established in Philadelphia at the office of the American Friends Service Committee. As the NJASRC, staff made contacts with hundreds of colleges, pursued financial aid for students, and oversaw the process of securing governmental clearance for the second generation. By the time the NJASRC shut down its operation in 1946, about 4,000 Nisei had been able to begin or continue their college education.[64]

The NJASRC ran into assorted difficulties in securing placements for students. Sociologist Robert O'Brien of the University of Washington, who served on the staff of the council during the war, noted that Japanese American resistance to resettlement proved to be the biggest obstacle. Issei and Nisei worried about, among other things, the breaking up of families, the financial insecurity of settling in unfamiliar cities, and race prejudice. Many parents of college students also hesitated to send their children alone into uncharted areas of the country where people had no familiarity with Japanese Americans. O'Brien commented on the WRA program of early resettlement: "Although a minority awaited only the chance to leave the centers, the greater number of the evacuees either hesitated or resisted as the WRA tried various means to show the wisdom of relocation. It was to take three long years of education, persuasion, and even threats, to gain evacuee co-operation in fulfilling this program." In fact, however, the WRA never really succeeded in its push to resettle Japanese Americans. In a one-year period (June 1943–June 1944), only 18 percent of the camp population had cooperated, falling far short of predictions by one WRA staff member who suggested that twelve months would be sufficient time to resettle the camp population.[65]

Students who ventured from the camps to college embarked on a journey that took them out of confinement but into unknown territory. The NJASRC tried its best to ease those transitions, and council staff in the field visited students in the camps as well as on campuses. Many students and staff exchanged letters, sharing experiences and thereby keeping connected to one another.[66] Mary Ogi, a graduate student in the Library School at Denver University, recounted her travels and adjustment to life in Colorado. Cleared to leave Tanforan in the fall of 1942, the coed recalled her feelings: "The ride over the Bay bridge was glorious—all I could think of was that I was *free* and was actually back in S.F. again." She managed to squeeze in a visit to friends and former teachers at the University of California at Berkeley. During her train ride from Oakland to Denver, Ogi commented on the "barren lands of Nevada and the sagebrush and salt beds of Utah" and the wonders of the Colorado landscape.[67] Like so many of the "college Nisei," Ogi struggled to balance classes, living conditions, and adaptation to a new environment. It helped to have other Nisei around, and Ogi had met and formed friendships with other second-generation women at the University of Denver. The cost of living created enough of a strain on her that she decided to take on a domestic job to help ends meet. Ogi thought often of her family in the camp at Topaz and also worked to save funds so that she might visit them during her vacation.

The ties to family loomed large for many Nisei who aspired to continue their education. Chizuko Kitano declined her scholarship to Smith College. Her father had just returned from the Department of Justice camp in North Dakota, and her mother suffered from illness. "I feel responsible for my parents and family in this trying period of confusion, and I must see them through in the adjustment period in the Relocation Center," commented Kitano. "It hurts me harder than you can imagine to let this wonderful opportunity go, but I am sure that the recipient of this award will be a worthy one."[68]

Constance Murayama did manage to get to Smith College and, like many of her counterparts, felt thankful for the opportunity to study and yet also realized that many had been left behind. Murayama and a fellow Nisei student enjoyed life in New England and, after some initial reserve, found a measure of acceptance: "When people along our streets got used to seeing Helen and me trotting along every morning, the house-wives invariably screeched good-morning to us." Classes demanded much; Murayama said that she "was up to her ears" in readings from Leo Tolstoy and Thomas Hardy. Papers needed to be written and time seemed to fly by, but she enjoyed the frenzy of the school term. Despite the activity and pleasantries, the Smith student recognized her life differed from those of her classmates: "This sounds like all sweetness and light, doesn't it? Of course, I was agonizingly home-sick but when I thought that 'home' equalled camp, it's surprising how fast the nostalgia evaporated. But the one time I entertained dark and gloomy thoughts was when I was filling out some papers, which asked for my permanent home address. Gosh, it really pulled me up short when I realized that Newell, W.R.A. was home."[69]

Nisei who left their new "homes" for college entered different environments but hardly escaped their status as Japanese Americans. In those places unaccustomed to the presence of Nikkei, the second-generation students stood out, even as many tried their best to blend into their surroundings. Those outside the camps may have been conscious of public perceptions but often looked to each other for companionship and support. The socialization before the war and certainly during it reinforced racial-ethnic ties. One student at the University of Utah complained to the NJASRC that fellow Japanese Americans congregated together despite the admonitions of council staff and others not to draw attention to themselves as a group: "When the nisei [*sic*] will ever learn a lesson, God only knows! The 120 plus some students here are too obviously forming small cliques and groups disgustingly noticeable. A great number have more sense, but some of the fellows are loud in expressing their criticisms of the school in comparison with former ones. . . . Already there are signs indicating that we shall be labeled as damn Japs."[70]

In his charge of clannishness, the student highlighted the reality of the college Nisei: wherever they went, they represented Japanese America. As the war progressed into the spring of 1944, Frank Inouye stated: "We cannot afford to lose sight of the fact that we do have a great responsibility to those who still remain in the camps." The second generation needed to attest to the loyalty and to the plight of Japanese Americans. "Since they are for the most part unable to speak coherently on their problems," Inouye argued, "it is up to us, the college students, to speak for them." The second generation never simply attended school as students; they were always Japanese Americans whose families and friends remained behind guarded gates. The elite group who attended college took with them the assimilationist plans of administrators; but, given the context of the war and the persistence of anti-Japanese sentiments, they remained a people set apart.[71]

Whether in the camps or in settings outside, Nisei largely continued their schooling during the war. Ironically, the WRA tried to foster the process of Americanization through the schools while discounting the fact that tearing apart Nikkei from their homes and confining them in desolate places could only send the opposite message—prisoners by virtue of race and ancestry. Many students saw through the facade but still suffered the injustices and contradictions of school and life under extremely artificial circumstances.

In his valedictory speech at Topaz High School, Harry Kitano recognized the bleak outlook for himself and his classmates. Kitano addressed the fifty-one other graduates of the Class of 1944 and reminded them: "We Nisei must set an example for the peoples of the earth, by overcoming the bitterness caused by evacuation and continue on toward making a friendly understanding among the peoples of this nation. We must think, talk and act equally and friendly toward caucasians, negroes and other orientals [*sic*] as hate has never yet overcome the problem of hate."[72] Perhaps the real lesson learned by the Nisei during the war had to do with their conditional status as American citizens. An education might lead to new experiences, but it did not enable others, including teachers and administrators, to see beyond the color line. The world Harry Kitano dreamed about required a movement beyond assimilation to one in which peoples of all backgrounds could stand as equals.

Camp Religion

If schooling brought Nisei more fully into the realm of camp administrators, the temples and churches remained largely a racial-ethnic affair. While no single institution or interpretive frame could possibly capture the complexity of internment, Buddhist temples and Protestant churches offer important insights into the camps. Religious institutions acted as: (1) social service agencies; (2) sources of racial-ethnic solidarity; and (3) places of meaning and faith. Churches aided Japanese Americans in making the transition to the camps in concrete ways as ministers and lay leaders helped members pack and make other necessary arrangements. Temple and church buildings became storage centers, since internees were allowed only two suitcases per person. Religion also supplied psychological and physical space for ethnic identification and solidarity and provided a means for assessing the war. The tradition of independent Japanese American congregations, well established for decades, continued during the war years. Buddhists and Christians supplied their own leadership, and this allowed them to gather together for a variety of purposes under religious auspices. Finally, as expressions of faith, Christianity and Buddhism offered many Japanese Americans meaning, comfort, and hope—frameworks within which to respond to and interpret their lives.

By the time of Pearl Harbor and the subsequent events leading up to forced removal, Buddhist temples and Christian churches had already laid a firm foundation for themselves in their communities. Religious affiliation, according to a War Relocation Authority camp survey, stated 55.3 percent Buddhist, 28.8 percent Protestant, 2.0 percent Roman Catholic, 13.4 percent no affiliation or no answer and 0.5 percent other (see table 4).[73] The upheaval of war certainly affected the ethnic churches as it did all sectors of Japanese America. The legacy of social service, racial-ethnic solidarity, and religious faith, however, remained important for the churches and their congregants throughout the years of imprisonment.

Social Service

Given the suddenness of internment, the social needs of Japanese Americans far outstripped the ability of the churches to meet those needs. The arrests of many Issei leaders, including Takashi Uchida, exacerbated mat-

Table 4. Religious Affiliation by Nativity in
Concentration Camps

Tradition	Issei	Nisei
Buddhist	68.5%	48.5%
Protestant	21.8	32.4
Roman Catholic	1.2	2.4
None/No Answer	7.6	16.3
Other	0.8	0.4
	99.9	100.0

Source: U.S. Department of the Interior, War Relo-
cation Authority, Community Analysis Section, Report
No. 9, "Buddhism in the United States," 15 May 1944,
Washington, D.C., 8. Based on 25 percent sample of ten
WRA camps.

ters. The Reverend Hideo Hashimoto of Seattle wrote: "The swift current of events following the outbreak of the present war has disrupted the lives of many of us. . . . I go about busily engaged in welfare work among needy families; soliciting funds and food for welfare; helping with registrations, disposal and storage of real and personal property; finding renters for houses and businesses; collecting junk; . . . providing nursery and recreational activities."[74] Hashimoto's letter underscored the frantic scramble of Japanese Americans who had been given days to settle a lifetime of hard work and investment. Buddhist temples and Christian churches not only supplied workers who assisted families in every facet of their preparations but also provided precious storage space in the sanctuaries, classrooms, and basements of church buildings.

The churches' task of helping members prepare for the move extended into the assembly centers and the camps. Lay leaders and clergy served as part of advance teams enlisted to ease the transition between the various stages of detention. Church networks assisted persons as they moved into their residential cubicles and adjusted to changes such as communal latrines, showers, and dining halls. Pastors took on roles as interpreters and middlemen between the administration and the internees in relaying policies and requests. In helping in such a wide variety of ways, the church leaders held positions that rivaled, if not surpassed, their prewar roles within the community. In dealing with day-to-day issues, Buddhist and Christian leaders did not forget their responsibilities to provide religious services. In June 1942, the Poston camp's First Christian Church sponsored a full program that began with an early morning prayer at 5:30 A.M., followed by a Nisei junior church at 8:30. After 9:15 Sunday school, adults and Nisei had simultaneous but separate services; this was repeated in the evening, when the second generation held a young people's gathering, and their parents met for Bible study. Nearly two years later, churches at Manzanar continued religious services with a reported 3,000 people in attendance at either the Buddhist temple or the Christian church. The Buddhist minister at Manzanar, the Reverend S. Nagatomi, also oversaw thirty-one memorials, one wedding, and five funerals during May 1944.[75]

In addition to formal worship services, churches allowed people to gather simply to talk about a wide variety of concerns, and these events complemented expressly religious programs. Church athletic leagues became an important part of camp life, as they drew many participants and huge crowds of observers. A baseball game might attract thousands of spectators to the stands. Camp newspapers carried results of the leagues in sports columns. Nisei lay leader Dave Nakagawa, who had been active with the YMCA in southern California, formed an athletic league at Santa Anita that continued at the camp in Amache, Colorado.[76]

Racial-Ethnic Solidarity

Helping internees cope with the daily struggles of existence occupied much of the energy of clerical and lay leaders, but religious institutions, by their very presence, also offered Japanese Americans a racial-ethnic institution with which they could identify. Temples and churches supplied space that enabled people to work through their trials. Religion helped create a sense of peoplehood.[77] On the theme of racial-ethnic solidarity, Gary Okihiro's study of the Tule Lake camp in northern California has argued that religion fueled resistance during the war and especially underscored the surge of Buddhist activity and folk beliefs/practices. According to Okihiro, Japanese Americans eschewed the Western tendency toward the compartmentalization of religion, and religious beliefs pervaded the culture and daily activities of the Nikkei, affecting both values and practice. In particular, religion helped combat the legacy of racism that predated the camps; it also tempered the attempts by the War Relocation Authority to use the camps as an opportunity to Americanize the internees. By upholding values such as filial piety, the family, and ethnic solidarity, religion affirmed key elements of the community, and it was the case that "resistance was rechanneled away from open rebellion into ethnic beliefs and practices, which, because of the nature of the oppression, themselves constituted resistance. Japanese religious belief, therefore, was both a vehicle for and an expression of the people's resistance."[78]

Okihiro's argument regarding the nature of religious resistance is helpful in understanding how temples and churches also acted as racial-ethnic centers of protest. At the camp in Jerome, Arkansas, Mary Nakahara offered her commentary through a church play. Entitled "The Exit We Search," the drama consisted of several flashback scenes to the period before the camps. Nakahara captured sentiments expressed in a variety of contexts, including a rural family, a college Nisei and her white American roommate, and a family gathered around the dinner table. The discussion of the family is especially noteworthy in its honesty and frankness regarding the diversity of perspectives that could strain family relations. Nakahara's fictional family consisted of a father, mother, and five children. The dialogue took place in the aftermath of Pearl Harbor as the family speculated what lay ahead for them and, by extension, other Japanese Americans:

> Father: You children don't realize what this war is going to do to you . . . and especially us, the parents. We'll be losing everything. The people here want to get us out of here. They might even start lynching us.
> Joe: Aw, Pop, don't be silly. America isn't that crazy. Besides, things like that don't happen.
>
> . . . .
>
> Father: It wasn't an easy life, son. The color of your skin makes a great difference. You can't ever be accepted as an American like the rest of the white people. You'll always be considered Japanese, no matter where you go, what you do, what you say. And you must be proud that you're a Japanese.
> Joe: Listen, Pop, I'm an American. I don't care what you say.
> May: I feel the same as Joe. Our teacher said America was made up of all nationalities. You know—a melting pot.
>
> . . . .
>
> Mother: But you children don't understand. Life at school and life after you finish school are two different worlds.
>
> . . . .
>
> Yutaka: I might be a Nisei, but I side up with Pop. We haven't got a chance here. I can tell you story after story of prejudice and stuff.
> Ayako: That's no way to talk. Let them make their choice for themselves. I want to see them live, really live . . . making their own decisions, not have parents and older ones like us tell them how to think and how not to think.
> Father: Ayako, why do you always talk like that? You look down on our judgment. You are a bad influence. You're the one that got Masao to volunteer.
> Masako: No, you're wrong. He's wanted to ever since Pearl Harbor. I'm glad he volunteered. Someday, you'll be glad, too.
> Mother: Masako, don't talk like that.

Father: He might be my son, but I'll never forgive him for that. To think that
he would fight against his own people.

Masako: But we're Americans, Pop. This is our country. We don't even know
Japan, nor do we ever care to go back there. I don't care. . . .

Ayako: Take it easy, Masa.

Joe: Masa, I'm with you.

Mother: Let's stop this.

"And thus, each day, friction in the family increased and developed. A
house divided," the play's narrator observed. "But the flaring words were
not embittered by hate; just a misunderstanding, but a misunderstanding
so great, that family ties were impossible."[79] Many of Nakahara's scenes
severely undermined notions of equality and justice. The camp audience
watching the play could hardly escape the irony of Joe's belief in his status as an American and his feeling that his country could never imprison
innocent citizens. The parents in the audience no doubt related to the play's
parents, who spoke of the Issei's struggles and advised their children on
the harsh realities of race in America.

Oberlin College students Dave Okada and Kenji Okuda picked up on
racial themes in the *Pacific Cable,* a nationally circulated Christian peri-
odical. In their article, Okada and Okuda pointed out that the camps represented an outgrowth of the historical legacy of racism against Japanese
Americans. That legacy, they argued, was responsible for their situation—
not "military necessity." At the time of the article (March 1943), FBI arrests and other investigations had failed to produce one instance of sabotage or disloyal activity, proving the case against Japanese Americans to
be bankrupt.[80] "M.B." used her pen to make a statement by contributing
a poem, "We Are But Refugees," to *The Pen,* a religious publication of
the Rohwer, Arkansas, camp:

> We are but refugees
>   in the land of the free,
> We're not from overseas,
>   this is our own country.
> We were born and bred here,
>   our parents, Japanese.
> Yet, within our own nation dear,
>   we are still refugees.
> America, we ask you why,
>   you leave us high and dry?

America, what is our sin?
  On you, our hopes we pin.
. . . .
Our loyalty to the nation
  cannot be a realization,
Until wrongs are somewhat righted,
  and rights reinstated.
Tomorrow may be a little late;
  for time may change our hearts.
Today, we want to know our fate,
  before our faith departs.[81]

Faith in country seemed to have departed already for the Reverend Royden Susu-Mago, who vented his anger through a letter written to a Dr. Richards, apparently a clerical colleague. He blamed well-meaning, European-American Christians for being naive and for sitting by while opponents of the Japanese in America mounted a drive that successfully "rounded up [Nikkei] like cattle and placed them in concentration camps." Susu-Mago wanted to know what had happened to due process of law and declared: "If these things constitute democracy I would like to know what the perpetrators of this [*sic*] unAmerican and Fascist tactics call what Hitler and his ilk do." In his eyes, the America that Japanese Americans experienced proved to be an impostor nation. The pastor decried a "prostituted America driven by hate, greed and racial animosity . . . the dictatorship of Roosevelt has undone all that we had learned to love and admire"; in response, he offered up a prayer: "God grant that the blinded eyes of our politicians may be opened that they may see the wrong that they have done and set it straight soon."[82] While few Japanese Americans voiced such fierce anger as Susu-Mago, his words and those of the others indicated some of the ways that Buddhists and Christians challenged their circumstances.

Resistance within the Christian circles also took shape in the reaction against a policy of "integration" that aimed to dismantle racial-ethnic churches. The WRA administrators hoped that geographic redistribution of Japanese Americans would break up ethnic ghettos of the West Coast so that other regions could absorb Issei and Nisei. Early resettlement of college-age students during the war, for instance, promoted the ongoing belief in education as a fundamental Americanizing influence. Many white American Protestant leaders did their part by encouraging Nikkei Christians to join white congregations. Historian Sandra Taylor has suggested that Protestant denominational policy meshed well with the assimilationist goals and objectives of the WRA.[83]

Japanese American Christians, however, largely rejected the plans for integration. The Reverend Paul Nagano stated that the churches played a pivotal role *because* they were centers of the ethnic community and sources of racial and ethnic identity.[84] According to Lester Suzuki, pastor of the Centenary Japanese Methodist Church of Los Angeles before the war, Japanese Americans carried out the bulk of the ministry in the camps. While denominations offered assistance from the outside, it consisted mostly of supplies and other supplementary aid.[85] Some Nikkei Christians, in fact, criticized white churches and denominations. Lay member Nobuko Lillian Omi, a resident at Santa Anita and Jerome, felt that white American Christians had let their fellow believers down. "I felt that God went with us and didn't desert us," Omi recalled. "As for our church, we could always build another one. I felt that there was a wall between American (White) churches and the ethnic churches, that we were deserted at a crucial time." Denominational leaders seeking to eliminate ethnic churches not only met resistance from Japanese Americans but from many within the white churches as well.[86]

In contrast to intra-Christian tensions, evidence exists that suggests that Buddhists and Christians experienced interfaith cooperation. Joint services of worship took place, and at one such event at the camp in Topaz, Utah, the Reverend J. K. Tsukamoto stated that the central geographic locations of both churches symbolized the role of religion in the lives of internees. Buddhist priest Zenkai Okayama added that in these difficult times, the community had to be guided by a religiously based morality and spirituality.[87] Both groups fell under the watchful eyes of the WRA, and this served as a link between Buddhists and Christians—suspects by virtue of race. Daisuke Kitagawa and "Jack Sato" attributed cooperation among the groups to the massive dislocation experienced by all the internees. Leaders of both groups sought to care for people within a religious framework, and the pressing needs of internees kept leaders fully occupied. In a state of emergency, the "instant" parishes and their leaders often just managed to get by and, hence, minimized potential conflicts that might have occurred.[88]

The changes brought about by internment undoubtedly contributed to positive relations between adherents of both traditions, but ethnic identification also played a crucial role. "John Ito" remembered that his father moved quite easily between ethnically based Buddhism and Christianity. Ito also saw race as the reason why Christians participated in cultural/

religious activities sponsored by the Buddhists. "Judy Nishimura" explained that she had attended Presbyterian, Methodist, and Buddhist churches for many years. For Nishimura, getting together with other Nisei represented the most important aspect of going to church and thus enabled her to switch between faith traditions without difficulty.[89]

A Place of Meaning and Faith

Resistance and interfaith cooperation illustrate how the churches acted as a base for ethnic solidarity. For many Japanese Americans, that sense of solidarity was enmeshed in religious faith commitments. Although highly diverse, religious beliefs sustained internees at various stages throughout the camps. Tashi Hori, president of the Manzanar YBA, reflected on how Buddhism had proven true during the trying times of the first year of the camps. "It has taught us to gain the highest perfection and preserverence [*sic*]," stated Hori. "This faith is a great gift in guiding our future life." In turning to their religion, Buddhists would find grounding in turbulent times.[90] Anthropologist Robert Spencer spent part of the war as a community analyst at the Gila River camp in Arizona. The social scientist noted that rites of passage such as birth, marriage, and especially death remained deeply connected to the faith tradition and practice of Buddhism. The observation of these rites formed an important part of the Buddhist legacy in the camps. At Gila River, clergy admonished Buddhists to do good, to love their neighbor, respect Amida, and have faith. Priests emphasized the need for community solidarity. Many of those incarcerated who had little previous affiliation with Buddhism attended services and religious activities during the war for social reasons but also for spiritual comfort.[91]

In his wartime autobiography, "Frank Higashi" recalled that his Christian journey had been one of searching for real faith rather than outward forms based on habits or customs. Raised in Protestant churches in San Francisco before the war, Higashi turned to his faith during his current trials: "To me, the Christian way of life was the highest and the most satisfactory way of life, and one that was the closest to the democratic and the American way of life. I knew it to be a hard way of life, but one that can achieve happiness because it was unselfish in nature and regarded man as fellow brothers and as equals."[92]

Faith during the war also meant looking to religious beliefs when facing death and great uncertainty over the welfare of loved ones. Naka Noguchi told about her prayer vigils for her sons, who were fighting in Europe with the U.S. Army. She placed a Bible in front of each child's picture and offered petitions many times each day. Given the fierceness of the fighting, Noguchi gave thanks to God for watching over her children and bringing them safely home. Buddhist M. Abe wrote to other Nisei in the camps from the front lines. In an article for the *Bussei Review* in June 1944, Abe had the following advice for the second generation: "If there is anything which I would like to impress into the minds of the Niseis in the various centers, it is their religion . . . be it Buddhist or Christianity. . . . war and its ugly nakedness of life will bring realizations that material things are useless in such times. Therefore, please tell my Bussei friends to attend churches so they will not be one of the many who are spiritually immature!"[93]

In turning to their faith commitments as Buddhists and Christians, Japanese Americans sought meaning. Nikkei also received from and gave to churches and temple life. Social service, ethnic solidarity, and religious faith had of course been part of the Buddhist and Christian witness within Nikkei communities long before the war had begun. The experiences and testing that the churches had endured in the decades prior to Pearl Harbor served them well during the trauma of the war years.

Legacy of the Camps

The many roads that led in and out of the camps changed the lives of Japanese Americans forever. Some felt the war's crushing blows in lost homes, businesses, and from the loss of loved ones and broken families. Nisei like Mitsuye Endo, Gordon Hirabayashi, Fred Korematsu, and Minoru Yasui challenged the injustice of incarceration through the court system. But these test cases painfully illustrated how wartime hysteria and a legacy of racism combined to dismantle constitutional rights. Regardless of age, gender, or social class, the camps spared no one along the Pacific Coast as all felt the effects of forced removal and incarceration.

By sending Nisei to the schools, Japanese Americans moved ahead with their lives, hoping to reconstruct their former lives as much as possible within the confines of the camps. As it had before the war, an education at least signaled hope for a brighter future for the next generation. WRA administrators used their power to push for Americanization, which would strip the second generation of "undesirable" vestiges of their ethnic background. Japanese Americans found help, solidarity, and solace in the racial-ethnic Buddhist temples and Christian churches that had for many years served the Nikkei. The daily vicissitudes of camp life proved quite challenging, and many drew on their religion for support and a space to call their own. The very context of the camps and the legacy of race prejudice, however, could do little to dispel the fact that Japanese Americans remained a marked population wherever they went. The second generation painfully faced these realities and experienced disillusionment as well as the resolve to push forward.

As the war drew to a close in 1945, Japanese Americans would leave the camps behind. Some returned to the West Coast, and others started anew in other regions of the country. Given the price paid, many Nikkei tried to bury the war and with it the pain and suffering that had wounded an entire people. And yet, in spite of the hardships and human costs, most individuals, families, and communities adapted, struggled, resisted, and survived this ordeal. America after 1945 might open up possibilities never before available; and yet, the sense of being Japanese American, in all its variations, remained an important part of the stories of the Nikkei after the war, as it had before. The war years proved beyond a doubt that, however difficult to distill, racial-ethnic identity mattered.

INSIDERS ON THE OUTSIDE:
NISEI JOURNALISTS AND WARTIME EDITORIALS

The news of the attack on Pearl Harbor that had disturbed the meal of the Uchida family in Berkeley, California, also made its way into the New York City living room of Nisei reporters Larry and Guyo Tajiri. The effect of what took place in picturesque Hawaii sent a ripple of shock, grief, and anger all across America. And yet, the events of that fateful Sunday held special significance for Nikkei, who now faced their worst nightmare: the United States and Japan at war. The Tajiris had relocated to New York City in 1940 to work with the *Tokyo and Osaka Asahi,* and, true to their calling, the journalist couple wanted to confirm what they had heard over the radio and headed uptown by subway to Times Square: "crowds milled on the sidewalks around the Times building, watching the bulletin boards. The first extras were out. The headlines were bold and black, the ink still wet. Hours later the crowd had grown, jamming the walks, pressing against the windows of the cafes and the haberdasheries which rim Times Square. Now a flickering tape of light circled the Times building, telling the story over and over again."[1] Like so many of the others sharing space on the cool and windy streets of Manhattan, the Tajiris were stunned—trying to comprehend what had happened in the Pacific and the implications for the future. With the United States joining a world at war, many Americans experienced both hardship and heartbreak, perhaps none more than Japanese Americans on the West Coast who endured the suffering of forced removal and incarceration.

Amid such cataclysmic change, journalists provided valuable information to their readers and, in time, represented a lifeline to the outside world for those inside concentration camps. This chapter views the war through the lens of Japanese American reporters who wrote during the period of transition after Pearl Harbor and into the war. Although incarceration shut down the immigrant press on the West Coast, fledgling newspapers in the interior of the United States, along with those that relocated, suddenly found a new and literally captive audience. Readers recognized that reporters' lives were inextricably bound with theirs and that they shared a fate that extended beyond the confines of barbed wire. As insiders on the outside, Nisei journalists, although monitored, knew a measure of freedom that enabled them to give voice to Nikkei concerns during a prolonged period of crisis.

In addition to providing a brief overview of the newspapers, this chapter focuses on three particular journalists who offered important insights into issues confronting Nikkei during the war. After Pearl Harbor, Larry and Guyo Tajiri accepted editorial positions with the *Pacific Citizen,* the Japanese American Citizens' League (JACL) paper that had relocated to Salt Lake City. They addressed a wide range of subjects but consistently took up the issue of race. The Tajiris not only drew on the lessons of the past but also placed the plight of those in the camps within a larger racial continuum, urging them to work together with others in America who also faced the pernicious effects of prejudice. Only in solidarity could lasting and positive change take place in the United States. Well ahead of their time, the Tajiris set a vision for the future that anticipated many of the concerns for social justice that emerged in the Asian American movement of the late 1960s.[2] A contemporary of the Tajiris, James Omura moved his base of operations from northern California to the Denver-based *Rocky Shimpo* and provided an alternative voice to JACL leadership. Omura questioned the right of the JACL to speak on behalf of Japanese America and also challenged Nikkei to exercise their rights in fighting the injustice they suffered at the hands of the U.S. government.[3]

The writings of the Tajiris and Omura constitute a reservoir of memory that offers fuller and more textured interpretations of the war and the camps. Their editorials aid the process of recovery of this infamous chapter in American history. The multiple voices speak against any claims to an authoritative or official narrative of the war and problematize notions such as loyalty and patriotism, unveiling in the process issues like resistance and internal conflict.[4] Although the camps swept up families and communities wholesale, they also represented a profoundly personal passage for the men, women, and children who endured incarceration.

Japanese American journalists who worked in the aftermath of Pearl Harbor provide especially compelling perspectives on the war and the camps because they formulated their views in the moment, without the historical distance afforded by hindsight. Nikkei newspapers also documented the home-front experiences of racial-ethnic peoples during World War II—a subject very much suffering from neglect. The writings of reporters testify powerfully to the irony embedded in the American effort to safeguard democracy abroad while, at home, Japanese Americans were carted off to concentration camps, and African Americans and Mexican Americans faced race riots in Detroit and Los Angeles. Commentators like the Tajiris and Omura not only called attention to the injustice of the camps but challenged the United States to fulfill its commitment to democracy and liberty for all of its citizenry. Accordingly, the Japanese American wartime press provides an important point of entry into this pivotal period of U.S. history.

The Press under Pressure

In the aftermath of Pearl Harbor, the press covered a community in chaos. Key Issei leaders had been arrested, thus creating a vacuum in communities along the West Coast. Nisei in Los Angeles gathered at the Maryknoll Catholic Mission under the banner of the United Citizens Federation on 19 February 1942, the same day President Franklin Roosevelt signed Executive Order 9066. Togo Tanaka, English-language editor of the *Rafu Shimpo,* estimated that 1,500 Nikkei attended the meeting, and organizers had to set up speakers outside the 800-seat hall for those unable to find seats. Despite the fact that Tanaka suspected that FBI and naval intelligence officers were in the audience, he stepped up to the podium and called the meeting to order, stating that the Nisei had nothing to hide. They met to bring coordination and unity to the various Japanese American groups who served the racial-ethnic community. Representatives from Buddhist and Christian churches, Local 1510 of the Fruit and Vegetable Workers Union, the Japanese American Citizens' League, and other organizations took their turn at the microphone.[5] The speakers affirmed their loyalty to the United States but, even under scrutiny, also stressed their rights as citizens. The Tajiris, native Californians, had since returned to their home state, and Larry spoke at the meeting. He urged his fellow Nisei to fight the efforts being made to herd them to the interior of the United States. "We need action and we need it now," declared Tajiri. "We are loyal to the American flag, but race hatreds are being stirred up in fascist pattern."[6] Among those doing the stirring, Los Angeles mayor Fletcher Bowron accused "all Japs"— including those born in American—as being capable of fifth-column activity and summarily dismissed city employees of Japanese descent. Nisei discovered that changing political winds could undermine support from "friends" in elective office. One participant at the meeting commented to

Tanaka: "I thought the Mayor was a liberal and a man who had scrupulous regard for human justice and honesty. He's more of a pompous jackass and hypocrite from what I can gather."[7] War often brought out the worst in people and governments; and, despite Larry Tajiri's call for action, Americans of Japanese ancestry had very little chance of halting the tide of hysteria, racism, and indifference that resulted in their incarceration.

Reporters on the West Coast lost their jobs since they and the newspapers that they worked for fell prey to forced removal, thus shutting down operations for the duration of the war. Some writers continued their work within the assembly centers and the concentration camps but found severe censorship to be the prevailing norm.[8] As Togo Tanaka found out, being a newspaper editor could be dangerous. After news of Pearl Harbor, the editor helped put out a special edition of the *Rafu;* the next day, FBI agents took Tanaka into custody. For the next eleven days, the journalist was moved to three different prison sites within the city of Los Angeles. After four days of being behind bars, Tanaka grew weary of noisome blankets and longed to take a shower: "Everybody is looking terribly seedy. No newspapers, no communication with the outside, and those terrible meals. Wrote another letter to Jean and gave it unsealed to the good-natured flat-foot who opens and shuts the cell door. He said he couldn't make any promises about when it would be mailed. . . . He said: 'How come you are in here, buddy? You don't talk like a Jap.' This gets me every time."[9] Tanaka's wife, Jean, knew only that the FBI had picked up her husband. The *Rafu* editor desperately sought to call home to check on his pregnant wife—only to be denied. In recalling those trying times, Tanaka wrote: "Never having been really churched, I found myself inexplicably turning to prayer in the quiet of the long night in those cramped jail cells, and discovered the meaning that when all else fails, truly, what else?"[10]

After Tanaka's release, he slowly made his way back to the paper whose key Japanese-language staff had also been arrested and continued to remain behind bars. The *Rafu* still managed to publish but especially felt the absence of publisher H. T. Komai. As Tanaka and others worked for Komai's release, the remaining Issei on staff worried that they might be next in line to be imprisoned. Adding to the tension, many readers facing financial difficulties canceled their subscriptions. By early March 1942, the *Rafu* had lost nearly 1,000 subscribers, cutting revenue already hurt by the severe drop in advertising dollars. Tanaka also noted that some of the Japanese-language staff had received anonymous threats: "Yoneo Sakai, Shiro Takeda and Joe Inouye seem to be the triumvirate coming on for most

Togo Tanaka, English-language editor of the *Rafu Shimpo* (Los Angeles Japanese
Daily News), testifies at a congressional hearing, c. 1942. (Security Pacific Collec-
tion/Los Angeles Public Library)

of this abuse. They are running the Japanese section for the most part now,
and they lean over backwards to make it pro-American in content and
spirit." The hostility toward some of the Japanese-language writers reflected a strain of Japanese nationalism that ran strong in certain segments of
the racial-ethnic community. Regardless of politics, however, all the im-

migrant papers along the West Coast were forced to shut down their operations in the spring of 1942. The silencing of the presses marked another way that life as Japanese Americans had known it underwent radical change. Tanaka's journal noted that after decades of reporting the news, the *Rafu* closed its doors on 4 April 1942.[11]

About a week earlier, the Tajiris, who had decided to stay in San Francisco and await orders to evacuate, had a sudden change of plans. The JACL leadership decided to move its headquarters from San Francisco to Salt Lake City and asked the couple to edit its fledgling in-house newspaper, the *Pacific Citizen*. Accepting the JACL's offer, the Tajiris had three days to get their things in order. Late in the afternoon of 27 March, the new editors of the paper hopped into the rust-colored Studebaker of Teiko Ishida, who had taken on the task of setting up the JACL shop in Utah. The army's decision to freeze all unrestricted travel outside military area number one on the West Coast expired at midnight and accounted for the frantic rush to get out of town. As the car raced through the streets, heading east, Larry Tajiri could not help but look back: "We saw San Francisco from the Bay Bridge, the city rising on its steep hills above the Embarcadero and the Bay was dramatic and breath-taking as always."[12]

In moving to Salt Lake City, the *Pacific Citizen* made another attempt to survive after many years of shoestring budgets, sporadic publication, and limited readership. The paper had started out in San Francisco as the *Nikkei Shimin* (Japanese American Citizen) in October 1929 and published exclusively in English. Its title changed to the *Pacific Citizen* in early 1930, the paper became designated as the official organ of the JACL in 1932. In financial trouble much of the time, the paper moved the next year to Seattle, where James Sakamoto of the *Japanese American Courier* took it over rather than see it cease publication. Sakamoto's run ended in 1939, when handling two struggling papers proved too much for the stalwart editor. The *Pacific Citizen* returned to San Francisco, and a local journalist, Evelyn Kirimura, edited the "monthly," four-page tabloid that published whenever it could. By the time the Tajiris took over in 1942, at the meager combined salary of $100 per month, the paper needed an overhaul that perhaps only journalists of their caliber and dedication could accomplish.[13] In one of the strange twists of fate, the paper, like the JACL, benefited from a newfound audience.[14]

Similarly, the large influx of Japanese Americans into the interior of the United States breathed new life into the struggling English-language sections of three other papers outside the restricted zones: the *Rocky Nippon*,[15] *Colorado Times*, and *Utah Nippo*. Published in Denver at 1328 29th Street, the *Rocky Nippon* launched its inaugural English-language edition on 3 October 1941 with the opening editorial proclaiming that the mission entrusted to them would not be in vain: "We shall be your voice, the voice of the niseis [*sic*]. We are here to bring better understanding between your ideas and those of your parents. . . . We are here to bring about a more amicable relationship between our fellow Americans and ourselves." Under editor Harry Matsunaka and assistant editor Mae Hirasawa, the paper had only a few months of existence before it began to serve a much broader base of readers. Having started out as a weekly, the *Rocky Nippon* by mid-1942 responded to the increased demand by publishing every two to three days.[16] An editorial published soon after Pearl Harbor indicated that the staff took its role as a voice for the Nisei seriously and noted that the second generation occupied a precarious position as American citizens whose "facial characteristics . . . even God cannot change." The writer called for a collective spirit since Japanese Americans faced a future marked by "bitterness, discrimination [and] self-pity." The editorial continued: "Our deepest pain, however, was that our fellow Americans did not understand that we were, if not more, deeply aware of the . . . [need] of Uncle Sam and we were willing to do more than our share. . . . we implore our fellow Americans of Japanese ancestry to not become bitter or to let our love for America become soured by epithets or discrimination."[17]

The *Rocky Nippon*'s counterpart, the *Colorado Times,* had little to say about Pearl Harbor in English as its Nisei section did not start until late August 1942. "In a Multitude of Knowledge," the paper's English masthead read, "There is Wisdom." Published triweekly, the English-language section of the *Times* provided news "by, for and of the Nisei." In addition to its new readers—courtesy of the U.S. government—the paper claimed to reach every Nikkei household in Colorado, New Mexico, Wyoming, and Nebraska. James Omura wrote briefly for the *Times,* and his first signed column, called the "Passing Parade," appeared 24 October 1942. Later during the war, Omura, the former editor of the journal *Current Life,* moved over to the *Rocky Nippon.* In a neighboring state, the *Utah Nippo* also had started an English-language section in the fall of 1939; by the end of 1940, it encountered the problem of so many immigrant papers: lack of financial resources. The relatively small pool of Issei subscribers could not underwrite the additional expenses of the Nisei section. A call went out for subscribers to contribute an extra dollar to their bills to help offset costs and to allow even minimal wages to be paid to the second-generation staff, who essentially had been working for free. After a lengthy absence during 1941, Sunao Ishio, the English editor, notified its readers in September that they had decided to go ahead with the English-language section. Little did Ishio know that events in a few months would catapult the paper into the status of major news source for thousands of Japanese Americans. Like the instant, tar-papered "cities" that sprang up in the deserts, war could generate major changes practically overnight. The *Pacific Citizen, Rocky Nippon, Colorado Times,* and *Utah Nippo* found themselves well-situated to report the news as it happened.

Editorializing a Vision

At the outbreak of war, English-language sections of Japanese immigrant papers had been covering the news for over a decade. Many second-generation Japanese Americans looked to the Tajiris, who had been at their trade for years. Larry Tajiri enjoyed a wide following among Nisei that dated to the early 1930s and his start in the profession. By the time Larry Tajiri became editor of the *Pacific Citizen* in Salt Lake City in the summer of 1942, a career in journalism had already taken him from Los Angeles to San Francisco to New York City. Enlisted by the JACL, Tajiri found himself in Utah, but he did not seem to be fazed, since he went where the news called him. Having started in high school journalism, Tajiri in 1931 edited the *Poly Optimist* during his senior year and guided it to recognition as the best school newspaper in southern California. The early exposure at Los Angeles Polytechnic High must have made an impression, since he left college his freshman year to take a full-time post at the *Kashu Mainichi* (Japan-California Daily News). The young Tajiri assumed the role of English-language editor for this Los Angeles immigrant daily and worked under its colorful publisher, Fujii Sei.[18]

In October 1934, Tajiri left the *Kashu* and headed north to accept a position on the English-language staff of the *Nichibei Shimbun* (Japanese American News), a much larger paper and arguably the leading Japanese American newspaper in the United States. He shared editorial responsibilities with veteran Nisei journalist Kay Nishida. Contributing to a regular column which he had brought with him from the *Kashu,* Tajiri's "Village Vagaries" reflected the reporter's broad interests, which included international politics, labor/union issues, and the arts. In particular, his strength as a writer lay in the ability to provide insight into how the news affected the lives of the Japanese in America. Tajiri's politically progressive views included support for unions as a means of improving the lives of Nisei and of fostering social change. At the same time, he recognized the complexities involved in events such as the 1936 Salinas lettuce strike, in which Nisei found themselves caught between Issei employers and union organizers who mobilized farmworkers in California.[19] Tajiri understood that issues of labor related directly to "race prejudice" (as it was called) since Japanese Americans, as racial-ethnic minorities, faced limited employment opportunities. During his years in San Francisco, Tajiri also helped form chapters of the Young Democrats (YDs) in the city and across the bay in Oakland. The YDs invited participation in the political process and worked toward building coalitions with other groups in American society.[20] Along with politics, Tajiri had a passion for the arts and literature that also included a critical eye toward the connections between Hollywood images and popular perceptions. Realizing the social barriers placed in the way of Nisei artists, the reporter used his position to provide an outlet and showcase for struggling writers and poets. He himself dabbled in fiction, and his writing appeared in Nisei literary journals.

Through the course of his work at the *Nichibei*, Tajiri met another reporter, Tsuguyo Marion Okagaki, who had graduated from the University of California at Berkeley, and also attended the prestigious School of Journalism at the University of Missouri. Muckraking ran in the family: Okagaki's father, Kichitaro, edited the San Jose branch of the *Shin Sekai*, the archrival of the *Nichibei*. Competition aside, Okagaki and Tajiri collaborated on a series of fictional romance stories that appeared in the *Nichibei* in February 1935. In a case of life imitating art, Tajiri and Okagaki created a romance of their own, marrying in the spring of 1937. The Tajiris worked closely together in the news business for many years—a match made in newsprint. The couple left San Francisco in 1940; and, after a stint at the *Tokyo and Osaka Asahi* offices in New York City, they headed back to California after Pearl Harbor.[21]

In surveying "Nisei USA," Tajiri's column for the *Pacific Citizen*, it is clear that he carried on his concerns developed before the war into his post at Salt Lake City. Tajiri addressed a broad set of issues, but race proved to be a thread running through much of his commentary. Despite the delicate nature of the times, he managed to ask difficult questions and express opinions that resonated with the second generation. Given Tajiri's record, it is noteworthy that he chose to work for the JACL and that the leadership invited him. Although he refrained from disparaging the JACL in print during his days in San Francisco, his political activities with the Young Democrats created an alternative to the conservative, business-oriented, and Republican tendencies of the JACL. Bill Hosokawa's in-house history of the Nisei organization suggests that the JACL recognized the outstanding talent of Tajiri and saw that he could help the struggling publication to achieve the potential that the founders of the paper had envisioned in the late 1920s.[22] In effect, war created the circumstances in which Larry Tajiri and the JACL could come together.

The accommodationist stance of the Japanese American Citizens' League did not prevent the Tajiris from doing their jobs as reporters. In effect, Larry Tajiri laid out both a critique and a vision of America through a Nikkei lens. Acting as a historian and teacher, Tajiri reminded his readers—with frequency and within varying contexts—of how race prejudice had deep roots in the Japanese American experience. The journalist exercised discretion but, in essence, connected anti-Japanese activity in the past to present woes. "So long as the Japanese remained a cheap, exploitable source of raw labor," according to Tajiri, "they were welcomed." As immigrants began to settle down "as individuals," however, discriminatory treatment followed. In the weeks preceding evacuation orders, political demagogues and those in the press whipped up a frenzy of prejudice against Japanese Americans. Senator Hiram Johnson became "one of the first politicians to capitalize on 'yellow peril.'" Although some Americans staunchly supported their Nikkei neighbors and friends, Tajiri wrote that "the public attitude which has generally condoned the evacuation of 65,000 Americans because their facial features are those of the enemy is rooted deep in California's long history of prejudice against the Oriental. The nisei [*sic*] is the unfortunate victim of these deep seated prejudices."[23] From his vantage point in January 1943, Tajiri obviously knew that Japanese Americans now lived behind barbed wire; and yet, even with the lessons from history, it still puzzled him that what had seemed impossible just a year earlier now indeed had become a cruel reality for over 120,000 people. The reporter placed major blame on publishing magnates like William Randolph Hearst and V. S. McClatchy.[24] Politicians, past and present, fared no better. The fanning of racist flames by Mayor Fletcher Bowron of Los Angeles after Pearl Harbor further added to the cries for the removal of Japanese Americans by the press and by special interest groups. Those in agriculture and in labor stood the most to gain from the incarceration of Japanese Americans: "It is a matter of historical fact that the resistance of white workers, particularly in the far west, to the Oriental immigrant laborer was instrumental in determining the government's attitude expressed in laws and prohibitions enacted and enforced during the period of immigration terminated by the 1924 Exclusion Act."[25] In targeting powerful publishers, politicians, and interest groups, Tajiri not only showed his understanding of the relationship between power and public opinion but vented his anger at an establishment elite that also drew the distrust and ire of many other Americans. At the same time, this strategy left intact a semblance of hope that the race prejudice heaped on the Nikkei did not necessarily reflect the true sentiments of the majority of their fellow Americans.[26]

The struggle for the hearts and minds of Americans also took place on Hollywood sets as the film industry joined the war through the production of propaganda movies.[27] Consistent with his interest in the arts, Tajiri kept an eye on the movie business. *Little Tokyo, USA* presented a worst case scenario; after seeing the film, Tajiri commented that "Hollywood has maligned peoples and nations before, but seldom has any race group been given the all out kicking around that the Nisei get." Set in Los Angeles, *Little Tokyo, USA* painted the second generation as homegrown fascists who worked with Nazi agents and the notorious Japanese Black Dragon Society to engage in espionage.[28] The white hero, police detective Preston Foster, is vindicated on 7 December 1941 for being falsely arrested for a crime he did not commit and saves the day by rounding up the traitorous Nisei. The film, by weaving actual historical events into its twisted plot, was all the more pernicious. For instance, the movie presented resistance to forced removal by Nisei as an effort to continue their treachery against the United States. The producers blurred the line between fact and fiction by using newsreel footage of Japanese Americans boarding buses and trains headed to Santa Anita and Manzanar. The closing shot of a deserted and boarded up Little Tokyo carried the warning: "Be vigilant, America."[29]

The frustrating and extremely dangerous element of film propaganda lay in its ability to reach mass audiences through a very powerful audio-visual medium. Tajiri noted that because of the tremendous expense and technical expertise, those harmed by motion pictures could not respond in like manner as one could with newspapers or magazines. Some eighty million Americans went to the movies weekly. The journalist predicted that the fallout from the film would affect all Asian Americans—not just Japanese—since studios used actors from other groups to portray the Nikkei. In short, the distinction might be lost on viewers. Tajiri noted the inhumane treatment of racial-ethnic minorities, arguing that Hollywood "has consistently failed to accept non-white races as ordinary, everyday human beings. The Negro is always shown as a menial or a buffoon. Until the Mexican government got tough about it, the Mexican was pictured as a 'dirty greaser.' The Chinese was either a pig-tailed comic or an evildoer filled with deviltry incomprehensible to the Occidental mind."[30] The Office of War Information's movie *Japanese Relocation* contained much less venom; but, because sponsored by the government, the film served as an apologia for incarceration. In reality, the Nikkei had been doing more than their share toward Allied victory. "The need is for a camera to record this participation," stated Tajiri. "The screen has already been used to spread the fiction of disloyalty about Japanese Americans. It can also be used to tell the truth." In the midst of lies and indifference, Japanese Americans truly needed a new deal from Hollywood.[31]

Like *Little Tokyo, USA*, decision-makers made little distinction between citizens and aliens, a fact that deeply troubled Tajiri and other Nisei. Much of the ensuing bitterness among the second generation resulted from a feeling of betrayal. In the past, "the fire and verbal brimstone were directed against an inarticulate alien group, while today the American children of those immigrants are the targets." Incarceration left little room for doubt about racial matters etched into the consciousness of so many Japanese Americans. "In California, the heat has been turned up so long against the Oriental" that its flames "singed" everyone in its path.[32] What had happened to Japanese Americans did not ferment overnight, and part of the cure rested in recognizing the problem: "Racial discrimination like venereal disease is an ugly subject, shunned by most people as a topic of conversation. . . . Perhaps racial discrimination as it exists today should be dragged out into the sunlight and examined. This war we fight today is, in one way, against racial discrimination the world over."[33]

Part of that world included California, and as the war progressed, Tajiri worried about activities of anti-Japanese forces that wanted to extend the ban into the postwar era. Already groups like the Home Front Commandos and the California Committee for Japanese Exclusion had joined a coalition of long-extant organizations that included the California Joint Immigration Committee and the Native Sons of the Golden West.[34] Exclusionists took proactive measures, for they knew that the war would not last forever. Indeed, by the end of 1944, with Allied victory in sight, the United States revoked its ban of Japanese Americans from the West Coast, effective at midnight, 2 January 1945. The reopening of restricted areas added another layer to an aggressive campaign by the WRA to resettle Nikkei into the midwestern and eastern parts of America. With military area number one no longer off limits, the WRA stepped up its pressures to get individuals and families to leave the camps. Along with the news of open return to California, the WRA issued notice that the camps would be phased out of existence by 1946.

The race baiting that had contributed to internment and continued during the war years remained a real concern for those who planned to return to California. Tajiri had kept readers abreast of hearings held by the

California state senate as well as actions taken by groups like floral grow-
ers to keep Japanese Americans out of the Golden State.[35] One Nisei allowed to return to the restricted area before the lifting of the ban had encountered hostile neighbors. In trying to move back home after clearance
had been authorized by the government, Japanese Americans in San Jose,
Lodi, Loomis, and Alameda County faced arson fires, threats, shootings,
and other acts of terrorism.[36] Regardless of what Nisei soldiers had done
in Europe or in Asia, uniforms studded with ribbons meant little if Japanese Americans could not walk safely down the streets of their hometowns.
Race prejudice, past and present, threatened America like a cancer and, if
allowed to persist, would lead to the death of democracy. In decrying discrimination in the realms of publishing, politics, economic interest groups,
and racist hate groups, Tajiri sought to expose the sources of the disease.
He wanted to make concrete something that often was left at a level of
abstraction. By unpacking race, Japanese Americans could better grasp its
internal dynamics and also determine the best ways to combat it: "Race
prejudice is not an 'inevitable and permanent feature of human nature.'
The nisei [sic] can accept race prejudice for what it is, a weapon in the hands
of selfish and greedy people. The nisei will find that race prejudice is not
the expression of all Americans or of the citizens of a functioning democracy. The nisei can fight race prejudice wherever it is found, as something
that is dark, ugly and vile. Race prejudice is un-American."[37]

Through his hard-hitting editorials, Tajiri focused much of his energy
and talent on the issue of race because war had underscored racial difference in ways that few could have anticipated. As a commentator mining
the past for clues, he saw the present travails as part of a continuum that
included other Asians like the Chinese and that also involved other racial-
ethnic minorities. Tajiri recalled a trip taken with his wife to New Orleans.
Staring out the train window, the couple found reminders of an America
still fettered by the chains of race. Housing developments separated by
railroad tracks and public facilities divided by color spoke loudly to the
state of race relations in the United States.[38] Tajiri linked the fate of the
Nikkei to others who faced similar barriers to full participation and access in American society. Only by seeing race prejudice in its larger context could there be any real hope of lasting change. The road had been and
continued to be hard for many others besides Japanese Americans:

> In attacking the fountainheads of anti-Semitism, of Jim Crowism and of prej-
> udice against other Orintal [sic] Americans and those of Mexican ancestry,
> the developing campaign against racial disharmony is reaching many of the

sources from which flow the bile of anti-nisei [*sic*] feeling. The hate campaign against Japanese Americans is but one of the racial questions which must be resolved in the sunkist valleys of California, but it is one which has been sharpened by the hysteria which is a consequence of war.[39]

The problems of America's religious and racial minorities needed to be seen as a whole. According to Tajiri, by isolating themselves, Nisei ran the risk of falling into the time-honored tradition of being pitted against other racial-ethnic minorities. Many well-intentioned European Americans had advised Nisei to divorce their problems from the general race issue that focused on African Americans. Through that separation, Japanese Americans stood the best chance to "advance" and attain the title of "honorary Aryans." Nisei might be tempted to embark on such a journey because of their own prejudices. The insightful Tajiri, however, counseled Nisei to move beyond bias, for "there can be no easy future for the Nisei if other racial minorities are not afforded similar equality of treatment."[40]

Tajiri's hope for the future of the Nikkei and for America looked a bit brighter as he assessed the first thirty-three months that had passed since Japanese Americans had been removed from the West Coast. Some Nisei had left the camps to find jobs and attend schools. It seemed only a matter of time (in November 1944) before Issei and Nisei would begin the process of reestablishing the lives they had known before the war began.[41] By 2 January 1945, the ban had been lifted, and the process Tajiri anticipated a few months earlier began with a trickle of Japanese Americans who made their way back to California. The reporter expressed the hope that the camps represented the "combustible remnants of Pacific Coast anti-Orientalism."[42]

Tajiri had certainly done his part in sharing his views with readers in the thick of the events as they happened. With wisdom, he drew on past experience—as an accomplished reporter and a student of history—to place the wartime experiences of Japanese Americans in perspective. He challenged his readers to understand racial politics and work for an America that lived up to its democratic ideals for Japanese Americans and for all other racial and religious minorities.

The Advice of "Ann Nisei"

Readers of the *Pacific Citizen* may have seen Larry Tajiri's byline as the editor, but Guyo Tajiri anchored the efforts to turn the newspaper into a staple of the wartime reading diet of Japanese Americans. An accomplished journalist in her own right, Guyo Tajiri played a pivotal if less visible role as part of the Tajiri team. Although assigned to the position of assistant editor and paid one-third the salary of her husband, Guyo Tajiri oversaw the day-to-day operations of the paper. In many ways, her management of the paper gave Larry considerable time and freedom to write. Although her voice often blended into the paper's coverage, Guyo Tajiri did contribute columns under the pseudonym "Ann Nisei." She addressed issues concerning second-generation women but also commented on broader themes such as family, resettlement, and telling the Nisei story that resonated with the writings of Larry Tajiri.[43] In the inaugural issue of the *Pacific Citizen* under the Tajiris, "Ann Nisei" noted the drastic changes that women faced regardless of whether they had been domestics, housewives, secretaries, or part of farming families. Women no longer had responsibilities for three meals a day; as Tajiri wrote, "now more than ever, she has work to do . . . her life is part and parcel of the greater community life, and she must be willing and anxious to share in it, that it may be closer to the ideals of beauty and truth she has always worked for in her own home." Guyo Tajiri encouraged her women readers to be of service to the community.[44] Many columns addressed practical concerns of women in the camps, suggesting tips for taking care of themselves and their loved ones. "Ann Nisei" provided information about easing the unappetizing fare of the dining halls through homemade soups and how to supplement diets through the preserving of foods in the barracks.[45]

While much of the advice dispensed by Guyo Tajiri did not directly challenge gender-role expectations of the times, she did address the barriers as well as the opportunities that the war presented to her women readers. As historian Valerie Matsumoto has pointed out, women's experiences during the war depended on a variety of factors such as age, generation, personality, and family background. Women encountered family strain, sexism, and racism but also received equal pay for equal work (in the camps).[46] "Ann Nisei" encouraged women to take jobs inside the camps and to venture outside them through the program of early resettlement. In part, Tajiri was combating stereotypes that undermined the humanity of women who had often been "pictured as part of the pale, frightened mass that was the Nisei. She was seen as vague, dull, stolid . . . exuding withal the faint odor of cherry blossoms." The events of the war had shown the falsity of such a picture as women made a new life in unfamiliar places like Chicago and New York with their families and on their own. As she shared stories of women thriving on the outside, Tajiri cautioned readers to be selective but supported those who desired a new start. Women who had left for jobs and for school could boast a "batting average this season [that] is very, very high."[47]

In dealing with life in and out of the camps, Tajiri addressed family issues such as the situation of wives of Nisei soldiers. She recognized the hardships of seeing husbands sent off to war but advised against following them to army bases. Life around military installations often included a lack of housing, jobs, and added burdens for the men preparing for combat. Instead, Nisei women could establish homes for men to return to after their tour of duty. For those whose situations allowed, women were encouraged to find employment, since hard work and friendships would help to pass the time in constructive ways. Guyo Tajiri recognized that married life during a war presented some rather unique situations. With regard to male companionship, Tajiri recommended that her married readers avoid going out on dates although there was nothing inherently wrong with having male friends or spending time with them. News of such friendships might trouble spouses.[48] Tajiri also tackled the subject of child rearing by calling on a sense of duty. Although children proved to be the most malleable of the Nikkei population, they also stood to suffer from socialization in the extremely artificial context of the camps. Both mothers and fathers needed to take up their responsibilities. The concern for the welfare and future of the next generation of Japanese Americans also implicitly undercut notions of children as members of a larger family unit and ethnic community, instead stressing the child as an individual with rights. Perhaps the suspension of liberties made Tajiri more conscious of promoting what she deemed a bill of rights for the youngest of the Nikkei:

— Your child has a right to expect protection from your natural impulses to spoil him.
— Your child has the right to expect such social training as he needs.
— Your child has the right to expect emotional and mental security in his home.
— Your child has the right to make certain decisions for himself.
— Your child has the right to be free from ridicule and sarcasm.
— Your child has the right to expect humor, sympathy, tact, and understanding at all times.[49]

While sensitive to issues of gender, Tajiri placed Nisei women in the larger context of the racial-ethnic community. She held out a vision of America in which Nikkei saw themselves as one minority among others. Only by facing race prejudice head-on and in solidarity with others could it be dismantled. In her opinion, even the war and concentration camps could not stamp out the perseverance and tenacity of the Nisei to move forward. In taking their rightful place in America by aiding the war effort and securing employment, Nisei women worked toward the realization of a United States that offered a high quality of life to all its citizens. She advised those in and out of the camps to get involved in reading groups, join civil rights organizations, work in interracial settings, and check discrimination wherever it surfaced.[50]

In her writing and through her work as a journalist, Guyo Tajiri set her sights on the days ahead. She encouraged her readers to envision a time different and far better than what they knew in the present. In spite of and also because of the devastation of the war years, the second generation would emerge from the camps with a resolve to hold America accountable to its proclaimed ideals of equality and democracy for all. She looked forward to a day when Nisei would write those accounts and certainly did her part for people living under extraordinary circumstances.[51]

A Voice in the Wilderness

In their own ways, Larry and Guyo Tajiri interpreted the war and sketched a vision for the future. During the Tajiris' tenure at the *Pacific Citizen,* their commentary rarely addressed the policies of their employer, the Japanese American Citizens' League. Sensitive to the fact that the paper served the JACL membership, they seemed content to leave that to others. Perhaps most vocal was James Omura of the *Rocky Shimpo,* who provided readers with an alternative to what he perceived to be the hegemonic perspective of the Nisei organization.

After a decade of trying to merely stay afloat, the JACL in 1942 experienced a sudden influx of power and influence.[52] Although the generational shift from Issei to Nisei had its roots in the passage of the 1924 exclusion act, not until after the bombing of Pearl Harbor did the process accelerate. With the void created by arrests of the Issei, the JACL stepped into the gap and promoted itself as the voice of the racial-ethnic community. The federal government's blessing boosted the JACL's stock, and groups who had previously been very critical of the organization joined in strange alliances peculiar to times of severe crisis. Japanese Americans with ties to socialism and communism worked in tandem with the JACL because both groups had pledged themselves against the Axis powers and agreed to cooperate with the removal of Japanese Americans.[53] Communist activist Karl Yoneda recalled:

We, Kibei, Nisei and Issei Communists and sympathizers decided not to fight or speak out against the "evacuation order," even though it violated our Constitutional and basic human rights. Our rationale was we would lose all rights if the German-Italy-Japan fascist Axis powers were victorious. The menace of worldwide fascism was knocking at our nation's doorstep. We had to do everything to insure Allied victory. We had no choice but to accept the racist U.S. dictum at that time over Hitler's ovens and Japan's military rapists of Nanking. We would thrash out the question of our rights after victory.[54]

At the other end of the political spectrum, the JACL embraced the iconoclastic World War I veteran Tokutaro Nishimura Slocum. According to Togo Tanaka, Slocum had been "disowned, discredited and shunned by the JACL" but now returned as a prodigal son at a meeting of the organization's Southern [California] District. Slocum enjoyed the limelight as a veteran and ultrapatriot. With Nisei loyalty in doubt after Pearl Harbor, Citizens League leaders like Fred Tayama and Kay Sugahara asked Slocum to address a mixed crowd that included the head of local naval intelligence, Lieutenant Commander Kenneth Ringle. The irony was not lost on Tanaka: "The fact that JACL-ers who before the war were calling Slocum such choice names as 'drunken bastard,' 'wife-beater,' 'bird dog,' [and] 'sonuvabitch' now accept him as a leader and elect him as chairman of committees is a pretty good indication of the confused and muddled state of JACL leadership." As the former soldier took to the podium, he expressed his satisfaction that the JACL had finally come around in embracing "real Americanism." The veteran proudly proclaimed that he had worked closely with government agents on the night of 7 December: "I was personally responsible for the arrest of Central Japanese Association members who are today in the safekeeping of the FBI."[55]

With the help of those like Slocum, the U.S. government stripped the Japanese American community of its Issei leaders and, in turn, thrust the Nisei into positions of power. In part due to timing and in part because of disposition, the federal government and JACL leadership worked together, each side promoting the "representativeness" of the JACL for its own purposes. According to historian Paul Spickard, the meteoric rise of the Japanese American Citizens' League brought with it resentment from Nikkei who believed that the organization pushed for its own interests ahead of those of Japanese Americans.[56] That criticism, which predated the war, would gather steam through the testimony of JACL representatives before the Tolan Committee in late February and early March 1942. Presided over by Representative John Tolan (D-California), the congressional committee conducted hearings in San Francisco, Los Angeles, Port-land, and Seattle that helped garner public support for the decision to intern.[57]

On the morning of 23 February 1942, Mike Masaoka appeared before the committee and from the opening question demonstrated his eagerness to prove his loyalty. In identifying himself, Masaoka declared: "Just to show you how Americanized we are, I have an English name and a Japanese tag-end there. Mike Masaoka, I am the national secretary and field executive of the Japanese American Citizens' League." A prepared statement, for the record, claimed that the JACL represented 20,000 members, 62 chapters, and nearly 300 Japanese American communities.[58] In early portions of the testimony, the national secretary expressed the willingness of Nikkei to cooperate with forced removal (if deemed necessary by the military for national security) but also stated that the JACL opposed internment on the basis of political and economic motives.[59] Masaoka's overriding concern to cooperate left him vulnerable to the ways that the committee sought to marshal opinion and build a case justifying internment. At one point in the hearing, Masaoka fielded a question about Pearl Harbor:

> The Chairman: What about your people at Pearl Harbor? Did they remain loyal Americans?
>
> Mr. Masaoka: Well, there seems to be some conflicting reports to that. In other words, frankly, Secretary of the Navy Knox himself admits that there were some Japanese who turned their guns on the invaders. Then, on other hand, the reports would seem to indicate another thing—sabotage. But I would like to make this a point, which I think ought to be considered. Here in the United States of America we are distinctly a minority group. We can be sin-gled out because of our characteristics. In the Hawaiian Islands or Philip-pine Islands the Japanese are either in a majority or look like the majority, and therefore, I think they could hide more easily in the general identity of the mass than we could here. Furthermore, I think we are further removed from the domination of the Imperial Japanese Government and I think that most of us are cognizant of the things that America has to offer.
>
> The Chairman: There are authentic pictures during the attack showing hun-dreds of Japanese old automobiles cluttered on the one street of Honolulu so the Army could not get to the ships. Are you conversant with these things?
>
> Mr. Masaoka: Only insofar as the general public is also informed, I believe.[60]

As the proceedings continued into the morning, Masaoka fielded a wide array of questions from the committee about Japanese Americans; from the interchange, it became clear that Representative Tolan and others paint-ed the JACL as representatives of the entire Nikkei community:

The Chairman: As the spokesman for the Japanese here today, would you say each and every one of that 93,000 [the total Japanese American population in California] is loyal to this country?

Mr. Masaoka: No, not each and every one. I think that would be impossible of any group. . . . We are also interested in finding out who those people are, because if we don't find them out they are going to wreck our entire society. We American citizens, especially, are not so much concerned with ourselves as with our children. We would like to commend you officially, publicly, and in every way for your appreciation of the fact that after all this is over we must once again live together as neighbors and fellow Americans.[61]

If any doubts lingered about the intentions of the U.S. government, Representative John Sparkman of Alabama erased them in a telling exchange:

Mr. Sparkman: . . . Do I understand that it is your attitude that the Japanese-American citizens do not protest necessarily against an evacuation? They simply want to lodge their claims to consideration?

Mr. Masaoka: Yes.

Mr. Sparkman: But in the event that the evacuation is deemed necessary by those having charge of the defenses, as loyal Americans you are willing to prove your loyalty by cooperating?

Mr. Masaoka: Yes. I think it should—

Mr. Sparkman (interposing): Even at a sacrifice?

Mr. Masaoka: Oh, yes; definitely. I think that all of us are called upon to make sacrifices. I think we will be called to make greater sacrifices than any others. But I think sincerely, if the military says "Move out," we will be glad to move, because we recognize that even behind evacuation there is not just national security but also a thought to our own welfare and security because we may be subject to mob violence and otherwise if we are permitted to remain.

Mr. Sparkman: And it affords you, as a matter of fact, perhaps the best test of your own loyalty?

Mr. Masaoka: Provided that the military or the people charged with the responsibility are cognizant of all the facts.

Mr. Sparkman: Certainly. That is assumed.

Mr. Masaoka: Yes.[62]

In assuming the mantle of community spokespersons, the JACL leadership took on a task that they would be remembered for during the war. Even supporters of the organization realized that Masaoka had fumbled before the congressional representatives. A group of transplanted San Francisco Nisei in New York City expressed their concern through a letter to a compatriot in the Tanforan Assembly Center:

The whole tenor of feeling among the nisei [*sic*] in the East is that the nisei should have put up a stronger stand—boy, that Tolan Committee Hearings testimony of the JACL burns everybody up. The "sabotage in Hawaii" business was poorly handled—Mike and Dave accepted the accusation and tried to point out that the mainland Japanese were different. And the answer to the question whether the nisei were willing to be evacuated was almost a categorical "yes." Well, of course, perhaps nothing they might have said might have made a difference at that. However I think that we should have let them know that we considered evacuation unfair and unjust in light of the facts, regardless of whether anyone considred [*sic*] it a "military necessity."[63]

The English-language section of the *Utah Nippo,* once edited by Masaoka, also offered a critique. An editorial by "T.M." suggested that the JACL served as a central organization but also pointed out areas that made such representation difficult. For one, the reporter felt that the leadership allowed for very little input from members, leaving decision making in the hands of a few established leaders who seemed uninterested in consulting with fellow Nisei. Moreover, the JACL did not serve the community in basic areas of need like housing and jobs, leaving many wondering why they should contribute their money.[64] The JACL had been successful in grabbing power, but the leadership found their standing in the community severely undermined by the time the Nikkei passed through the camp gates. Many studies have documented how those associated with the JACL earned the label of "inu" (literally "dog") or "informant" and became targets of attacks and beatings.[65]

Neither the writers from the *Utah Nippo* nor from New York City mentioned that a second group of Nisei testified before the Tolan Committee several hours after the JACL. Ernest Iiyama, president of the Nisei Democratic Club of Oakland, and Michio Kunitani of Berkeley tried to undercut charges of sabotage at Pearl Harbor. They also stressed the need for equal treatment, arguing that Japanese Americans should not be singled out from Italians or Germans. The most pointed testimony, however, came from James Omura, who spoke as the publisher and editor of the magazine *Current Life.* Omura requested a hearing because, he stated, "I am strongly opposed to mass evacuation of American-born Japanese. It is my honest belief that such action would not solve the question of Nisei loyalty."[66] He opposed what some of the other representatives of the ethnic community had said. "I refer specifically to the JACL," Omura declared. "It is a matter of public record among the Japanese community that I have been consistently opposed to the Japanese American Citizens' League." The problem did not lie in the organization's principles but rather in its direction—one that the journalist felt had been misdirected. In addition to his distaste for the JACL, Omura minced no words when it came to the Tolan Committee:

> Has the Gestapo come to America? Have we not risen in righteous anger at Hitler's mistreatment of the Jews? Then, is it not incongruous that citizen Americans of Japanese descent should be similarly mistreated and persecuted? . . . Are we to be condemned merely on the basis of our racial origin? Is citizenship such a light and transient thing that that which is our inalienable right in normal times can be torn from us in times of war? We in America are intensely proud of our individual rights and willing, I am sure, to defend those rights with our very lives. I venture to say that the great majority of the Nisei Americans, too, will do the same against any aggressor nation—though that nation be Japan.[67]

Although Omura's words fell on deaf ears, his testimony, along with others on the afternoon of 23 February 1942, confirmed that opinions varied about the events surrounding the wartime imprisonment of Japanese Americans. Omura carried on his crusade during the war at the *Colorado Times,* a Nikkei paper he left in the fall of 1942 when it "transformed into a pro-JACL organ by colluding with the government's propaganda shop, the Office of War Information (OWI)." He later discovered that the *Times* had been subsidized by the OWI and had thus fallen even deeper into the government's hip pocket.[68]

After leaving the *Colorado Times,* Omura moved over to the *Rocky Shimpo,* where he continued in his critique of the JACL. His zeal equaled what he viewed as the organization's "clutching and grasping for power like the inexorable will of the octopus, relentlessly crushing out the honest criticisms of the ordinary man." Omura did not believe that the fate of the Nisei should rest in "the hands of a few egoistic Nisei."[69] The journalist anticipated questions that may have entered the minds of his readers: "You have perhaps wondered why I have been so strongly opposed to the JACL. I am convinced that the national officers let the Nisei down. They were eager to 'yes' the army. They did not fight for the rights of the U.S.-born. Instead of looking at the evacuation from a broader standpoint those JACL leaders attempted to profit on the distress of U.S. Japanese as individuals and as an organization. It was first JACL and second, the cause."[70]

James Omura also established the Pacific Coast Evacuee Placement Center in Denver, a civil rights organization that doubled as a clearinghouse of employment information for Nisei. An early article describing the center did not make any direct mention of Omura but stated that "it has no connection with any Nisei organization—is at bitter odds with the National headquarters of the Japanese Americans Citizens League—and is free from influence or subsidization." Working with the War Production Board, the War Manpower Commission, and the War Relocation Authority, the center offered its clients services free of charge. In touting the center, however, Omura actually spoke little about it as an employment service. Rather, the organization seemed to serve as another vehicle to showcase what seemed to be a voice in the wilderness crying out against the injustice of the camps, the self-aggrandizement of the JACL, and the indifference of other Nisei.[71] In March 1943, Omura took his views to a JACL meeting near Fort Lupton, Colorado, in which he and an anti-JACL faction challenged Mike and Joe Masaoka and the JACL. Tempers flared and a near-brawl ensued.[72] One year later, after another clash with JACL leaders, Omura had been warned: "Keep out of the alley late at night." According to Omura, threats, insults, and false charges indicated that there was "no honor among the JACL (pronounced JACKAL) tribe."[73]

In the course of the war, Omura joined forces with Nisei at the Heart Mountain, Wyoming, camp who had demanded clarification of their citizenship status. The government imposed a loyalty registration in the camps as part of the reinstitution of the military draft in January 1944. Earlier, in the fall of 1943, internee Kiyoshi Okamoto had formed the Fair Play Committee of One to protest what he considered "un-American" practices in the camp as well as a growing sense of injustice over incarceration. Others joined him and challenged their captors on the ground that incarceration violated their constitutional rights as U.S. citizens. The draft raised once again the specter of loyalty. The government attempted to crush the "rebellious" American-born Japanese. In Denver, Omura got wind of the events at Heart Mountain and, through editorials, supported the efforts of the Nisei to assert their constitutional rights. It no doubt gratified Omura that those at Heart Mountain stood in direct opposition to the JACL's wholehearted endorsement of Nisei volunteers for the U.S. military.[74]

By the spring of 1944, matters had heated up over the draft; as part of the government's efforts to quell resistance, Project Director Guy Robertson asked War Relocation Authority Director Dillon Myer to investigate the *Rocky Shimpo,* since Robertson considered Omura's editorials to be tantamount to sedition. The Alien Property Custodian, it turned out, controlled the paper, since it had been owned by noncitizen Issei. Government officials soon took possession of Omura's correspondence and records, and the Alien Property Custodian fired him and his staff. Joining the attack, the Heart Mountain camp paper, the *Sentinel,* blasted Omura as the "number one menace to the post-war assimilation of the Nisei." By the end of April 1944, the editor's future looked bleak.[75]

Omura and the Heart Mountain people faced charges for unlawful conspiracy to counsel, aid, and abet violations of the draft. Authorities arrested Omura and seven Nisei from Heart Mountain in July 1944. The trial resulted in guilty verdicts for all except Omura, the only party found innocent.[76] As he later recalled, the verdict of not guilty mattered little in the eyes of the many Nikkei who had branded him a troublemaker and a traitor. It took Omura months to find work with an employer who would disregard efforts to impugn him. The long arm of the JACL entered into Omura's troubles, and he recounted that sedition remained the "pet charge" of the organization—one that the JACL had tried to lodge against him before the Heart Mountain incident.[77]

After years of fighting, Omura's commentary ended with the trial. Taking on the JACL and the U.S. government proved costly, especially during a time of war. In his own combative style, Omura represented another dimension of Nisei wartime experience, one too often overshadowed by the postwar dominance of the JACL. Part of the breaking of silences has meant that James Omura and those at Heart Mountain have gotten to tell their side of the story and thus highlight the tremendous diversity of Japanese American journeys through the war.[78]

A Legacy in Newsprint

Although they did not suffer the fate of the camps directly, these three Nisei journalists felt a strong kinship to those behind barbed wire who were held responsible for the events of 7 December 1941. The failure by the government and many Americans to distinguish between Japanese Americans and Japan spelled disaster for the Nikkei. Although the hardships of the camps were extraordinary, Japanese Americans had suffered discrimination because of their racial-ethnic background for many decades. Within these contexts, Nisei reporters brought familiar voices and shared perspectives to a process marked largely by oppression, hostility, and alienation.

The legacy of Nisei journalists underscores the need to explore how war translated into the lives of those relegated to the margins of American society and history. Those stories will no doubt alter our readings of World War II and the home front, complicating images of the "good" war. For those who suffered the consequences of racism, the war crystallized the longstanding injustice that racial-ethnic Americans had endured and sowed the seeds for the protest and social change that would emerge in the following decades. In the case of Japanese Americans, reporters like Larry and Guyo Tajiri and James Omura offered their readers a frame of reference to interpret the events unfolding before them. Their critiques as well as their vision challenged Japanese Americans and all Americans to work to realize a better future marked by racial justice. Then, perhaps, the war fought to safeguard democracy abroad could finally be brought home.

RECORDING NISEI EXPERIENCES:
THE KIKUCHI LIFE HISTORIES

Journalists Larry and Guyo Tajiri called on the past to sketch out a vision for their readership concerning the present and future of Japanese America. Similarly, life histories, recorded between April 1943 and August 1945, provide valuable insights into the wartime and prewar experiences of the second-generation women and men who left the camps and resettled in Chicago. As participants in the Japanese [American] Evacuation and Resettlement Study (JERS), sixty-four Nisei told their stories to JERS staff member and fellow Nisei Charles Kikuchi. While only a small sample, the cases—because of their volume, depth, detail, and timing—constitute important historical documents. The outpouring of memories in recent years, in contrast, stands separated by several decades from the events described. As powerful as testimonies and oral histories have been, they suffer the distance that time can create in opening up a given historical period.[1] The interviews conducted by Kikuchi are distinctive in that they took place amid the war and the resettlement process. The cases formed a portion of the massive documentary efforts of JERS, which was headed by Dorothy Swaine Thomas of the University of California at Berkeley. The Kikuchi life histories complement demographic information gathered on Japanese Americans and describe the transition from camp to life in the Midwest. Excerpts from fifteen of the cases, along with statistical data on Japanese Americans, were published in 1952 by Thomas with the assistance of Kikuchi and JERS staff member James Sakoda.[2]

This chapter focuses on the Kikuchi life histories and makes two main arguments regarding their significance. The first is that the content of the documents complicates perceptions, engendered in part by JERS, that the resettler population somehow represented the "success" story of the concentration camps. Tellingly, Thomas chose to title the resettler study *The*

Charles Kikuchi, c. 1935, Vallejo, California (Yuriko Kikuchi)

Salvage, indicating her belief that those Japanese Americans who chose to relocate to sites like Chicago offered a positive side to forced removal and incarceration. In contrast, the first published account of JERS, *The Spoilage,* focused on that segment of Japanese America "whose status in America was impaired." Included in this group were Issei who returned to Japan after the war, Nisei who renounced their U.S. citizenship, those who had been sent to the segregated camp at Tule Lake for "disloyals," and Nikkei who had been involved in protest movements in various camps.[3] Although she read and edited the life histories collected by Kikuchi, including the fifteen published cases in *The Salvage,* Thomas apparently did not detect the ways in which their content undermined the simplistic and problematic dichotomy she introduced. Definite traces of the "spoilage" seeped into the "salvage" population, raising the question of whether Thomas could appreciate the costs incurred by those who resettled. She concluded that "the net effect of forced migration and selective resettlement was, therefore, the dispersal beyond the bounds of segregated ethnocentered communities into areas of wider opportunity."[4] If anything, time has shown how deeply wartime experiences and the camps left their mark on the entire Japanese American community, resettled or otherwise.[5] More recent scholarship on the concentration camps has also demonstrated how labels attached to various groups of Nikkei during the war spoke as much to propaganda, perceptions, and the power to define as they did to some external reality.[6] The content of the life histories presents a more complex image of the resettler population. Although commonly viewed as unquestioning patriots who professed undying loyalty to the United States, the individuals interviewed by Kikuchi in actuality offered a range of perspectives, including criticisms of American democracy and of the treatment of Japanese Americans as racial-ethnic minorities.

The second argument is that although the life histories were intended to document the adjustment of the second generation from the camps to life outside, they in fact reveal far more, representing a rare opportunity to listen to Japanese Americans in their own words. The expressly nondirective, open-ended format of the interviews, moreover, enabled interviewees to offer their opinions on a range of topics, including major themes in this study: race, generation, and identity formation. Kikuchi saw the importance of accurately recording the full expression of Nisei experience, suggesting that "no one really knew what the Nisei were thinking or feeling."[7] The interviews allowed Nisei to look back on their entire life history during an important period of transition in which they had just emerged from the camps and now faced the prospect of rebuilding their lives in a new and unfamiliar setting. It is not clear what lasting influence the interviews had on those who participated; but, from the histories themselves, it seems safe to conclude that Japanese Americans constructed narratives that gave meaning to their lives even as they sought to make sense of them. The chance to pour out their thoughts created an important outlet for these Japanese Americans to reflect on where they had been and where they might be headed. Contemporary readers benefit in observing how this cross-section of men and women constructed their past as historical agents in the midst of cataclysmic change. What emerges from these narratives is a wealth of material that defies any easy or simple categorization of the second generation and instead attests to the remarkable diversity that characterized Nisei resettlers and, by extension, Nisei in general. As Kikuchi himself noted in the early 1940s: "I learned that there was no such thing as a 'typical' Nisei."[8]

Given the thousands of pages that comprise the life histories, this chapter can only selectively analyze their content and will do so in light of several themes that reflect larger concerns of the study. Before delving into the raw data, however, it is important to place the documents and their recorder, Charles Kikuchi, within the broader context of JERS. A discussion of the cases as historical documents, moreover, is warranted. Their use as evidence of Nisei experience was entangled with the very process by which researchers gathered the information. JERS, despite the aspirations of its director, was hardly nonideological, and a brief analysis of the project as well as of the career of the life history and its connection to the study is helpful in situating and positioning the documents under study. As a member of the JERS staff and also as a Nisei, Kikuchi not only proved to be a fascinating figure but in some ways an unlikely chronicler.

The discussion of the content of the life histories examines patterns that emerged from the various interviews. In particular, the emphasis is on Nisei interpretations in three areas: (1) of how race affected their lives; (2) commentary on issues of identity formation; and (3) perspectives on American democracy. Although these themes hardly capture the breadth or depth of the interviews, they do, in part, illuminate the information and perspectives embedded within these narratives. In this respect, the analysis offered here suggests something of how Japanese Americans created their own history and is an indicator of the enduring value of these documents. As a recording of human experience, the Kikuchi life histories extend beyond the confines of Japanese American history and engage central themes in U.S. history, including immigration, the nature of race relations, the home front during World War II, and the formation of American identity.

The JERS Project

Social demographer Dorothy Swaine Thomas was a professor of rural sociology at the University of California at Berkeley at the time of Pearl Harbor. Although Thomas had no previous scholarly interest in Japanese immigration to the United States or in Japanese Americans, she envisioned the events leading to forced removal and eventual incarceration as an opportunity to study "enforced mass migration." Hence, the Japanese [American] Evacuation and Resettlement Study was proposed, perhaps serving as a point of comparison for Thomas's previous research on the subject of internal migration. Thomas benefited from having served on the research staff of Gunnar Myrdal's study of African Americans, which had been funded by the Carnegie Corporation. Her ties to philanthropic organizations paid dividends as Thomas secured over $100,000 from the Rockefeller, Columbia, and Giannini foundations and from the University of California. Based in California throughout the war, Thomas recruited Berkeley undergraduates and graduate students as research assistants and sent them into the concentration camps to serve as field investigators. Japanese American and European-American students who had some background in the social sciences engaged in participant observation. The Nikkei in particular occupied a liminal position that blurred the distinction between insider/outsider status since they and their families, apart from JERS, underwent the trauma and upheaval of removal and incarceration. Berkeley colleagues from anthropology, social welfare, economics, and political science who had originally agreed to work with Thomas to guide the project were unable to participate due to war-related demands, leaving Thomas with sole responsibility for overseeing the study.[9]

Consistent with her training as a demographer, Thomas throughout the JERS project focused her energies on understanding the social phenomena taking place in empirical terms. In that regard, JERS-generated materials and the published findings based on the study constitute a major statistical resource about Japanese Americans during the war. At the same time, given the scope and the scale of JERS, it may seem surprising that Thomas rarely offered interpretive analysis to accompany impressive demographic information. The apparent refusal to place the study within the framework of social theory was a cause of frustration for more than one of her fieldworkers. With little patience for what she considered "unrealistic and fanciful" theories that enchanted social scientists, Thomas directed her team of researchers to the straightforward task of recording the effects of incarceration and the eventual reentry of Japanese Americans into American society. It seems fairly clear that life histories entered into the project largely through the influence of W. I. Thomas, Dorothy's spouse and an influential figure in the sociological tradition developed at the University of Chicago earlier in the century.[10]

The publication of W. I. Thomas and Florian Znaniecki's seminal five-volume study *The Polish Peasant in Europe and America* (1918–20) paved the way for the Chicago school of sociology that stressed, among other things, the importance of studying experience from the subject's point of view. Interviews, personal documents (e.g., letters), and life histories became part of a methodological tradition in which the subjective dimension of experience factored heavily into social scientific analysis. W. I. Thomas and Chicago colleagues such as Robert E. Park and E. Franklin Frazier conducted extensive research along these lines, in effect viewing the city of Chicago as a human laboratory. By the 1940s, however, the Chicago school's influence had waned as sociology turned to grand theory and survey data analysis.[11] Despite such shifts in the field, W. I. Thomas played an important role in shaping the direction of JERS research as staff members were instructed to keep diaries and field notes and to gather other kinds of information about how Japanese Americans were experiencing the war and the camps. Thomas's imprint is perhaps most evident in the life histories collected by Charles Kikuchi. In the excerpts that appeared in *The Salvage,* Dorothy Thomas's brief introductory remarks indicate that the case studies directly complement the demographic material in the first part of the book, providing readers with actual examples of how macro-level phenomena factor into individual lives. Throughout the JERS project, Dorothy and W. I. Thomas were clearly more interested in the perspectives of the subjects under study than they were in the theoretical musings of the field investigators.

In addition to the conditions in the camps, the study, true to its name, also was concerned with the transition of Japanese Americans from incarceration to life on the outside. The interest in resettlement corresponded with the vision that War Relocation Authority (WRA) administrators considered to be at the heart of their responsibility: the rapid assimilation of Nikkei into American society. While some may have questioned the means, the ultimate goal of pulling Japanese Americans out of their enclaves on the West Coast and dispersing them into the rest of the country seemed to be an ideal way of integrating this population. The efforts to resettle those in the camps met with initial bureaucratic red tape in 1942, but the disastrous loyalty registration in early 1943 helped open the gates. Between March 1943, when the registration program ended, and 2 January 1945, when the order to exclude Nikkei from the West Coast was rescinded, some 35,000 Japanese Americans had left the camps for sites in the Midwest and the East.[12]

Of the various cities, Chicago became home to the largest number of resettled Japanese Americans. According to one estimate, some 20,000 Nikkei made the Windy City their new home during the war. An urban study by Michael Albert, however, notes that many of those leaving the camps had initially hoped to move to Denver, a locale within close proximity of most of the WRA camps (except Arkansas). The early influx of

Nikkei in Denver created negative publicity within the city; and, in an effort to stem criticism, WRA officials blocked settlement in the intermountain West. With Denver no longer an option, many Japanese Americans flocked to Chicago since it provided access to a major job market and was closer to the camps than many other cities. Though there were some reports of job discrimination, the need for wartime labor enabled many Japanese Americans to find work in Chicago. Housing proved to be a different matter. Overcrowding brought on by migration to urban areas during the war strained many cities, but Japanese Americans, like African Americans and other racial-ethnic minorities, faced the added hardship of de facto segregation based on race. Many Nikkei recalled being turned away despite "For Rent" signs in windows. Ironically, despite WRA efforts to disperse the resettlers, over two-thirds of the Chicago Japanese population was concentrated in two sections of the city: the Near North Side and Oakland/Kenwood (South Side). The North Side neighborhood had a history of being an early stop for immigrants in Chicago, and the South Side areas were undergoing a transition from a European-American to an African-American enclave.[13]

It is not clear whether under different circumstances the goal to integrate Japanese Americans into the mainstream of America would have been accomplished. As social scientist Setsuko Matsunaga Nishi has pointed out, while most Japanese Americans paid lip service to assimilation, that process did not bear much on the actual experience of most resettlers. Survival was a far more pressing concern; not surprisingly, many Japanese Americans turned to one another in negotiating life in new surroundings. Resettlers looked to each other for information about jobs and housing, and most Nikkei were part of social networks comprised of other Japanese Americans.[14] Though hardly a homogeneous population, Japanese Americans in Chicago, despite their internal diversity, did remain a people set apart by race and experience.

The fact that the plans of WRA administrators did not fully materialize also suggests that resettlement was not simply a government-sponsored policy, but also an opportunity for men and women to shape their own journeys. Some sought to escape the oppressive conditions of life behind barbed wire while others desired a chance to find work or continue their education. Regardless of resettlers' motives, leaving the camps represented an opportunity to move forward with life. Ever diligent in documenting the wartime experiences of Japanese Americans, JERS staff accompanied those headed for Chicago, and Dorothy Thomas arranged for them to base their operations at the University of Chicago.

Charles Kikuchi

In March 1943, Charles Kikuchi left the camp in Gila, Arizona, for Chicago; he had drawn the attention of the Thomases through his dedication as a diarist and his voluminous field reports.[15] Unlike some of the other researchers, Kikuchi had no predilections toward social scientific theory, an advantage in the eyes of the director, but a fact that at times made Kikuchi question the value of his contribution to the project. Any such doubts were answered by the Thomases' enthusiastic reception of Kikuchi's work, and as JERS shifted to resettlement issues in Chicago, Kikuchi seemed to be the ideal person to conduct the life history component. For the next thirty months, the native of San Francisco's Bay Area devoted himself to the task of collecting Nisei life histories.[16]

Given his own background, Kikuchi must have thought it strange at times that he had become a recorder of Nisei experience. The second child and eldest son of eight children, Kikuchi, born in 1916, spent his early years in Vallejo, California, where his father worked as a barber. Poverty, overcrowded family housing, and his father's drinking created a difficult home environment; unfortunately, Charles served as a lightning rod for his father's frustration and anger. The situation grew so bad that his mother felt that it would be best for Charles to leave and arranged for him to be placed in an orphanage at age eight. He would spend the next nine years as the only Japanese American within an interracial setting in which he had the distinction of being an orphan with parents. Not until he began his studies at San Francisco State College in the fall of 1935 did Kikuchi reestablish contact with Japanese Americans and his immediate family. He keenly sensed his own status as a stranger in both contexts.[17]

Perhaps it was Kikuchi's unusual childhood and adolescence that caused well-known author Louis Adamic to feature him in his book series on immigrants and the American-born generation. Although Adamic had made a number of contacts within the Nikkei community, it was Kikuchi's life history, first submitted as an undergraduate sociology paper, that was published in 1939 as "A Young American with a Japanese Face." After a meeting in San Francisco and based on drafts supplied by Kikuchi, Adamic rewrote Kikuchi's story but kept the narrative in the first person—in effect, assuming Kikuchi's voice. Adamic established a clear and simple divide between the generations with narrator Charles (read Adamic) trumpeting the wonders of assimilation. At the same time, Adamic did not hesitate in providing observations on the degradations of Japanese immigrant culture. Despite the ways that Adamic used the account to further his own agenda, the story contains glimpses of a remarkable young man who struggled to work through his racial-ethnic and generational identity. In this regard, Adamic publicized the conditions that many Nisei faced at the time and, in an interesting way, enabled Kikuchi to venture further down the road of self-discovery.[18]

There is no indication that Kikuchi enjoyed any fame from his featured story, and as for fortune, the college graduate quickly discovered that a diploma meant very little as he accepted a string of odd jobs for meager wages and with no prospects for the future. In 1941, Kikuchi must have considered himself fortunate to land a job for forty cents per hour with the California State Employment Service. As his entry point into Japanese America, the post required him to research the background, characteristics, and problems of the Nisei in San Francisco. The 157-page report that Kikuchi wrote began his education as a student of the second generation and prompted him to return to school. He would earn a master's degree in social welfare so that he could work with minority populations. Kikuchi was enrolled at the University of California at Berkeley when the United States entered the war. Tamotsu Shibutani, also a student at Berkeley and a member of the JERS staff, recommended Kikuchi to Thomas based on contacts established when compiling the report on the Nisei.

Kikuchi was drawn initially to JERS as a job and a chance to make some money; but, in retrospect, he would realize the lasting influence that his association with the study had for him personally as a second-generation Japanese American. Unlike some of the other Japanese American JERS staffers, Kikuchi did not translate his work for the project into an academic career but instead found in the process a way to identify himself as part of the second generation.[19] From his diaries and scattered correspondence, it becomes clear that, in studying and listening to the Nisei, Kikuchi shared an affinity with those he interviewed. On one hand, this is hardly surprising given his own status as a Nisei and a peer of those whom he interviewed. On the other hand, his rather unusual childhood and subsequent experiences placed him on the very margins of the second-generation world that he had uneasily interacted with before the war. In this respect, his story can be placed alongside the others, illustrating how the process of collecting life histories of Nisei transformed the person responsible for chronicling the experiences of others. At a conference held on the Berkeley campus of the University of California in 1987, Kikuchi reflected on his journey that had begun over forty years earlier: "It never occurred to me that the wartime experience and my activity with JERS were a therapeutic contribution to my process of becoming an emotionally balanced Nisei, capable of coping with occasional, overt racism and the wider social problems of American society."[20]

Life Histories

When asked by Dorothy Thomas to conduct the life histories, Kikuchi had hoped to cast a wide net, covering age-sex groupings, educational-generational classes, religious and other cultural criteria, and occupational status for the entire Nikkei community. Those initial plans, however, gave way to a more modest design; and, for reasons not stated, a decision was made to limit the interviews to 100 Nisei men and women in Chicago. While the sixty complete and four partial Kikuchi life histories represented only a fraction of those who comprised resettled Japanese Americans, they were able to depict a cross-section of Nisei in terms of gender, region, class, and other factors. Kikuchi based his selection on the contacts he had made in Chicago and through a variety of other networks such as acquaintance/friends from California and from referrals from fellow JERS staff members. The interviews generally took place in the evenings or at other off-work times, often lasting several hours and involving follow-up sessions as well. Kikuchi not only wrote out detailed notes during the sessions but, soon after the interviews, rearranged his material to conform to the life history outline that guided his work.[21] While JERS provided Kikuchi with a salary to cover his basic expenses, his zeal for the project extended beyond the confines of a mere job. He spent many eighteen-hour days over the course of thirty months (spring 1943–summer 1945) interviewing Nisei.[22] In reading through the documents, one is struck by the sheer volume as many of the individual cases exceeded 100 typed pages with some running as long as 250 pages. In addition to the official casework, Kikuchi kept an observation journal as well as a personal diary that provided separate spaces to include his own thoughts to guard against his personal views from detracting from the objectivity of the histories.[23]

The interviews are remarkable in their ability to open up individual experience, especially for Japanese Americans whose history has long been silenced by neglect. As sociologist Dana Takagi has suggested, the life histories reveal the adaptive mechanisms and personality features by which racial-ethnic minority persons in America have managed their daily lives. An emphasis on macro-level analysis within the social sciences has meant that issues of particularity and historical contingency often have dropped out of view, providing very little access into the actual experiences of men and women.[24] Because World War II and the concentration camps represented arguably the most pivotal juncture of Japanese American history, the life histories enable us to engage Nisei men and women as active interpreters of their own experience in the thick of events. Their reflections place contemporary and prewar activity, social forces, and relationships into a historical framework.

A strength of the cases as historical documents is that they are written in plain language, unadorned by much commentary. True to the Chicago school form, the interviews, as much as possible, are left to speak for themselves. W. I. Thomas, in an exchange of correspondence with Kikuchi, sent him a seventeen-page typed address that the senior scholar gave during the war at the University of California at Berkeley. Entitled "The Employment of the Behavior Document in the Social Sciences," the lecture outlined Thomas's belief in the importance of environmental factors in human behavior and how the task of the social sciences was "to inquire into the relation of forms of social organization to individual and group adjustment." Life histories proved to be a crucial source in this process; regarding their format, Thomas wrote: "The life-history is an autobiographic narrative, which should be unguided except for inventories of items to assist the subject in a complete recall of experience. The psychoanalytic technique . . . has most frequently had the vicious feature of indoctrinating the subject by suggesting, consciously or unconsciously, replies corresponding with the particular theory of the analyst."[25] Thomas recognized pitfalls such as factual reliability, selectivity, and bias but nevertheless concluded that, in forming decisions about human behavior, we were forced to use the statements of others and their representations of reality. In that respect, highly subjective, delusional, and even fabricated accounts were significant in their ability to provide insights into individual and collective behavior. There is no doubt that Kikuchi received direct guidance on the life history process from W. I. Thomas; and correspondence between the two included a note from Thomas based on his review of Kikuchi's early work on the Nisei interviews in Chicago. Kikuchi had wanted to make sure that his efforts were in line with the JERS project and must have been pleased by a letter dated 18 October 1943 in which Thomas responded: "[I] have been astonished at both the quantity and quality of your work. I could suggest no changes in your procedure."[26]

While the Thomases envisioned JERS as bearing the merits of academic detachment, the study in fact operated from an assimilationist framework that envisioned enforced migration into Anglo-/European-American society. The fifteen cases that Dorothy Thomas edited and abridged for publication in *The Salvage,* while largely faithful to the full account, in places omitted materials that deviated from the assimilation formula.[27] In addition to her spoilage/salvage perspective, Thomas also offered a generalized profile in the summary/preface to the life histories that glossed over material within the narratives that made such a composite sketch problematic. To cite just one case, Thomas suggested that the religious orientation of the resettled population, like the dominant majority of the United States, was either Christian or of no formal religion—a sign of their assimilation. In reading the Nisei interviews for religion, however, it becomes clear that many Nisei interviewed showed a remarkable flexibility regarding religion that spoke to a sense of racial-ethnic identity and/or to social needs as much as it did to adherence to a particular religious tradition. A number of individuals moved easily between Buddhism and Christianity, suggesting less of a distinction between the two traditions than might be expected.[28] Moreover, how might self-identified Buddhists (who, in effect, were so in name only) fit into the schema that Thomas outlined?[29]

In contesting Thomas's reading of the documents, the point is that texts do not speak for themselves but await interpretation. Nor are the Kikuchi cases free from the interchange between interviewer and interviewee or from a host of other issues that factored into the overall process of their production. Nevertheless, a close reading can uncover themes or patterns that assist in deciphering the content of the narratives. I highlight three areas that suggest the ways in which the Nisei who participated in the JERS project made sense of their times. First, there is a discussion of how Japanese Americans interpreted racial issues. A second related area has to do with how interviewees negotiated matters of identity. Construction of the self, as one would expect from autobiography, took as many forms as there were interviews, but what emerges is an opportunity to delve into that creative process. Finally, the commentary of Nisei on U.S. democracy, based on their experiences, testifies to how these individuals thought about their place in America in a time of war and as they faced the future.[30]

The Role of Race

The concentration camps left little room for doubt that race was a major factor in the lives of Japanese Americans. This was, of course, hardly news to most Nisei, but the war, forced removal, and incarceration brought the issue to the fore much more than may have been the case in earlier years. For some, race took the form of memories of growing up on the West

Coast; for others, it was figured by more recent events. Responses under-scored a range of views from decidedly pro-American to that of growing bitterness and cynicism, but all recognized that Nisei would have to con-front their ongoing status as a persecuted racial-ethnic minority in the United States. Given the profile of these resettlers as assimilationist, it is noteworthy that numerous Nisei espoused distinct anti-European-Ameri-can attitudes. The camps no doubt had something to do with these views; but for some, the anger and resentment were not limited to the war.

Many Nisei discussed incidents of racism that they had encountered in their past. Tommy Hamada,[31] a resident of San Francisco's Bay Area, re-membered an incident in high school when he allowed a European-American student to copy his paper during final exams. Identical answers must have tipped off the teacher who then accused Hamada of cheating, adding that he was a "low Jap." Hamada in turn called his teacher a "whore," which apparently led to a minor scuffle. In negotiating the conflict, the principal of this elite public high school apparently did not bother to investigate the accusation and instead scolded Hamada for not being a model student like the other Nisei. All would be forgotten if he agreed to a transfer. Hamada recalled that he was in store for some lessons: "I thought they [fellow Nisei] were crazy when they said the white man was against us. I didn't see how they could be when we had our American citizenship."[32] Frances Nishimoto also drew on her school experiences in central California and conveyed that although the school was predominantly European American, she only as-sociated with her Japanese American classmates. She recalled: "I didn't have any Caucasian friends at all. I guess this was because I felt different from them." It also did not escape Nishimoto's notice that Nisei were not elect-ed to student government positions or given access to other leadership posts despite their exemplary record.[33]

In assessing the racial contexts that they faced and how they would re-spond, some Nisei voiced a pro-American stance that appeared to support the status quo. On closer examination, however, they also included com-mentary that tempered their profession of loyalty and belief in the Amer-ican way. For instance, James Terada, a Hawaiian-born Nisei who came to Los Angeles as a youth, pledged his allegiance to the United States and yet added that he was disgusted with politics since Nikkei did not receive a "square deal." "We just have to sit back and get kicked around. You know how it is, a Jap is a Jap, and they won't give you much of a chance." Terada's reflections were based in part on his experiences as a barber who had encountered discrimination in the years prior to the war. He remem-bered how difficult it was to secure a state license to practice his trade.

Terada attributed his troubles to his race: "my face was yellow and I did not pass the test of being a white man. Don't ever believe that there is no discrimination out there."[34] Although Hazel Nishi had experienced the effects of gender bias in Japan and racism in the United States, she did not want to dwell on it since it made her miserable. Instead, as Kikuchi noted in his diary, the Santa Cruz native thought she would be better served by moving forward in spite of the circumstances. At the same time, doubts lingered as she knew too well the presence of prejudice, and she expressed a desire not to be in denial about her situation.[35] Chizu Sanada seemed to be the all-American resettler who spent her evenings and other spare moments writing to Nisei soldiers and hosting them in Chicago when they were on leave. It bothered her that other Japanese Americans neglected the war, too concerned with themselves to serve others. While she espoused strong support for the Allied cause and for America, she did not hesitate to explain that her pro-American actions and attitude were in direct response to the prejudice and discrimination that she felt surrounded Japanese Americans. Focusing on the wrongs borne by the Nisei, according to Sanada, would foster frustration and self-pity—qualities that undermined the chances of the second generation succeeding in America.[36]

Other interviewees were more pointed in their views on race. Hisao Shimada, a Nisei who was attempting to continue his education in the Midwest, could not understand why an institution of higher learning that claimed to accept Nikkei in effect used other means to keep them out. Shimada, from a rural farming family in California, commented: "I am finding it harder and harder to appease the feelings of cynicism (perhaps bitterness to some extent) which is beginning to develop." His grades and background check had been approved. Qualifications, not skin color, the aspiring student claimed, ought to determine his fate at the university. Shimada noted the irony of a society that did not place color barriers on the draft and combat duty but did so when it came to educational opportunities: "What the hell, does my skin color mean that much to them?"[37] According to Ikuko Maruyama, many Nisei not only had grown cynical but exhibited pro-Japanese as well as pro-American sentiments. She sensed that many Americans of Japanese ancestry realized how precarious a position they occupied in the United States, and she noted that some Nisei might even face deportation. Given the current climate, Maruyama argued, "it is not very safe to express opinions these days. . . . the best thing to do is to go along and to hope for the best."[38] Such advice might work for some, but Chizu Sanada, despite her patriotic efforts, was not very optimistic about what lay ahead:

Americans has [*sic*] respect for most "white blood," but it has not been too willing to accept "colored blood" as part of America too. . . . there are plenty of groups in this country who never want to accept us as loyal Americans. They are so prejudiced that I don't know how they will ever be convinced differently. . . . The present generation of Nisei may have to fight until they go to their graves in order to win their point, but I think it will be worth it for the sake of the coming generation of Japanese American children.[39]

Not only did Nisei convey their concerns over the entrenched nature of racial discrimination, but some of these prime candidates for assimilation told Kikuchi of their distrust and even hatred of European Americans. Charles Kikuchi had known Tommy Hamada before the war and thought of him as a "typical" all-American Nisei; but the camps, Kikuchi noted, had raised Hamada's race consciousness: "he takes the rather common attitude that the 'white bastards' are too prejudiced and so what's the use." Hamada had done not only his time in camp but also worked farm details in which Nisei were released to harvest crops during the war. This program, portrayed by the WRA as a chance to aid the war effort and demonstrate loyalty, disillusioned Hamada. On one trip, Hamada and other Nisei who had toiled all day went into town to have dinner only to be stared down and refused service. "Then and there, I knew that I hated all white men."[40] At the Stockton Assembly Center, Barry Shimizu was part of a gang that stole from the center canteen and general store. In addition to other motives, Shimizu highlighted the fact that they did not like the *hakujin* (European-American) manager, who apparently had been inflating prices and pilfering goods. The manager was an example of the corruption in the camps; from Shimizu's perspective, their stealing helped to even the score. What would normally be seen as illegal and antisocial behavior was justified in racial terms.[41]

Blackie Najima had been at Tanforan Assembly Center, where an elderly Issei man died after a soldier used a rifle butt to batter his head. Najima stated: "I felt like running and taking the bayonet away from the *keto* [white bastard] soldier and running it through his guts. I hated the thought of being surrounded by these bastards." Najima's anger was not limited to the soldier; it extended to the whites that he had known growing up in San Francisco and who he blamed for being responsible for running Japanese Americans out of town. It angered him that European Americans could not only be so cruel but so self-righteous in the process. "The goddam *ketos* think that their s—— don't stink."[42] A Nisei from Stockton, Lester Kimura, who captured Kikuchi's attention because of his penchant for zoot suits, gave his frank assessment of European Americans who he perceived to be in positions of authority. These were the people who wanted Nisei to serve in the armed forces. By dying on the battlefield, Japanese Americans could prove their loyalty to the nation, but Kimura would have none of it since being "six feet under" posed no future. As he walked the streets of Chicago, Kimura recounted the insults that he and others endured: "Sometimes I walk by some *hakujin* and they mutter something about 'dirty Japs' under their breath. . . . I get so mad that I would like to knock them down and grind my heels into their dirty faces . . . [but] I don't want to let those *hakujin* know that they get me down because of my pride."[43]

As had been the case before the war, Nisei reflections on race encompassed a wide range of views; and yet, regardless of the differences, the interviewees by virtue of their words testified to the continuing legacy of race in their lives. The traumatic nature of the camps and the tenuousness of life in Chicago only accentuated racial concerns among Japanese Americans. Those who shared their stories with Charles Kikuchi added an ironic twist to the saga of resettlement that intended to foster their assimilation into American society.

Issues of Identity

Although the life history interviews allowed Nisei to explore an array of topics, much of the content in one way or another constituted a formulation of individual and collective identity. Women and men spoke of their personal journeys but also often placed their stories within larger contexts. An interesting facet of the interviews included Nisei who attempted to pass as other Asian Americans, and this strategy represented one response to the process of finding a sense of self. Other interviewees spoke about the implications of being white and, in so doing, also commented on their status as Japanese Americans. In reflecting on their sociocultural world, Nisei also addressed what they perceived as a divide that separated them from their fellow Americans.

In the effort to reestablish himself as a barber in Chicago, James Terada approached a Filipino American barber who offered to rent Terada a chair in his shop. Given the tensions between the two groups over the war, Terada sought to pass as a Chinese American. The tactic apparently did not work very well since Filipino American customers questioned his identity and suspected that he might indeed be Japanese American. Terada did not explain why or how such suspicions were started; in any case, he soon quit to relieve the owner, who was being harassed for harboring the "enemy."

While his ability to pass as a Chinese American met with limited success, Terada, oddly enough, was viewed as a Filipino American by European-American customers.[44] Terada's experience paled in comparison with the most intriguing case of passing, in which Bill Katayama made a career of sorts in assumed identities; his ruse began in 1941 and stretched into his post-camp life in Chicago. Before the war, Katayama, a Nisei from San Francisco, aspired to an entertainment career and received his first break as a singing bartender in a chic Chinatown club. Assuming the persona of Bill Loo, a Korean American, Katayama worked the late shift, mixing drinks and crooning tunes. He earned enough money to live apart from his family and shared an apartment with female Korean American roommates. Things were going well; and yet, in establishing his new identity, Katayama sensed an uneasiness and discovered that being Japanese American was more than skin deep. Especially after Pearl Harbor, he knew that the problems facing his community were also his, even though his assumed identity provided a credible cover. The internal struggle within Katayama grew stronger as tensions mounted; and with the United States at war, he found it difficult to remain silent. Katayama told his roommates that he was actually half Korean and half Japanese, a creative response to a conflicted situation. Eventually, however, Katayama revealed the real story to his roommates, whom he described as sympathetic. Those at work were less kind as self-doubt apparently undermined his ability to pass. Growing suspicion that he was not a Korean American led to his dismissal. Katayama was able to find another job by passing as a Korean; and in his new post, he ran into other Nisei like Kim Low, who passed as a Chinese American singer. According to Katayama, a number of Japanese Americans assumed the identities of other Asian Americans.[45]

Although not a strategy often utilized, passing provided Nisei with a means of dealing with their identity even if it meant shedding their status as Japanese Americans. Inventing oneself, however, had its limits. Racial markers only enabled a certain amount of movement along the spectrum of possible American identities. Katayama's career as an entertainer foundered despite his change in ethnicity since Hollywood cared little about which particular Asian American group an individual claimed. After the camps, Bill Katayama did manage to find a job in Chicago as a bartender in a Chinese restaurant, once again as a Korean American, but he was soon forced out when he could not converse with an elderly Korean American customer who was excited about finding a fellow countryman. Later, Katayama passed as a Chinese American and found work in a European-American restaurant as a bartender, but he resented being placed out of sight in a back room where tips were nonexistent and working conditions poor. To add insult to injury, Katayama still had to pay full union dues even though Asian Americans were barred from membership. The job did not last long as Nisei wanting to get access to the exclusive club tried to use their connections to Katayama and, in the process, exposed his identity. Kikuchi noted that Katayama finally sought relief by leaving Chicago for New York City.[46]

If some Nisei reinvented themselves as Korean or Chinese American, other second-generation men and women contemplated "whiteness." In a society in which they occupied a racially subordinate position that in wartime translated into mass incarceration, it is not surprising that some interviewees broached the topic of what being white meant in the United States. Yuri Kosamoto, for one, knew too well how race could fundamentally alter life chances. As such, she recognized that many Nisei wished that they were white or at least envied white people because of the power and access that such status could confirm. "Being a Japanese does limit your opportunities and it bars you from so many things, and it also changes the whole course of your life," commented Kosamoto. Having struggled to put herself through a vocational business school in northern California, Kosamoto could not find secretarial work after graduation. Most firms simply did not hire Japanese Americans. As a result, she joined so many of her Nisei cohorts who entered menial, low-paying, and backbreaking work. Despite the complex nature of identity issues, they seemed relatively simple to Kosamoto, who stated: "If I were a white person I could have gone into an office job before the war and not been forced to take a domestic job because of the discrimination against Japanese in California."[47] At times, Frances Nishimoto also envisioned being a European American so that she could find jobs and housing more easily, but she did not wish it often: "I was just made to be born a Japanese and I can't help it so I might as well make the best of it." A trace of resignation emerged from Nishimoto's interview as she accepted the fact that a racial-ethnic hierarchy existed in the United States. Japanese Americans occupied a secondary status; and, in spite of the camps, Nishimoto figured that being a Nikkei was still "better than being a Negro or Filipino."[48]

While some may have wanted to enjoy the privileges and opportunities that came with being white in America, few if any interviewees expressed any real desire to be rid of their ancestry. Nisei stated that immigrant parents and communities inculcated a sense of racial-ethnic pride. Japan's ascendancy in Asia as a modern power no doubt fueled strains of nationalism. While Chie Yamazaki had experienced discrimination because of her identity as a Japanese American, she did not suffer from an inferiority complex: "I regard my Japanese ancestry with pride and think we are a great people. I have never wished that I were white." In part, her feelings were based on the assessment that "white" races had always exploited "colored" races. The persistence of that exploitation, according to Yamazaki, was a blight on the United States; and until there was true equality between the white and colored races, America would never be able to live up to its ideals.[49] Coming out of the camps, Nisei could hardly be impressed by the state of race relations. Margaret Suzuki interpreted attitudes of second-generation men and women toward whiteness as one way of dealing with the difficulties of their situation. As historian Vicki Ruiz has argued, racial-ethnic minorities at times have engaged in imitative behavior of the dominant society as psychological ballast against the damaging effects of racism.[50] In the case of Japanese Americans, Suzuki explained to Kikuchi: "I know that many of the Nisei secretly wish that they were white but they will never admit to it. They try to make themselves like the crowds as much as possible in other ways like the hair styles and clothes and habits. It is not because I think that I am inforior [*sic*], because I think that I am just as good as the next person. But with a Japanese face, we are not accepted as individuals for what we can do. In a way all the Nisei long for escape from their discomforts."[51]

Nothing could really provide escape from the contexts that Nisei faced before the war, in the camps, and even as they came out on the other end in Chicago. And yet, in these various settings, Japanese Americans turned to each other. They created a subculture within U.S. society in response to the racism that they encountered and because their shared history gave the second generation common ground to negotiate their life circumstances. In the life histories, many Nisei attested to the separate nature of their existence from the world around them despite being very much a part of their larger surroundings. In school before the war, Richard Moto remembered: "Not very many of the Nisei mingled freely with the *hakujin* students. It was just accepted that we should be separated . . . and we just didn't think about it often." Moto felt different from his non-Nisei classmates, and he also mentioned that his father often lectured him about the "white bastards."[52] Some Nisei noticed that, as they got older, a distance came between them and their other classmates that seemed less evident in earlier years. Japanese-language schooling and ties to the immigrant community had something to do with this distancing, according to Johnny Masaki, but it also had to do with a growing sense of alienation when issues of race and sexuality became more explicit.[53] As an undergraduate at the University of California at Los Angeles in 1940, Bill Katayama recalled that the Nisei had their own enjoyable social life and that "it was like going to a separate school."[54]

In his interview, Katayama told Charles Kikuchi: "You know, I would never tell a *hakujin* all the things I told you." Katayama was quite candid in his views and, near the end of his comments, suggested that although those in authority might not approve, the second generation, when it came to matters of identity, really wanted their own social world. Few Japanese Americans sought to move into what he termed "pure Caucasian society." Although Katayama could hardly speak for all Nisei, other interviewees did echo his sentiments. Some officials grew concerned that resettled Nikkei in Chicago were not following orders to disperse into the heartland of America but instead were replicating patterns that existed on the West Coast before the war. Though the shape of Japanese America in Chicago stood in stark contrast to Little Tokyo, the second generation did indeed establish networks that proved vital in terms of housing, jobs, and social life. In turning to each other, Japanese Americans were extending the ties that had their roots in prewar communities as well as those that had been forged in the camps. Despite the complex ways that members of the second generation appropriated their identity, the vast majority would agree with Bill Katayama's insight that "Nisei need each other to make adjustments to life."[55]

Democracy, American Style

Part of the adjustment expressed in the life histories had to do with making sense of an American democracy that allowed U.S. citizens to be ordered from their homes and communities and incarcerated solely on the basis of their ancestry. The interviews enabled individuals to look back on their own past as well as to try to process what was still unfolding before them. These Nisei were supposed to be among the most assimilated and had been "cleared" by authorities as fit for resettlement. At the same time, they carried with them the scars of the camps, which in turn triggered questions about what they had been taught about the founding principles of the United States. A pattern of disillusionment emerged, not surprising given what Nisei had experienced but still telling since these women and men represented the "salvage" population within Japanese America.

In looking back on her experiences, Chizu Sanada remembered the swelling of resentment and bitterness among those sent to the Santa Anita Assembly Center during the spring of 1942. Though most people were concerned about daily survival, some Nisei sensed very deeply that they had been betrayed and branded as citizens who could not be trusted. Not only did morale drop rapidly, but there was very little incentive to prove one's loyalty to the United States since good citizenship and other efforts before and after Pearl Harbor had no effect.[56] Like many other interviewees, Mike Mizuno, a mechanic from Santa Maria, saw politics at work in their incarceration. He cited agricultural interests that eyed Japanese American farmland as well as politicians who could use anti-Nikkei sentiment to boost their campaigns and their careers: "it was a hell of a deal all around . . . [and] the Constitution and democracy didn't mean a damn thing when it came down to the pinch."[57]

The war and the camps brought disillusionment on an unprecedented scale. It became clear to many Nisei that the democracy they learned about in school was nowhere to be found. Fresh from the camps, interviewees spoke about this disjuncture in ways that have seldom been heard, since so much of the focus on the war years has been on the patriotism of Japanese Americans. Struggling to survive in Chicago, Bill Katayama, assessing the future in light of the present and the past, commented on the irony of it all: "I think Democracy, ha! Especially now in a time of war when we are supposed to be fighting for equality! But then, I supposed discrimination is inevitable and I try to look at it philosophically, but I still can't swallow it."[58] Blackie Najima found it difficult to take such a detached attitude and recalled: "When I first got to camp I thought my American citizenship was only a paper to wipe my behind with. These *keto* out here don't even know we have it. I wouldn't give a damn if I lost my citizenship either. It doesn't make any difference."[59] Chie Yamazaki summed it up well when she told Charles Kikuchi that democracy was "just an ideal" that had no practical import on her life. She predicted that life after the war would be just as difficult for Japanese Americans as it had been before, since the root cause of incarceration ran deeper than the war itself. Even as a child, Yamazaki realized that she lived in a country in which differences such as race would be used as a means of discrimination.[60]

The failure of American democracy and its tragic implications for Japanese Americans gave Nisei much to ponder. In the case of Mike Mizuno the reader has an opportunity to see how this particular Nisei struggled over the issue. Sprinkled throughout his life history were examples from the immediate and more distant past of how Mizuno experienced racism and subsequent hardships. It is clear that he believed that the United States failed him at a critical time, and yet, by the end of the interview, Mizuno commented that he was in the army and hoped to hasten the end of the war. Even so, he did not consider the state of his citizenship worth fighting for and added that dictatorship was just as viable in a democracy as it was in a fascist state. Mizuno did, however, still hold out hope that the United States might be able to change; and though slim, that chance for a different future was what enabled him to support the cause. He ended the interview by restating his strong disillusionment, and though he sensed that his attitude might not be appreciated, he did not mind admitting it.[61]

In an eloquent reflection, Mizuno offered his insights and commentary on democracy, race relations, and his thoughts for the future. The quote below, taken from Charles Kikuchi's diary, did not appear in the excerpt of Mizuno's life history that appeared in *The Salvage:*

> I don't think there is any such thing as democracy the way I understood the term in school. The biggest cause for its failing is racial prejudice. It's the old idea that the white man [is] superior to everyone else in the world. This war won't eliminate that kind of thinking too much. It may gradually diminish because a lot of colored boys are fighting for this country. They won't come back and be willing to be shoved around. They will be given some privileges but not as much as they have earned. Some of the *hakujin* guys say that if you give the Negro an inch, they will take a mile. That is as it should be until they get equal rights. The same goes for the Nisei. But it won't come fast enough for me and I have to worry about earning a living for my family. It may come in another generation or so I think."[62]

Part of the pain of the war and the camps for many Nisei was the realization that the country of their birth and allegiance had failed them miserably. Although plenty of incidents prior to the war revealed the flaws in American society and government, the second generation had some measure of hope in the belief that, if they worked hard enough and proved to be exemplary citizens, things might change. The concentration camps caused many Nisei to become disillusioned about the core nature of American democracy. Women and men in Chicago may have left the physical aspects of camp behind, but nearly all carried with them the emotional and psychological freight of having been prisoners of their own country.

The Life Histories as Witness

The Kikuchi life histories provided Nisei with a rare opportunity to reflect on their own lives, in which their early years, war, concentration camps, and resettlement came together in the form of raw and relatively uncensored material. Rich in detail and suggestive of the state of mind of a subset of Nisei, the life histories are remarkable documents. The presentation in this chapter has merely offered a selective glimpse into the interviews;

but, having said this, what emerges from the analysis is perhaps a surprising picture of the resettlers, especially given that Dorothy Swaine Thomas characterized them as "the salvage." With respect to race, identity, and American democracy, the histories might more appropriately have been placed with the spoilage.

In disrupting standard categories, the narratives that Nisei constructed illustrate that the wartime experiences of Japanese Americans were far more complex than might be construed from the narrow renditions that have until recently dominated the popular perceptions.[63] Documents like the life histories are invaluable records that allow contemporary observers and even those who endured this historical period to recognize that the war produced a multiplicity of stories. Recognition of this fact alone can lead to rethinking the period as well as Japanese American history. The hope is that in recognizing and listening to an ever widening chorus of voices, a more accurate and inclusive understanding of the past will continue to unfold.

Perhaps most importantly, the life histories allow their readers access to the thoughts and feelings of Nisei men and women as historical agents. These documents help reclaim a buried part of the past, enabling Japanese Americans to speak in their own words about their journeys. Humorous, mundane, poignant, and troubling, the interviews attest to a group of Japanese Americans who struggled to rebuild their lives and find a sense of meaning and hope in the wake of their time spent in concentration camps. The thousands of pages of text illustrate the tremendous diversity even within this relatively small sample of the resettled Nisei population in Chicago. And yet, Japanese Americans also shared the effects of this moment in their life courses—binding as well as cutting across the differences among them. The Kikuchi life histories bear witness to a people in transition and to the dawn of a new era for Nisei in a postwar, cold war America.

EPILOGUE

It is likely that neither Mitsuye Endo, the Nisei plaintiff from Sacramento, nor her attorneys, Saburo Kido and James Purcell, could have anticipated that their habeas corpus petition would effectively end the wartime incarceration of Japanese Americans. Filed in San Francisco on 12 July 1942, the Endo case would test the legality of the U.S. government detaining American citizens solely on the basis of race. After considerable delays by lower courts and a tortuous trail through the legal system, the case was heard before the highest court in the land. On 18 December 1944, the U.S. Supreme Court decision in ex parte endo ruled that the War Relocation Authority (WRA) did not possess the authority to detain U.S. citizens who qualified for its leave policy. The Court's ruling, while skirting the issue of the constitutionality of the incarceration itself, marked the beginning of the end of the concentration camps. Not coincidentally, the day before the Court's finding was made public, the War Department released a statement indicating that except for those deemed disloyal, all persons of Japanese ancestry would be given the same freedom of movement throughout the United States as other citizens and alien residents, effective 2 January 1945.[1] Hence, as those in the camps prepared for the new year, they did so with the realization that they would soon reenter American society. WRA officials stepped up their efforts to drive out those in the concentration camps as vigorously as others had lobbied to put them there. At the end of 1945, all of the camps except Tule Lake had been closed; and by 1 July 1946, the last camp and the WRA had shut down operations.[2]

The months and years spent in concentration camps represented a major turning point for Japanese Americans. The shift between generations, already in process before war, accelerated after Pearl Harbor as federal officials placed authority for the racial-ethnic community into Nisei hands. In addition, a majority of the second generation came of age in the camps and, by 1945, had entered their young adulthood. In contrast, Issei saw a lifetime of sweat and sacrifice erased by the forced removal that had robbed them of farms, businesses, and homes. The economic losses had been staggering—an estimated $370 million in wartime dollars; a more recent estimate (based on 1983 dollars) placed the loss at somewhere between $2.5 and 6.2 billion.[3] Now elderly, Issei faced a future with few resources, outside their families, to rely on. Most Japanese Americans eventually made their way back to California, Oregon, and Washington. Nisei carried the responsibility of caring for their parents, their own budding families, and for establishing new careers. Economic opportunities unavailable to qualified and credentialed Japanese Americans before the war slowly opened up and enabled more Nisei to find better jobs. State and federal courts struck down longstanding measures such as restrictive housing covenants and antimiscegenation laws, and new legislation such as the McCarran-Walter Act of 1952 finally lifted the longstanding ban on naturalization for all Asian Americans. By no means had racial barriers fallen, but signs pointed to an easing of the most blatant forms of discrimination.[4]

The changes ushered in by the war and the camps meant that Nisei re-entered a world different from the one they had known during the 1920s and the 1930s. Little Tokyos and Japantowns resurfaced, but no longer would racial-ethnic enclaves so fully contain Japanese America. Changes took place as the second generation moved to different parts of town and as they took advantage of their education and entered careers beyond the ethnic economy. As a consequence, the loci of home, work, and social life were less likely to be centered in one place, reflecting the growth and sub-urbanization of cities like Los Angeles. An era had passed with incarceration. WRA officials, however, might still be troubled with how resilient and adaptable racial-ethnic ties proved to be under these new circumstances. Identities forged within contexts of prejudice, discrimination, and concentration camps could not be easily forgotten. If Nisei chose not to highlight their racial-ethnic difference, they did so because their history offered ample evidence of how such markers could used against them.

Such evidence, however, was not limited to the past. Japanese Americans returning to the West Coast, as well as those who dispersed to other parts of the country, faced outward and more covert forms of racism. In addition, Nikkei witnessed racism at work in the sensational "Tokyo Rose" trial of 1949. In a case replete with symbolic meaning, a Nisei named Iva Toguri d'Aquino, trapped in Japan during the war, had been charged with treason for her work on a Radio Tokyo propaganda program. Although purportedly aimed at settling war crimes, in reality the trial was a show of force by the Truman administration, which needed to boost its image as a defender of democracy during the cold war. Media attention and widespread name recognition of "Tokyo Rose" among American soldiers made the high-profile case a potential gold mine for positive publicity. The federal government translated displaced wartime anger and deep-seated prejudice into political capital.[5]

Born on 4 July 1916 in Los Angeles, Iva Toguri d'Aquino hardly fit federal prosecutor Tom De Wolfe's description of her as a "female Benedict Arnold."[6] Quite the contrary, the eldest daughter of Jun and Fumi Toguri viewed herself very much as an American. She attended public schools in southern California and later enrolled at the University of California at Los Angeles, graduating in 1940 with a degree in zoology. Her plans to attend medical school never materialized, however, as she left for Japan in July 1941 as the family representative to pay respect to a dying aunt.[7] Due to the urgency of the situation, d'Aquino left without a U.S. passport, instead obtaining a certificate of identification—a technicality that would prove momentous. At the time d'Aquino set sail, U.S.-Japanese relations had gone from bad to worse. As conflict seemed imminent, Jun Toguri wired her daughter in the fall of 1941 to return to California, but Iva ran into bureaucratic red tape because of her lack of a U.S. passport. Although her certificate of identification and her birth certificate should have been more than sufficient to establish her citizenship, she found herself snared within immigration policies that were discriminatory toward Asians and Americans of Asian ancestry. There was nothing she could do as time slipped by. Pearl Harbor left her stranded in Japan.[8]

During the war (and certainly afterward), d'Aquino paid dearly for her fierce sense of loyalty to the United States. She steadfastly refused to renounce her U.S. citizenship, despite ongoing harassment by the Japanese secret police. Her refusal also meant that she would have to set out on her own to Tokyo because of the pressures placed on her relatives, who were accused of harboring the enemy. Alone and effectively illiterate in the Japanese language, d'Aquino struggled to survive, suffering from malnutrition and other health problems. As an American, she was not eligible for ration cards. In the face of such hardships, d'Aquino sacrificed even more for her country by using her own meager resources to purchase food and medicine for Allied prisoners of war while also supplying them with accurate news of the war. The ultimate irony is that had d'Aquino given up her citizenship, she would have been shielded from the treason charges (as were the Nisei who testified against her at the trial).[9]

During the war, d'Aquino found part-time work as a typist at Radio Tokyo. Her stint as a broadcaster began when the station conscripted d'Aquino, some twenty other women, and a few Allied prisoners of war to use their English-language skills for propaganda purposes. Testimony during the trial, including the prosecutor's witnesses, made it clear that the "Zero Hour" program provided little more that entertainment. The end of the war came before the show had a chance to launch its propaganda campaign.[10] At the war's end in August 1945, Iva lived with her husband, Felipe d'Aquino, a Portuguese national of Japanese ancestry whom she had met at the radio station. Reporters who accompanied occupation forces into Tokyo desperately sought out the "Tokyo Rose" that American servicemen had created in their fantasies. Finding a woman who could bring the fictive temptress to life would represent a major coup. Through a series of events, two reporters got a tip that led them to d'Aquino. Lured by a huge advance and unreliable information, d'Aquino was transformed, literally overnight, into "Tokyo Rose."[11] The legend now had a face and a name, and d'Aquino's life would never be the same.[12]

Infamy had its price, and d'Aquino became embroiled in cold war politics that led to two lengthy arrests and a highly problematic trial. During these events, actions by federal officials displayed a flagrant disregard for the rights of a U.S. citizen. Initially arrested in 1945, d'Aquino spent over a year in prison in occupied Japan without ever being charged only to have her case dismissed due to a lack of evidence. U.S. attorneys, responding to pressure applied by the likes of radio personality Walter Winchell, rearrested d'Aquino in 1948 and shipped her to America to stand trial for treason. She had been trying to get back into the United States since her release in 1946. D'Aquino had received word that her mother had died in the Gila, Arizona, camp. Understandably, she longed to see her family and also very much wanted the child she was carrying to be born on American soil. D'Aquino was finally heading home but as a prisoner of her own country.[13]

On 5 July 1949, a day after d'Aquino's thirty-third birthday, the treason trial began in San Francisco, a venue federal attorneys chose for its long history of anti-Japanese activity and sentiment. At the end of the thirteen-week ordeal (the most expensive federal trial to date), the jury returned one guilty verdict (of eight counts) that claimed that d'Aquino had muttered a line about U.S. ships sunk at the Allies' resounding victory at the Battle of Leyte Gulf. Despite the lack of any evidence actually linking d'Aquino to the radio voice, the U.S. government spent more than one-half million dollars to prosecute a myth. Apart from the cost, it took deal making, perjured testimony, and prejudicial instructions from the bench to force the verdict desired by federal officials.[14] Pro bono defense lawyers Wayne Collins, Theodore Tamba, and George Olshausen appealed the decision but to no avail. Iva Toguri d'Aquino received her sentence in November 1949: ten years in prison and a $10,000 fine. D'Aquino told reporters: "My conscience is clear. I can't help what the jury felt. I still feel that I didn't do anything wrong."[15] She served about six years and two months of her sentence, receiving time off for good behavior, but upon her release was continually hounded by federal agents, deportation actions, and efforts to collect the fine. Justice finally was served in 1977, when President Gerald Ford granted a full and unconditional pardon.[16]

While Japanese Americans like Clifford Uyeda of San Francisco played an instrumental role in coordinating the pardon campaign for d'Aquino during the 1970s, very few Japanese Americans supported her during the trial itself. Perhaps 1949 proved to be too soon for Nikkei to be able to embrace d'Aquino's case as their own. No doubt, many men and women were struggling to reconstruct the lives that had been ripped apart by the war. A Nisei on trial for treason could only lead to further trouble. Exceptions to the rule, Larry and Guyo (Marion) Tajiri did provide extensive coverage of the trial in the *Pacific Citizen*. While the bulk of the articles reported factual and procedural information, they also recognized that d'Aquino's troubles were not unconnected to Japanese Americans in general. The Tajiris, as they had done before and during the war, encouraged their readers to see the larger significance of the situation at hand.[17]

Both journalists noted the role of race. In an editorial, Larry Tajiri argued: "Despite statements to the contrary in the public press this week, race prejudice is a definite factor in the trial of Iva Toguri d'Aquino." Tajiri pointed to the jury selection process, in which the prosecution used its peremptory challenges to remove every potential racial-ethnic juror (African American and Chinese American) from the pool. Consequently, an all–European American jury was chosen (six men, six women, and two women alternates). Tajiri suggested that the prosecution in this action might be trying to subvert any plans the defense might have in raising the issue of race.[18] Apart from the jury issue, Tajiri also commented that prejudice had "touched and shaped the lives of all persons of Japanese ancestry who lived in California before the war." That prejudice had been responsible for the lack of opportunities for Nisei, some of whom then turned to Japan for possible jobs. Many second-generation men and women who had gone to Japan for such reasons found themselves stranded during the war.[19]

Guyo Tajiri's more extensive coverage of the trial, while evenhanded, reflected a sympathy for d'Aquino's plight. In signed articles, Tajiri portrayed the defense in positive terms, noting how they had weakened the prosecution's case. She also commented on the fact that d'Aquino had pledged with other Nisei in Japan not to renounce their U.S. citizenship regardless of the circumstances. Another story noted with concern the poor treatment of d'Aquino in jail that directly contributed to her intestinal influenza, requiring a recess in the trial while she recuperated. One could also sense a sensitivity to the defendant's difficulties in the coverage of d'Aquino's own testimony. As a seasoned journalist, Tajiri moved beyond the simple facts to offer her readers insight into the trial. Articles commented on the prosecution's use of the testimony of Nisei who had renounced their U.S. citizenship and worked for Radio Tokyo. In the story conveying the guilty verdict, considerable space was given to the fact that potentially prejudicial instructions from the bench swayed the jurors, who at one point overwhelmingly favored acquittal. In a final editorial, Guyo Tajiri commented: "there were, however, the inevitable traces of racism, some of them obvious, some evident only to the hypersensitive." Tajiri wryly quoted from prosecuting attorney Tom De Wolfe's closing testimony, in which he claimed that prejudice had nothing to do with the trial since the case was being tried in a western community by a group of westerners; as Tajiri recorded, De Wolfe stated: "You and I know . . . we have no prejudice against the Japanese." With only a slim hope of a successful appeal, Tajiri realized that d'Aquino would likely become—"in the opinion of most Americans, including the Nisei"—the seventh traitor in the history of the United States. And yet, Tajiri wondered whether Nisei "might feel a slight tugging at the back of their minds—could it have been I?"[20]

By ending her observations with a question, Guyo Tajiri was in effect asking her Nisei readers to think about how they and d'Aquino had far more in common than it might first appear. For political motives steeped in race prejudice, the U.S. government had punished d'Aquino for something she did not do—just as it had incarcerated Nikkei during the war. Similarly, a shared racial-ethnic background had enabled the government to paint d'Aquino and Japanese Americans as the enemy. D'Aquino also found out, a little later than the rest, that the principles of democracy and justice did not apply equally to all Americans. Had circumstances been slightly different, any Nisei could have stood in d'Aquino's place just as she would have been with her family at the Gila River camp. Japanese Americans likely failed to rally to d'Aquino's side because her case so powerfully symbolized the ordeal that the Nikkei had just emerged from. In that sense, the drama that transpired in the courtroom extended beyond the fate of a sole individual, even if one Nisei ultimately paid the price. Metaphorically, one could interpret the case as Japanese America on trial; the verdict confirmed the sentence that they had served. It is not surprising, then, that Nikkei sought to distance themselves from d'Aquino.

The "Tokyo Rose" trial may have demonstrated the ongoing racial subordination of Japanese Americans, but the case only captured part of the story. Despite the harsh realities of race prejudice, Nisei had always managed to shape and infuse meaning into their own lives. In that regard, *Growing Up Nisei* has documented a history that needs to be told—for the sake of successive generations and as part of a larger "community of memory."[21] Like other children of immigrants, Nisei underwent the dynamic and constructive process of "becoming Americans." Understanding how this took place informs our understanding of self and nation. The richly textured world of the Nisei undermines dismissive characterizations of the second generation as assimilationist. The experiences of Nisei illustrate the highly contextual natures of race, generation, and identity formation. Far from a uniform picture, what surfaces is a montage that blurs the lines between categories that have so often been applied to the migration and settlement process in America. The internal complexity contained within this study helps us to move away from cardboard figures and toward a portrayal of Japanese Americans as fully human.

No single study could possibly explain what it meant to grow up Nisei in California during the period stretching from exclusion in 1924 to the "Tokyo Rose" trial of 1949. The focus of this story has been on a number of important institutions in the development and growth of a Nisei subculture before and during the war. The foundations laid during the 1920s and the 1930s would help many Nisei adjust to the upheaval of the camps. A case has been made for the continuity of Japanese American history in which events and issues such as identity formation must be seen as part of a larger frame of experience. A relatively distinct cohort of Americans came of age under extremely trying circumstances, and their journeys speak to the powerful role that race has played in our national history. Although often viewed as an aberration, the concentration camps in fact were an outgrowth of longstanding discriminatory efforts aimed at Japanese Americans since their arrival at these shores.

To the extent that this study has been successful in portraying the history of one second-generation group, more work is needed on this cohort, especially among racial-ethnic groups, since their experiences challenge us to rethink traditional interpretations of migration, settlement, and national identity. While the increasing calls for comparative work are well-heeded, a simultaneous stance should also be made for the value and integrity of works that focus on a single group. That stance is important not because of any inherent flaw in comparative work but rather since the push for comparison is often a coded way of suggesting that groups like Japanese Americans do not by themselves merit the kind of historical attention that others (namely, European Americans) routinely receive. The hope is that scholarship will move in the direction of an innovative tandem of comparative and single-group studies.

The need for such work seems especially compelling given the fact that, as we approach the twenty-first century, the color line has hardly disappeared. Although racial formations have undergone change, the recent debates and political battles in California over immigration, affirmative action, bilingual education, and the place of ethnic studies bear resemblance to the nativist perspectives of earlier periods, including those that the Nisei experienced. A careful examination of our history, it seems, is wise counsel. Whether or not we as a nation can ever fulfill the creeds we uphold will depend on learning from our past to envision a different kind of future.

For Nisei poised at the beginning of a new era, the years following World War II were filled with uncertainty. No reminders were necessary of how racial-ethnic difference had deeply affected life chances regardless of hard work, ability, or education. These children of immigrants, moreover, carried with them the memories of incarceration—memories that time would not erase. And yet, those who were able moved ahead, determined to stake their claim as Americans in the fullest sense of the word.

NOTES

Introduction

1. Japanese Americans use terms to denote generational status, "Nisei" being the second generation or children of immigrants. "Kibei" are Nisei who were typically sent to Japan as young children to live with relatives. "Nikkei" is an inclusive term for all Japanese Americans. For more information, see Brian Niiya, ed., *Japanese American History: An A to Z Reference from 1868 to the Present* (New York: Facts on File, 1993). Sociologist Emory Bogardus used the term "Hansei" to describe those who were born in Japan but who came to the United States at an early age and who, for all intents and purposes, were Nisei. Emory Bogardus, "Culture Conflicts in Relocation Centers," *Sociology and Social Research* 27 (May 1943): 381–90.

2. Toshio Mori, "Sweet Potato," in *The Chauvinist and Other Stories* (Los Angeles: Asian American Studies Center, University of California, 1979), 107–10.

3. Rudolph Vecoli provides a helpful discussion and overview of the historiography of the field in "From *The Uprooted* to *The Transplanted*: The Writing of American Immigration History, 1951–1989," in *From "Melting Pot" to Multiculturalism: The Evolution of Ethnic Relations in the United States and Canada*, ed. Valeria Gennaro Lerda (Rome: Bulzoni Editore, 1990), 53.

4. Dorothy S. Thomas, Charles Kikuchi, and James Sakoda, *The Salvage* (Berkeley: University of California Press, 1952), 574–79, 596, 610.

5. Ibid., 596–97, 600–605. One percent of the employed Nisei did not report their occupation. Agricultural workers by sex: 5,611 male/1,340 female. Nearly a thousand (960) women worked as unpaid labor, while 4,704 men worked as farmers, managers, or paid laborers. Clerical, sales by sex: 1,983 male/1,175 female. Women domestics numbered 1,475, while 1,078 men worked in unskilled labor.

6. An interdisciplinary group of scholars have explored the issue of lifecourse that I have found instructive: Glen Elder Jr., John Modell, and Ross D. Parke, eds., *Children in Time and Place: Developmental and Historical Insights* (Cambridge: Cambridge University Press, 1993), especially the essay by William Tuttle; John Modell, *Into One's Own: From Youth to Adulthood in America, 1920–1975* (Berke-

ley: University of California Press, 1989); Harvey J. Graff, *Conflicting Paths: Growing Up in America* (Cambridge, Mass.: Harvard University Press, 1995).

7. Deborah Dash Moore, *At Home in America: Second Generation New York Jews* (New York: Columbia University Press, 1981); Donald Weber, "Reconsidering the Hansen Thesis: Generational Metaphors and American Ethnic Studies," *American Quarterly* 43 (June 1991): 326. Weber alludes to Marcus Lee Hansen's three-generation hypothesis, which suggests that what the son wishes to forget (i.e., ethnic identity), the grandson strives to remember. See Peter Kivisto and Dag Blanck, eds., *American Immigrants and Their Generations* (Urbana: University of Illinois Press, 1990), which explores the contributions and legacy of Marcus Lee Hansen.

8. Yuji Ichioka, "Coming of Age," *Amerasia Journal* 13 (1986–87): ix–xiii. Also see John Modell, "The Japanese American Family: A Perspective for Future Investigations," *Pacific Historical Review* 37 (Feb. 1968): 67–81.

9. This study builds on the work of others who have examined mainland Japanese America during the prewar period, including: John Modell, *The Economics and Politics of Racial Accommodation: The Japanese of Los Angeles, 1900–1942* (Urbana: University of Illinois Press, 1977); Jerrold Takahashi, "Japanese American Responses to Race Relations: The Formation of Nisei Perspectives," *Amerasia Journal* 9 (1982): 29–57; Roger Daniels, "Japanese America, 1930–41: An Ethnic Community in the Great Depression," *Journal of the West* 24 (Oct. 1985): 35–49; Yuji Ichioka, "A Study in Dualism: James Yoshinori Sakamoto and the *Japanese American Courier*, 1928–42," *Amerasia Journal* 13 (1986–87): 49–81; Valerie J. Matsumoto, "Desperately Seeking 'Deirdre': Gender Roles, Multicultural Relations, and Nisei Women Writers of the 1930s," *Frontiers* 12.1 (1991): 19–32; idem, *Farming the Home Place: A Japanese American Community in California, 1919–1982* (Ithaca, N.Y.: Cornell University Press, 1993); Lon Yuki Kurashige, "Made in Little Tokyo: Politics of Ethnic Identity and Festival in Southern California, 1934–1994" (Ph.D. diss., University of Wisconsin at Madison, 1994); Brian Masaru Hayashi, *"For the Sake of Our Japanese Brethren": Assimilation, Nationalism, and Protestantism among the Japanese of Los Angeles, 1895–1942* (Stanford, Calif.: Stanford University Press, 1995); Paul Spickard, *Japanese Americans: The Formation and Transformation of an Ethnic Group* (Boston: Twayne, 1996). The literature on the war years is extensive; and a good introduction to the literature, though in need of updating, is the section on internment in Hyung-chan Kim, *Asian American Studies: An Annotated Bibliography* (Westport, Conn.: Greenwood Press, 1989).

10. To give a sense of the development of this wide-ranging literature, the following works have been listed in chronological order (by date of publication): George Kagiwada, "The Assimilation of Nisei in Los Angeles," in *East across the Pacific: Historical and Sociological Studies of Japanese Immigration and Assimilation*, ed. Hilary Conroy and T. Scott Miyakawa (Santa Barbara, Calif.: ABC-Clio Press, 1972), 268–78; Stanford Lyman, "Generation and Character: The Case of the Japanese-Americans," in Conroy and Miyakawa, *East across the Pacific*, 279–

314; Christie W. Kiefer, *Changing Culture, Changing Lives* (San Francisco: Jossey-Bass, 1974); John Connor, *Tradition and Change among Three Generations of Japanese Americans* (Chicago: Nelson-Hall, 1977); Darrel Montero, *Japanese Americans: Changing Patterns of Ethnic Affiliation over Three Generations* (Boulder, Colo.: Westview Press, 1980); Gene Levine and Colbert Rhodes, *The Japanese American Community: A Three-Generation Study* (New York: Praeger, 1981); Sylvia Yanagisako, *Transforming the Past: Tradition and Kinship among Japanese Americans* (Stanford, Calif.: Stanford University Press, 1985); Evelyn Nakano Glenn, *Issei, Nisei, War Bride: Three Generations of Japanese American Women in Domestic Service* (Philadelphia: Temple University Press, 1986); Mei Nakano, *Japanese American Women: Three Generations, 1890–1990* (Berkeley, Calif.: Mina Press, 1990); Stephen S. Fugita and David J. O'Brien, *Japanese American Ethnicity: The Persistence of Community* (Seattle: University of Washington Press, 1991); Donna K. Nagata, *Legacy of Injustice: Exploring the Cross-Generational Impact of the Japanese American Internment* (New York: Plenum Press, 1993); Yasuko I. Takezawa, *Breaking the Silence: Redress and Japanese American Ethnicity* (Ithaca, N.Y.: Cornell University Press, 1995).

11. S. Frank Miyamoto, *Social Solidarity among the Japanese in Seattle* (1939; rpt., Seattle: University of Washington Press, 1984); Bill Hosokawa, *The Nisei: The Quiet Americans* (New York: William Morrow and Co., 1969); Eileen H. Tamura, *Americanization, Acculturation, and Ethnic Identity: The Nisei Generation in Hawaii* (Urbana: University of Illinois Press, 1994); Jerrold Takahashi, *Nisei/Sansei: Shifting Japanese American Identities and Politics* (Philadelphia: Temple University Press, 1997).

12. Roger Daniels, "The Japanese," in *Ethnic Leadership in America*, ed. John Higham (Baltimore: Johns Hopkins University Press, 1978), 37–38.

13. Stanford University professor Edward K. Strong guided a four-volume study of Japanese Americans: Edward K. Strong, *Vocational Aptitudes of Second-Generation Japanese in the United States* (Stanford, Calif.: Stanford University Press, 1933); idem, *Japanese in California* (Stanford, Calif.: Stanford University Press, 1933); idem, *The Second-Generation Japanese Problem* (Stanford, Calif.: Stanford University Press, 1934); Reginald Bell, *Public School Education of Second-Generation Japanese in California* (Stanford, Calif.: Stanford University Press, 1935). Graduate students at Stanford and at USC (under the supervision of sociologist Emory Bogardus) also wrote many master's and doctoral theses on this subject; this body of work will be addressed in chapter 1 (on Nisei education and schooling). Stanford historian Yamato Ichihashi also produced his seminal work *Japanese in the United States: A Critical Study of the Problems of the Japanese Immigrants and Their Children* (Stanford, Calif.: Stanford University Press, 1932). See also Gordon H. Chang, ed., *Morning Glory, Evening Shadow: Yamato Ichihashi and His Internment Writings, 1942–45* (Stanford, Calif.: Stanford University Press, 1997). During the war, the government compiled a tremendous amount of data on Japanese Americans who had been incarcerated. Of the numerous works, see

U.S. Department of the Interior, War Relocation Authority, *The Evacuated People: A Quantitative Description* (Washington, D.C.: Government Printing Office, 1946).

14. One study was conducted by social scientists at the University of California at Berkeley under the direction of faculty member Dorothy Swaine Thomas. This extensive collection, the Japanese [American] Evacuation and Resettlement Study (JERS), is housed at the Bancroft Library, University of California at Berkeley. Edward A. Barnhart's *Japanese American Evacuation and Resettlement: Catalog of Materials in the General Library* (Berkeley: General Library, University of California, 1958) is a detailed guide to the collection. Published studies based on JERS include: Thomas et al., *Salvage;* Dorothy S. Thomas and Richard S. Nishimoto, *The Spoilage: Japanese-American Evacuation and Resettlement during World War II* (Berkeley: University of California Press, 1946). For a critical overview of the collection and the ethical dimension of JERS, see Yuji Ichioka, ed., *Views from Within: The Japanese Evacuation and Resettlement Study* (Los Angeles: Asian American Studies Center, University of California, 1989) and Richard S. Nishimoto, *Inside an American Concentration Camp: Japanese American Resistance at Poston, Arizona,* ed. Lane Ryo Hirabayashi (Tucson: University of Arizona Press, 1995). In another study, the War Relocation Authority (WRA) sponsored anthropologists, who served as "community analysts." For an insightful overview of this project, see Orin Starn, "Engineering Internment: Anthropologists and the War Relocation Authority," *American Ethnologist* 13 (Nov. 1986): 700–720. Much of the government material is housed at the National Archives and Record Service in Washington, D.C., Record Group 210, Records of the WRA.

15. Ronald Takaki, *Strangers from a Different Shore: A History of Asian Americans* (Boston: Little, Brown, 1989), 7–8.

16. Much of the literature written before the 1960s focuses on the excluders rather than the excluded. See Roger Daniels, "Westerners from the East: Oriental Immigrants Reappraised," *Pacific Historical Review* 35 (Nov. 1966): 373–84; idem, "American Historians and East Asian Immigrants," *Pacific Historical Review* 43 (Nov. 1974): 449–72.

17. For a helpful overview, see Virginia Yans-McLaughlin, ed., *Immigration Reconsidered* (New York: Oxford University Press, 1990). Also of interest is the forum on ethnicity and immigration in Kathleen Neils Conzen, David A. Gerber, Ewa Morawska, George E. Pozzetta, and Rudolph Vecoli, "The Invention of Ethnicity: A Perspective from the USA," *Journal of American Ethnic History* 12 (Fall 1992): 3–63.

18. For further discussion: Lyman, "Generation and Character," 157–76; S. Frank Miyamoto, "Problems of Interpersonal Style among Nisei," *Amerasia Journal* 13 (1986–87): 29–45; Fugita and O'Brien, *Japanese American Ethnicity.* My initial research indicates that while Issei men dominated first-generation organizations, the Nisei experienced more balance in terms of gender. Women held key positions in the YBA and the YPCC, for instance. The YWCA and its Buddhist

counterpart (YWBA), moreover, gave Nisei women important opportunities to serve in leadership roles.

19. Lisa Lowe, *Immigrant Acts: On Asian American Cultural Politics* (Durham, N.C.: Duke University Press, 1996), 6.

20. Elliot West and Paula Petrik, eds., *Small Worlds: Children and Adolescents in America, 1850–1950* (Lawrence: University Press of Kansas, 1992), 1–8. Also see Selma Cantor Berrol, *Growing Up American: Immigrant Children in America Then and Now* (Boston: Twayne, 1995).

21. Graff, *Conflicting Paths,* 304.

22. Leading "ethnicity school" texts include: Nathan Glazer and Daniel Moynihan, eds., *Ethnicity: Theory and Experience* (Cambridge, Mass.: Harvard University Press, 1975); Stephan Thernstrom, Ann Orlov, and Oscar Handlin, eds., *The Harvard Encyclopedia of American Ethnic Groups* (Cambridge, Mass.: Harvard University Press, 1980); Werner Sollors, ed., *The Invention of Ethnicity* (New York: Oxford University Press, 1989). For reviews and critiques: Alexander Saxton, "Nathan Glazer, Daniel Moynihan, and the Cult of Ethnicity," *Amerasia Journal* 4 (1977): 141–50; M. G. Smith, "Ethnicity and Ethnic Groups in America: The View from Harvard," *Ethnic and Racial Studies* 5 (Jan. 1982): 1–22; Stephen Steinberg, *The Ethnic Myth* (Boston: Beacon Press, 1981). For a very helpful debate between Ronald Takaki and Nathan Glazer on "race" versus "ethnicity," see Takaki, ed., *From Different Shores* (New York: Oxford University Press, 1987), 11–37. My discussion of race and ethnicity relies heavily on E. San Juan Jr.'s insightful analysis and critique, *Racial Formations/Critical Transformations* (Highlands, N.J.: Humanities Press, 1992), chaps. 1–3.

23. San Juan, *Racial Formations,* 31–41. Historian Alexander Saxton has done much to contextualize and untangle the role and use of "race" in American history. See *The Indispensable Enemy: Labor and the Anti-Chinese Movement in California* (Berkeley: University of California Press, 1971) and *The Rise and Fall of the White Republic* (London: Verso Press, 1990).

24. Michael Omi and Howard Winant, *Racial Formations in the United States* (New York: Routledge, 1986), 61, 68. Omi and Winant provide a helpful overview of various theories of race in America. Robert Blauner authored an important early study that places race squarely in the center of analysis, *Racial Oppression in America* (New York: Harper and Row, 1972).

25. See Evelyn Brooks Higginbotham, "African-American Women's History and the Metalanguage of Race," *Signs* 17.2 (Winter 1992): 251–75; Barbara J. Fields, "Ideology and Race in American History," in *Region, Race, and Reconstruction: Essays in Honor of C. Vann Woodward,* ed. J. Morgan Kousser and James M. McPherson (New York: Oxford University Press, 1982), 143–78.

26. Peggy Pascoe, "Miscegenation Law, Court Cases, and Ideologies of 'Race' in Twentieth-Century America," *Journal of American History* 83 (June 1996): 48. See also Robert J. C. Young, *Colonial Desire: Hybridity in Theory, Culture, and Race* (London: Routledge, 1995), 27–28, 94.

27. Renato Rosaldo, *Culture and Truth* (Boston: Beacon Press, 1989), 21, 131–32.

28. Tomas Almaguer, *Racial Fault Lines: The Historical Origins of White Supremacy in California* (Berkeley: University of California Press, 1994), 2–3, 7, 183–204.

29. The Fourteenth Amendment extended citizenship to African Americans, but Issei, except for select World War I veterans, were not eligible for naturalization until 1952, under the McCarran-Walter Act.

30. For background on the anti-Japanese movement, see Roger Daniels, *The Politics of Prejudice: The Anti-Japanese Movement in California and the Struggle for Japanese Exclusion* (Berkeley: University of California Press, 1962).

31. Two standard works on Japanese American immigrants are: Yuji Ichioka, *The Issei: The World of First Generation Japanese Immigrants, 1885–1924* (New York: Free Press, 1988), which deals with the mainland; and Yukiko Kimura, *Issei: Japanese Immigrants in Hawaii* (Honolulu: University of Hawaii Press, 1988). Ichioka discusses Abiko in detail. Valerie J. Matsumoto's community study *Farming the Home Place* details the Cortez colony that Abiko helped establish.

32. Ichioka, *Issei*, chap. 7, details the effects of the 1924 Immigration Act. Many immigrants saw the act as the culmination of their rejection by the United States.

33. Phelan quoted in Roger Daniels, ed., *Japanese Immigration* (New York: Arno Press, 1978), 3, 25. For background on Phelan, see Robert E. Hennings, *James D. Phelan and the Wilson Progressives of California* (New York: Garland, 1985); Kevin Starr, *Americans and the California Dream, 1850–1915* (New York: Oxford University Press, 1973), 249–53.

34. Ichioka, *Issei*, 253–54.

Chapter 1: The ABCs of a Nisei Education

1. Kazuo Kawai, "Three Roads, and None Easy: An American-Born Japanese Looks at Life," *Survey Graphic* 9 (May 1926): 164.

2. Ibid., 164.

3. Charles Wollenberg, *With All Deliberate Speed: Segregation and Exclusion in California Schools, 1855–1975* (Berkeley: University of California Press, 1976); Irving Hendrick, *Public Policy toward the Education of Non-White Minority Group Children in California, 1849–1970* (Riverside: School of Education, University of California, 1975).

4. Tamura, *Americanization, Acculturation, and Ethnic Identity;* see also Eileen H. Tamura, "The English-Only Effort, the Anti-Japanese Campaign, and Language Acquisition in the Education of Japanese Americans in Hawaii, 1915–40," *History of Education Quarterly* 33.1 (Spring 1993): 37–58. Also of interest: Thomas James, *Exile Within: The Schooling of Japanese Americans, 1942–45* (Cambridge, Mass.: Harvard University Press, 1987).

5. Bell, *Public School Education*, 7. The students in Los Angeles County numbered about 13,500.

6. Kawai, "Three Roads," 166.

7. Paula Fass, *Outside In: Minorities and the Transformation of American Education* (New York: Oxford University Press, 1989), chap. 1.

8. Lawrence Cremin, *The Transformation of the School: Progressivism in American Education, 1876–1957* (New York: Alfred A. Knopf, 1961). Also of interest is Steinberg, *Ethnic Myth*.

9. Fass, *Outside In*, 33–34.

10. Irving Hendrick, "California's Response to the 'New Education' in the 1930s," *California Historical Quarterly* 53 (Spring 1974): 25–40, esp. 25–31. Hendrick notes that the heyday of the movement in California was 1915–40. An older—but standard—history is Roy Cloud's *Education in California* (Stanford, Calif.: Stanford University Press, 1952), esp. chaps. 20–31; also relevant is David B. Tyack, *The One Best System* (Cambridge, Mass.: Harvard University Press, 1974), esp. chaps. 4–5.

11. Hendrick, "California's Response," 26, 28. For background on schools during the Depression: David Tyack and Elisabeth Hansot, *Public Schools in Hard Times* (Cambridge, Mass.: Harvard University Press, 1984).

12. Judith Raftery, *Land of Fair Promise: Politics and Reform in Los Angeles Schools, 1885–1941* (Stanford, Calif.: Stanford University Press, 1992), 3–4.

13. Fass, *Outside In*, 37–39.

14. Edward Hartmann, *The Movement to Americanize the Immigrant* (New York: Columbia University Press, 1948), 8 (quote), 269–70.

15. David Herman, "Neighbors on Golden Mountain: The Americanization of Immigrants in California and Public Instruction as an Agency of Ethnic Assimilation, 1850 to 1933" (Ph.D. diss., University of California at Berkeley, 1981), xvi, 329, 347–50.

16. Ibid., xvii–xx, 263, 347–50, 354, 624. The "Americans All" program in intercultural education that sponsored curriculum and national radio broadcasts represented a serious effort to view the process of Americanization as mutual exchange. See Nicholas V. Montalto, "The Intercultural Education Movement, 1924–41: The Growth of Tolerance as a Form of Intolerance," in *American Education and the European Immigrant, 1840–1940*, ed. Bernard J. Weiss (Urbana: University of Illinois Press, 1982), 142–60.

17. Alice Osborne McKenna, "Americanizing the Foreign Home," *Los Angeles School Journal* 9 (28 Sept. 1928): 13–14; Harry M. Shafer, "Tendencies in Immigrant Education," *Los Angeles School Journal* 9 (5 Oct. 1925): 9–11.

18. Although Americanization programs were run by women and geared toward women, I did not find any articles that specifically dealt with Nisei women in areas such as home education. For a general overview, John F. McClymer, "Gender and the 'American Way of Life': Women and the Americanization Movement," *Journal of American Ethnic History* 10 (Spring 1991): 3–20.

19. Gertrude M. Allison, "Japanese Unit of Study for Fourth and Third Grade," *Los Angeles School Journal* 13 (17 Mar. 1930): 11. Answers included quality of life and better government.

20. Lucile Regan, "Nisei: The Second Generation," *Los Angeles School Journal* 19 (1 June 1936): 15, 48–51.

21. Strong, *Second-Generation Japanese Problem*, 5, 18, 20, 59, 258–59. See also Strong, *Vocational Aptitudes*.

22. Emory Bogardus, "Some Causes of Prejudice," *Los Angeles School Journal* 12 (31 Dec. 1928): 16–17.

23. Ibid.; Stow Persons, *Ethnic Studies at Chicago, 1905–45* (Urbana: University of Illinois Press, 1987), 60–61, 67–69, 71–72. Bogardus dedicated *Immigration and Race Attitudes* (Boston: D. C. Heath and Co., 1928) to Robert E. Park.

24. Gretchen Tuthill, "Study of the Japanese in the City of Los Angeles" (master's thesis, University of Southern California, 1924), 48 (quote from unnamed interviewee), 86–90.

25. Ruth M. Fowler, "Some Aspects of Public Opinion Concerning the Japanese in Santa Clara" (master's thesis, Stanford University, 1934), 244–51.

26. Saikichi Chijiwa, "A Social Survey of the Japanese Population in Palo Alto and Menlo Park" (master's thesis, Stanford University, 1933), 52–53, 66.

27. Emory Bogardus and Robert Ross, "The Second-Generation Race Relations Cycle: A Study in Issei-Nisei Relationships," *Sociology and Social Research* 24 (Mar.–Apr. 1940): 357–63. Stow Persons comments that Bogardus did not follow up the idea of "marginal man" culture (what I term a Nisei subculture) as an alternative—that is, a culture composed of marginal men and women reconciled to their marginality (*Ethnic Studies at Chicago*, 71–72, 108). I think that the Nisei during the prewar years did create their own culture by choice and by necessity. Prior to his formulation of the second-generation cycle, Bogardus elaborated on Park's cycle in suggesting that the behavior of "native" Americans toward the Chinese, Japanese, Filipinos, and Mexicans involved seven phases. See "A Race-Relations Cycle," *American Journal of Sociology* 35 (Jan. 1930): 612–17.

28. Index, Survey of Race Relations, Hoover Institution Archives, Stanford University, Stanford, Calif. (hereafter cited as SRR); *A Survey of Race Relations on the Pacific Coast* (n.p., n.d.), 3, in the Graduate Theological Union Library Archives, Berkeley, California. The survey included Chinese, Japanese, Koreans, Filipinos, Asian Indians, Mexicans, and others. Elliot Mears's *Resident Orientals on the Pacific Coast* (Chicago: University of Chicago Press, 1928) turned out to be the only official publication of the Race Relations Survey. Many of those involved in the project completed theses and monographs from their fieldwork and continued with work on race relations after the project ended, including William C. Smith, *Americans in Process: A Study of Our Citizens of Oriental Ancestry* (Ann Arbor, Mich.: Edward Bros., 1937); Forrest E. LaViolette, *Americans of Japanese Ancestry: A Study of Assimilation in the American Community* (Toronto: Canadian Institute of International Affairs, 1945).

29. Robert E. Park, *Race and Culture* (Glencoe, Ill: Free Press, 1950), 164.

30. Ibid., 158–65. A copy of the guidelines given to researchers can be found in SRR, box 6. On the role of life histories and their connection to Japanese Ameri-

cans, see Dana Takagi, "Life History Analysis and JERS: Re-evaluating the Work of Charles Kikuchi," in *Views from Within: The Japanese Evacuation and Resettlement Study*, ed. Yuji Ichioka (Los Angeles: Asian American Studies Center, University of California, 1989), 197–216.

31. Park, *Race and Culture*, 159–60; Park has not received much credit for his commitment to the study of race or life history. In his biography of Park, Fred H. Matthews suggests that the sociologist's views on race relations and assimilation were far more nuanced and subtle than critics have acknowledged. See *Quest for an American Sociology: Robert E. Park and the Chicago School* (Montreal: McGill-Queen's University Press, 1977), chap. 6.

32. Robert E. Park, "Behind Our Masks," *Survey Graphic* 9 (May 1926): 135.

33. Interview with "UZ", 21 Aug. 1924, SRR, box 35, file 53.

34. L. Toyama, "My Life History," SRR, box 37, file 459, 3 (including the passage quoted).

35. *Shin Sekai*, 6–10 Oct. 1931. Horiuchi carried on his analysis in debate format and included a very lukewarm, pro-college perspective. See ibid., 4 and 6–7 Nov. 1931.

36. *Rafu Shimpo*, 12 June 1938.

37. Kibei—or Kibei Nisei, as they were called—represent another dimension of the Japanese American experience. See "Kibei," in Hyung-chan Kim, *Dictionary of Asian American History* (Westport, Conn.: Greenwood Press, 1986), 347–48. Karl Yoneda's autobiography tells the story of a fascinating—if quite atypical—Kibei; see *Ganbatte: Sixty-Year Struggle of a Kibei Worker* (Los Angeles: Asian American Studies Center, University of California, 1983).

38. Toyotomi Morimoto, "Language and Heritage Maintenance of Immigrants: Japanese Language Schools of California, 1903–1941" (Ph.D. diss., University of California, Los Angeles, 1989), xii, 8, 78–79, 122; Strong, *Second-Generation Japanese Problem*, 201.

39. Horace Chansler, "The Assimilation of the Japanese in and around Stockton" (master's thesis, College of the Pacific, 1932), 43.

40. Chotoku Toyama, "The Japanese Community in Los Angeles" (master's thesis, Columbia University, 1926), 21–27; Morimoto, "Language and Heritage Maintenance," 9, 63.

41. Michiji Ishikawa, "The Japanese in California" (master's thesis, Columbia University, 1928), 85–90; Morimoto, "Language and Heritage Maintenance," 67–68.

42. Paul Hirohata, ed., *Orations and Essays by the Japanese Second Generation of America* (Los Angeles: Los Angeles Japanese Daily News, 1932), i–iii.

43. Goro Murata, "American Government and Idealism," in Hirohata, *Orations and Essays*, 67–69.

44. Kay Sugahara, "Foreword," in Hirohata, *Orations and Essays*, iii.

45. Haruko Fujita, "Why Japanese Came to America," in Hirohata, *Orations and Essays*, 117–18.

46. The bridge concept enjoyed support from many quarters, including Issei leaders, Japanese diplomats, and Americans involved in education, trade, and religion. The immigrant newspapers gave a lot of attention to the idea. Sociologist Jerrold Takahashi and historian Yuji Ichioka both provide helpful overviews of the political contexts for the bridge concept. See Takahashi, "Japanese American Responses," 29–57, and *Nisei/Sansei;* see also Ichioka, "Study in Dualism," 49–81.

47. *Rafu Shimpo,* 20 June 1937.

48. Morimoto, "Language and Heritage Maintenance," 110–21.

49. For background on the first study tours, see Yuji Ichioka, "*Kengakudan:* The Origin of Nisei Study Tours of Japan," *California History* 73.1 (Spring 1994): 30–43.

50. *Japanese American Courier,* 4 Apr. 1936.

51. The Nisei spoke of the bridge in diverse ways, including the more traditional forms heralded by diplomats and others, especially in essay contests (see *Nichibei Shimbun,* 1 Jan. 1934). My point is that the bridge also served as a way of negotiating the tensions that accompanied being Japanese American.

52. Isamu Nodera, "A Survey of the Vocational Activities of the Japanese in the City of Los Angeles" (master's thesis, University of Southern California, 1936), 114–17; Modell, *Economics and Politics,* 127–32. Modell's chapter 6 is a helpful overview of the vocational situation of the Nisei in Los Angeles. He touches on issues and concerns facing many Nisei throughout California. He also looks at areas such as retail produce, the back-to-the-farm movement, and unionization among the Nisei in agriculture. *Nichibei Shimbun,* 5 Sept. 1938, reported Onoura's findings. The poll is from *Rafu Shimpo,* 20 June 1937.

53. Morimoto, "Language and Heritage Maintenance," 130–32.

54. *Rafu Shimpo,* 20 June 1937; Ichioka, "Study in Dualism," 67.

55. The school newspaper of Roosevelt High School, the *Rough Rider,* 27 Sept. 1934, carried news about alumna Alice Sumida. I thank Mr. Joseph Zanki, a longtime faculty member of Roosevelt, for providing me access to bound copies of the *Rough Rider.*

56. "The Second Generation Japanese," SRR, box 33, folder 354.

57. During the mid-1930s, the *Nichibei Shimbun* printed stories about Sannomiya's activities and her speaking tours to the United States.

58. Eriko Yamamoto, "Struggle of a Frontier Nisei: A History of Japanese-Americans through Mrs. Kikuchi's Words" (master's thesis, Claremont Graduate School, 1982), chap. 4; see also idem, "Miya Sannomiya Kikuchi: A Pioneer Nisei Woman's Life and Identity," *Amerasia Journal* 23 (Winter 1997–98): 73–102.

59. Sannomiya letter to Dr. Robert A. Wilson, 13 Jan. 1968, in Japanese American Research Project (JARP), Special Collections, University Research Library, University of California at Los Angeles, no. 2010, box 160, folder 13.

60. *Nichibei Shimbun,* 22–23 Apr. 1930.

61. Alice Shikamura, "The Vocational Intentions of the Second-Generation Jap-

anese Students in Three California Universities" (master's thesis, Stanford University, 1948), 3 (quote), 23.

62. *Rafu Shimpo*, 20 June 1937; *Nichibei Shimbun*, 28 June 1937. Although technically born in Japan, Kawai came to the United States as a young child and, for all intents and purposes, experienced life as a Nisei growing up in Los Angeles. See *Nichibei Shimbun*, 16 Feb. 1932; *Shin Sekai*, 16 Feb. 1932. The Survey of Race Relations also contains biographical information about Kawai.

Chapter 2: Keeping the Faith

1. The vast majority of Buddhists belonged to the Pure Land sect; most Christians were Protestants. There were, of course, others—including Roman Catholics, adherents of other branches of Buddhism, and practitioners of other religions—but this chapter will focus on Pure Land Buddhism and Protestant Christianity. For general background, see Ichioka, *Issei*; Tetsuden Kashima, *Buddhism in America* (Westport, Conn.: Greenwood Press, 1977); Ryo Munekata, ed., *Buddhist Churches of America: 75 Year History, 1899–1974* (Chicago: Nobart, 1974); Shigeo Kanda, "Recovering Cultural Symbols: A Case for Buddhism in the Japanese American Communities," *Journal of the American Academy of Religion* 44 (Dec. 1978): 445–75; Hayashi, "*For the Sake of Our Japanese Brethren*"; Sumio Koga, ed., *A Centennial Legacy: History of the Japanese Christian Missions in North America, 1877–1977* (Chicago: Nobart, 1977); Ryo Yoshida, "A Socio-historical Study of Racial/Ethnic Identity in the Inculturated Religious Expression of Japanese Christianity in San Francisco, 1877–1924" (Ph.D. diss., Graduate Theological Union, Berkeley, Calif., 1989).

2. Takako Fuchigami, "Both Buddhism and Christianity Are Vitally Important to the Second Generation," *Bhratri* 2 (July 1934): 17–18. I thank Dr. Ryo Munekata of Los Angeles, as well as the staff of the Institute of Buddhist Studies, in Berkeley, for allowing me access to issues of this publication.

3. The literature includes: Timothy L. Smith, "Religion and Ethnicity in America," *American Historical Review* 83 (Dec. 1978): 1155–75; Martin Marty, "Ethnicity: The Skeleton of Religion in America," *Church History* 41 (Mar. 1972): 5–21; Jay P. Dolan, "The Immigrants and Their Gods: A New Perspective of American Religious History," *Church History* 57 (Mar. 1988): 61–72; Catherine Albanese, *America: Religions and Religion* (Belmont, Calif.: Wadsworth, 1981); Peter Williams, *America's Religions* (1990; rpt., Urbana: University of Illinois Press, 1998).

4. For a sense of the breadth of American religion, see Charles H. Lippy and Peter W. Williams, *Encyclopedia of American Religious Experiences*, 3 vols. (New York: Scribner's, 1988); Gordon Melton, *The Encyclopedia of American Religion*, 3d ed. (Detroit: Gale Research, 1989).

5. Will Herberg, *Protestant-Catholic-Jew* (Garden City, N.Y.: Doubleday, 1955). I thank Roger Daniels for pointing out the fact that the notion of the triple melt-

ing pot dates back to Ruby Jo Reeves Kennedy's work on intermarriage in New Haven, Conn. See "Single or Triple Melting-Pot? Intermarriage Trends in New Haven, 1870–1940," *American Journal of Sociology* 49 (Jan. 1944): 331–39.

6. Patricia Nelson Limerick, Clyde A. Milner II, and Charles E. Rankin, eds., *Trails: Toward a New Western History* (Lawrence: University Press of Kansas, 1991); Clyde A. Milner II, ed., *A New Significance: Re-envisioning the History of the American West* (New York: Oxford University Press, 1996), especially Gail Nomura's essay ("Significant Lives: Asia and Asian Americans in the U.S. West," 135–57).

7. In recent years, a number of essays have taken up the topic of religion in the American West, providing helpful overviews of the existing literature; yet, most authors have recognized the need for more research in this area. See Laurie Maf-fly-Kipp, "Eastward Ho! American Religion from the Perspective of the Pacific Rim," in *Retelling U.S. Religious History,* ed. Thomas A. Tweed (Berkeley: University of California Press, 1997), 127–48; Ferenc M. Szasz and Margaret Connell Szasz, "Religion and Spirituality," in *The Oxford History of the American West,* ed. Clyde A. Milner II, Carol O'Connor, and Martha Sandweiss (New York: Oxford University Press, 1994), 356–91; D. Michael Quinn, "Religion in the American West," in *Under an Open Sky,* ed. William Cronon, George Miles, and Jay Gitlin (New York: W. W. Norton, 1992), 145–66; Carl Guarneri and David Alvarez, eds., *Religion and Society in the American West* (Lanham, Md.: University Press of America, 1987).

8. Raymond Brady Williams, *Religions of Immigrants from India and Pakistan* (Cambridge: Cambridge University Press, 1988), 3, 11–13, 24, 31.

9. Kimura, *Issei;* Ichioka, *Issei.*

10. The discussion will be limited to Jodo Shinshu Buddhism; within this school, the subdivisions of the Hompa or West Hongwanji and the East Hongwanji have been most prominent among Japanese Americans. See Nishi Utsuki, *The Shin Sect: A School of Mahayana Buddhism* (Kyoto, Japan: Publication Bureau of Buddhist Books, 1937). For studies of Buddhism in Hawaii, see Louise H. Hunter, *Buddhism in Hawaii: Its Impact on a Yankee Community* (Honolulu: University of Hawaii Press, 1971); Tamura, *Americanization, Acculturation, and Ethnic Identity,* 203–10. Also of interest: Mark R. Mullins, "The Organizational Dilemmas of Ethnic Churches: A Case Study of Japanese Buddhism in Canada," *Sociological Analysis* 49 (1988): 217–33.

11. For background on Shin Buddhism in America, see Munekata, *Buddhist Churches of America;* Kashima, *Buddhism in America;* Kanda, "Recovering Cultural Symbols"; William C. Rust, "The Shin Sect of Buddhism in America: Its Antecedents, Beliefs, and Present Condition" (Ph.D. diss., University of Southern California, 1951); Minimai Ratanamani, "History of Shin Buddhism in the United States" (master's thesis, College of the Pacific, 1960); Donald Tuck, *Buddhist Churches of America* (Lewiston, N.Y.: Edwin Mellen Press, 1987). For inclusive studies of Buddhism in the United States, see Emma McCloy Layman, *Buddhism*

in America (Chicago: Nelson-Hall, 1976); Charles Prebish, *American Buddhism* (North Scituate, Mass.: Duxbury Press, 1979).

12. Munekata, *Buddhist Churches of America*, 44–46.

13. Kashima, *Buddhism in America*, 12–14.

14. Munekata, *Buddhist Churches of America*, 45–47.

15. U.S. Department of the Interior, War Relocation Authority, Community Analysis Section, Report No. 9, "Buddhism in the United States," 15 May 1944, Washington, D.C., 3. A small number of European Americans adopted Buddhism. See Thomas A. Tweed, *The American Encounter with Buddhism, 1844–1912* (Bloomington: Indiana University Press, 1992).

16. Strong, *Japanese in California*, 168–70. Strong's survey projected that 51.5 percent of the second generation were Christians, while 39 percent were Buddhist. Also, 3.5 percent (Issei) and 7.5 percent (Nisei) indicated no affiliation, while a total of 13.2 percent (7.6 percent Issei; 16.1 percent Nisei) did not answer the question on religious affiliation. Strong's figures applied to those fourteen years of age and older. U.S. Department of the Interior, *Evacuated People*, 79. The WRA study included all persons evacuated and so included Japanese Americans outside of California. The remaining 16.3 percent from the WRA survey consisted of no response and other religions like Tenri-Kyo (0.04 percent). There is also some question as to the accuracy of reporting for the WRA survey; some internees felt that Christian affiliation might be a safer claim given the wartime hysteria against them, Japan, and all things Japanese. Strong's study and a later, separate study by sociologist Dorothy Thomas (based on selected internment camps) analyzed religious affiliation along other axes beside nativity, including the Hawaiian population, the Kibei population, rural/urban, and male/female. See Thomas et al., *Salvage*, 65–71.

17. The North American Buddhist Mission was reorganized as the Buddhist Churches of America in 1944 in a formal cutting of ties with Japan. See Kashima, *Buddhism in America*, 59–61.

18. Kosei Ogura, "A Sociological Study of the Buddhist Churches in North America with a Case Study of Gardena, California, Congregation" (master's thesis, University of Southern California, 1932), 34–36, 85.

19. Ibid., 34–36, 85.

20. Isao Horinouchi, "Americanized Buddhism: A Sociological Analysis of a Protestantized Japanese Religion" (Ph.D. diss., University of California at Davis, 1973), 119; Robert F. Spencer, "Japanese Buddhism in the United States, 1940–46" (Ph.D. diss., University of California at Berkeley, 1946), 77–82.

21. Kashima, *Buddhism in America*, 23, 137–39. Ryo Munekata, tape-recorded interview by the author, Los Angeles, Calif., 21 July 1995.

22. Horinouchi, "Americanized Buddhism," 115–16, 155, 187–88. He states that cost factors, as much as anything else, also entered decisions about architectural style. See also Kashima, *Buddhism in America*, 41; Spencer, "Japanese Buddhism," 57.

23. Kashima, *Buddhism in America,* 129. Horinouchi coined the term "Protestantization" in his study of Buddhism.

24. Frank E. Reynolds and Charles Hallisey, "Buddhist Religion, Culture, and Civilization," in *Buddhism and Asian History,* ed. Joseph M. Kitagawa and Mark H. Cummings (New York: Macmillan, 1987), 3–28; Tamaru Noriyoshi, "Buddhism in Japan," in Kitagawa and Cummings, *Buddhism and Asian History,* 159–74; Araki Michio, "The Schools of Japanese Buddhism," in Kitagawa and Cummings, *Buddhism and Asian History,* 267–75.

25. Hajime Nakamura, "The Basic Teachings of Buddhism," in *Buddhism in the Modern World,* ed. Heinrich Dumoulin (New York: Macmillan, 1976), 3.

26. Noriyoshi, "Buddhism in Japan," 167–68; Michio, "Schools of Japanese Buddhism," 272–73; Utsuki, *Shin Sect,* 1–15; Munekata, *Buddhist Churches of America,* 28–35; Tuck, *Buddhist Churches of America,* 202.

27. "Instructions to the Ministers of the Mission," North American Buddhist Mission, 1927 Annual Conference Minutes, rpt. in Rust, "Shin Sect," 344–47.

28. Ichioka, *Issei,* chap. 7.

29. Fred Nitta, "The YBA Movement in America," 1966, personal archives of Dr. Ryo Munekata, Los Angeles, Calif.

30. Ibid., 3–5.

31. "History and Constitution of the North American Federation of the YWBA Leagues," July 1928, Institute of Buddhist Studies (IBS) Archives, Berkeley, Calif. Many thanks to Kimi Hisatsune and Margaret Yam at the IBS for unearthing materials for me.

32. Valerie J. Matsumoto's work on the farming community of Cortez touches on the role of religious groups as spaces for socialization. See *Farming the Home Place,* 53–54, 77–86. Although conferences during the early years were technically single sex, it was quite common for either the YMBA or the YWBA to send members to the other's conferences.

33. *Bhratri* 2 (July 1932). (This journal published only occasionally, and volume numbers, pagination, and other citation information varies from issue to issue.) See also Nitta, "YBA Movement," 3, 19–21.

34. *Bhratri* 2 (July 1932); Nitta, "YBA Movement," 11–12.

35. Nitta, "YBA Movement," 2.

36. Gary Y. Okihiro notes that, in Hawaii, Bussei organizations fostered leadership skills that translated into labor organizing. See *Cane Fires: The Anti-Japanese Movement in Hawaii, 1865–1945* (Philadelphia: Temple University Press, 1991), 68.

37. *Bhratri* 2 (July 1934): 81; *The Campanile Review* 1 (Dec. 1932): 5. For more on the Pacific Era, see Ichioka, "*Kengakudan,*" 30–43.

38. *Bhratri* 2 (July 1934): 81; *The Campanile Review* 1 (Dec. 1932): 5; Nitta, "YBA Movement," 4. For more on Nisei as cultural bridges, see Takahashi, *Nisei/Sansei;* Ichioka, "Study in Dualism," 49–81.

39. *Bhratri* 2 (July 1934): 22.

40. *Berkeley Bussei* (Fall 1939).

41. *Sangha* (Feb. 1941), in IBS Archives, Berkeley, Calif.

42. *Berkeley Bussei* (Spring 1941); ibid. (Fall 1941).

43. *Sangha* (Feb. 1941).

44. Tamura, *Americanization, Acculturation, and Ethnic Identity,* 198. This perspective runs throughout the monograph.

45. On Americanization, see Hartmann, *Movement to Americanize.* For a California perspective, see Herman, "Neighbors on Golden Mountain."

46. *Bhratri* 2 (July 1932): 21–22.

47. Ibid.: 7–10.

48. *Berkeley Bussei* (Spring 1941).

49. Ibid.

50. *Pacific Citizen,* June 1941.

51. Ichioka, *Issei,* 16–28

52. William Bryant, ed., *The Church's One Hundred Years in the Japanese American Community* (San Francisco: Christ United Presbyterian Church, 1988), ii–23; Koga, *Centennial Legacy,* 46–47, 62–97, 108–252; *Official Journal* (Pacific Japanese Mission of the Methodist Episcopal Church), 1924; *Official Journal* (Pacific Japanese Provisional Annual Conference Methodist Episcopal Church), 1940. The northern and southern branches of the Methodist Episcopal Church in the United States, which had split over the issue of slavery, reunited in 1939. See Donald Fujiyoshi, "A Study of the Educational Program of the Church School of the Japanese Christian Church and Institute of Los Angeles" (master's thesis, University of Southern California, 1942), 20.

53. Koga, *Centennial Legacy,* 36.

54. Hirochika Nakamaki, "The History of the Japanese Christian Churches and the Consciousness of Japanese Christians in Sacramento, California," in *Japanese Religions in California,* ed. Keiichi Yanagawa (Tokyo: Department of Religious Studies, University of Tokyo, 1983), 258–65.

55. Yoshida, "Socio-historical Study," 5–9, 350–51. Brian Hayashi's monograph *"Our Japanese Brethren"* deals centrally with the issues of nationalism and assimilation.

56. Yoshida, "Socio-historical Study," 60–61, 152.

57. Ibid., 60–61; Michael J. Kimura Angevine and Ryo Yoshida, "Contexts for a History of Asian American Presbyterian Churches: A Case Study of the Early History of Japanese American Presbyterian Churches," ms., Dec. 1989, 23–24, 27. I thank the Reverend Angevine for giving me a copy of his paper.

58. Koga, *Centennial Legacy,* 37, 112–15.

59. Ibid., 37, 188–89.

60. Angevine and Yoshida, "Contexts for a History," 20.

61. Bryant, *Church's One Hundred Years,* 57–59; *Nichibei Shimbun,* 13–16 May 1933; ibid., 24 June 1934.

62. The church was founded in June 1896 under the name of the Japanese Meth-

odist Episcopal Mission of Los Angeles. In July 1926, the church took on the name Centenary Methodist Episcopal Church in honor of the centennial celebration of the denomination. See *Program of Progress Directory* (Los Angeles: Centenary Methodist Church, 1962), vi, in JARP, box 361. The church's newsletters in the 1930s sometimes refered to the church as the Los Angeles Japanese Methodist Episcopal Church.

63. Koga, *Centennial Legacy,* 194–95; scattered issues of the *Japanese Methodist Episcopal Church Weekly News* in JARP, boxes 292–93.

64. *Japanese Methodist Episcopal Church Weekly News,* 13 Apr. 1938.

65. Lester and Seda Suzuki, tape-recorded interview by the author, Berkeley, Calif., 15 May 1993.

66. Membership totals for 1923–24 to 1930–31 can be found in *Japanese Student Bulletin,* 10 (Oct. 1931): 9. The information given includes Nisei members of the JSCA but does not differentiate between them. (The numbering of the *Bulletin* issues is only approximately sequential; the month and year are more helpful for gaining a sense of the chronology.) I thank Timothy Tseng for sending me a nearly complete run of the *JSB,* which can be found in the Union Theological Seminary Archives, New York City.

67. *Directory of the Japanese Students in North America, 1925–26* (New York: Japanese Students' Christian Association in North America, 1925–26), 5, 8–13.

68. The first issues of the *JSB* actually predate the organization, and it appears that the *Bulletin* originated as part of the Friendly Relations Committee.

69. *JSB* 10 (Feb. 1932): 3; *JSB* 8 (Oct. 1930): 1–2. The total expenditures for the 1924–25 academic year were $3,000. The JSCA broke even for the year with income generated from the following: membership dues and financial drive, $2,000; subsidy from the Friendly Relations Committee, $1,000. By 1939–40, the operating budget was about $4,000 per year, and the JSCA managed to stay afloat financially, although the Friendly Relations Committee subsidy had dropped to about $500 per year. See *JSB* 4 (Oct. 1924): 2; *JSB* 17 (May 1940): 3. The JSCA, in sharing office space with the Friendly Relations Committee and the International YMCA, apparently benefited from clerical support and other perquisites. See *JSB* 3 (Oct. 1923): 2.

70. *JSB* 3 (Dec. 1926): 2; *JSB* 16 (Nov. 1938): 1; Hideo Hashimoto, "From University to Pastorate," ms., n.d. I thank Professor Hashimoto of Lewis and Clark College for making his manuscript available to me.

71. *JSB* 3 (Dec. 1926): 2; *JSB* 4 (Dec. 1927): 1. Despite casting a wide net in search of the *JSCA Pacific Coast Echoes,* I have not been able to locate it.

72. Akagi is mentioned in John J. Stephan's "Hijacked by Utopia: American Nikkei in Manchuria," *Amerasia Journal* 23 (Winter 1997–98): 10.

73. *JSB* 6 (Oct. 1929): 1; *JSB* 13 (May–June 1934): 7; *JSB* 5 (Feb. 1929): 3; *JSB* 4 (Jan. 1928): 1. Akagi later went to Manchuria as counselor to the South Manchuria Railway Company.

74. Roy Akagi, *The Second Generation Problem: Some Suggestions toward Its*

Solution (New York: Japanese Students' Christian Association in North America, 1926), 7–9.

75. Ibid., 7, 12.

76. Ibid., 12–13.

77. Ibid., 14–17.

78. Ibid., 18–33. I have only given a sampling of this section of the pamphlet.

79. Tadashi Fujita, "Biography of Rev. Suzunosuke Kato," ms., n.d. I thank Tadashi Fujita of Berkeley, Calif., for access to his personal papers.

80. Ibid.; Lester Suzuki, "The Significance of the NCYPCC," n.d., 2–5. I thank the Reverend Suzuki for copies of his work on Japanese American Christianity.

81. Suzuki, "Significance"; *Nichibei Shimbun*, 3 Nov. 1927; ibid., 16 Feb. 1930; ibid., 28 June 1930; ibid., 3 Feb. 1932; ibid., 14 Mar. 1932; ibid., 28 Sept. 1934. There is some discrepancy in the newspaper reports concerning the date of Morishita's marriage to the Reverend N. Oda, but it appears that that the wedding took place on 4 June 1932.

82. Michael Yoshii, "The Young People's Christian Conference: The Formation and Development of a Nisei Christian Youth Movement," ms., May 1985. I thank the Reverend Yoshii for giving me a copy of his paper.

83. "Grow in Living Faith," Northern California Young People's Christian Conference, 1938, Pine United Methodist Church Archives, San Francisco, Calif. I thank the Reverend Gary Barbaree of Pine United for loaning me archival materials.

84. Northern California Young People's Christian Conference program, 1939, personal papers of Tadashi Fujita, Berkeley, Calif.

85. Yoshii, "Young's Peoples Christian Conference," 19. Yoshii incorporates theologian Paul Tillich's concept of "vocational consciousness."

Chapter 3: Making the Headlines

1. Togo Tanaka, tape-recorded interview by the author, Los Angeles, Calif., 18 May 1992.

2. The theme of racial subordination is taken from Takahashi, *Nisei/Sansei,* chap. 3. Takahashi's work has been especially helpful in its discussion of racial responsibility.

3. Sally M. Miller, ed., *The Ethnic Press in the United States: A Historical Analysis and Handbook* (Westport, Conn.: Greenwood Press, 1987), xii–xvii; also Harry H. L. Kitano's chapter on Japanese Americans.

4. "The Vernacular Newspapers," Japanese [American] Evacuation and Resettlement Study (JERS), Bancroft Library, University of California at Berkeley, call no. 67/14c, folder **O10.16. The asterisks indicate that the identity of the author must remain confidential. For a detailed guide to the JERS Collection, see Barnhart, *Japanese American Evacuation.* For further reading on the ethnic press, see Robert E. Park, *The Immigrant Press and Its Control* (New York: Harper and Bros., 1922); Jean P. Grazier and Cecile Gaziano, "Robert Ezra Park's Theory of News,

Public Opinion, and Social Control," *Journalism Monographs* n.v. (Nov. 1979): 1–47; Louis Wirth, "Consensus and Mass Communication," *American Sociological Review* 13 (1948): 1–15; Morris Janowitz, *The Community Press in an Urban Setting*, 2d ed. (Chicago: University of Chicago Press, 1967); Warren Susman, "Communication and Culture: Keynote Essay," in *Mass Media between the Wars*, ed. Catherine L. Covert and John D. Stevens (Syracuse, N.Y.: Syracuse University Press, 1984), xi–xxii; William H. Taft, *Newspapers as Tools for Historians* (Columbia, Mo.: Lucas Bros., 1970).

5. Matsumoto, "Desperately Seeking 'Deirdre,'" 19–32. Matsumoto stresses the need to pay attention to the prewar years.

6. The more literal translation of "*Doho*" would be brethren or brotherhood, but the phrase "For equality, peace, and democracy" was used by the paper.

7. Ichioka, "Study in Dualism," 49–81.

8. This chapter is based on the detailed reading of these five newspapers throughout the prewar period, though many other newspapers could have been included as well. See also Dorothy A. Stroup, "The Role of the Japanese-American Press in Its Community" (master's thesis, University of California at Berkeley, 1960). Stroup's study compares the *Nichibei Shimbun* and the *Shin Sekai*. Chapter 2 includes a history of Japanese American newspapers.

9. *Nichibei Shimbun*, 7 July 1925.

10. Ibid., 1 Jan. 1992. Yuji Ichioka traces the history of the first Japan study tours (*kengakudan*) sponsored by the paper. Occasional English translations of Japanese-language editorials in the early 1920s preceded the regular English-language sections.

11. *Rafu Shimpo*, 21 Feb. 1926. For a detailed account, see Kaori Hayashi, "History of the *Rafu Shimpo*: Evolution of a Japanese American Newspaper, 1903–1942" (master's thesis, California State University at Northridge, 1990).

12. Togo Tanaka recalled that when he was interviewed by Komai for the position of English editor, Komai wanted to make sure that Tanaka clearly saw the United States—not Japan—as his home. Tanaka interview, 18 May 1992.

13. *Shin Sekai*, 18 Sept. 1929. In June 1935, the *Shin Sekai* merged with the *Hokubei Asahi* to become the *Shin Sekai Asahi* (New World-Sun Daily).

14. *Doho*, 10 June 1938. Ronald C. Larson's "*Doho*: The Japanese American 'Communist' Press, 1937–1942" provides further background on the newspaper. I thank Arthur Hansen of California State University at Fullerton for sending me a copy of Larson's paper.

15. Ichioka, "Study in Dualism." Sakamoto's strong ties with the national Japanese American Citizens League and its activities connected him with other influential Nisei throughout the West Coast.

16. *Nichibei Shimbun*, 1 Jan. 1992.

17. Stroup, "Japanese-American Press," 30–31. The *Nichibei Shimbun* strike of July 1931 involved disputes regarding personnel and unpaid wages among the Japanese-language staff. The strike debilitated the *Nichibei* from late July until mid-

October. Financial burdens, exacerbated by the strike, resulted in the Los Angeles branch being auctioned in December 1931. The English-language staff remained on the sidelines. For background on the strike, see the *Shin Sekai* during this time period. The *Shin Sekai*, the chief competitor of the *Nichibei*, supported the strikers who opposed Kyutaro Abiko.

18. These figures are taken from the *Newspaper Annual and Directory* (Philadelphia: N. W. Ayer and Son) for the years 1925, 1929, 1930, 1932, 1934, 1936, 1938, 1940–45. Unless otherwise noted, future circulation figures are derived from Ayer directories during these years. According to the 1925 *Newspaper Annual*, "circulation" is defined as "the average number of complete copies of all regular issues for a given period, exclusive of left over, unsold, return, file, sample, exchange and advertiser's copies" (6). No figures appeared for the *Doho*.

19. Ichioka, "Study in Dualism," 75. I could not find circulation figures for the *Doho*, though it is safe to assume that the figures were small given the paper's connection to the Communist Party.

20. JERS, **O10.16.

21. Tanaka stated that the Nisei retained their independence as tensions between staffs grew over events such as the Sino-Japanese War. See JERS **O10.16. In regard to the war and news from Japan, however, Tanaka and other Nisei journalists relied on dispatches from such Japanese outlets as the Domei News Service, an unofficial arm of the Japanese government.

22. This episode is taken from Togo Tanaka's journal, part of the JERS Collection, A17.06. Isami Arifuku Waugh's "Hidden Crime and Deviance in the Japanese-American Community, 1920–1946" (D.Crim. diss., University of California at Berkeley, 1978) documents an aspect of Japanese American history that is not easily recovered.

23. *Japanese American Courier*, 1 Jan. 1934.

24. Ibid., 24 Mar. 1928; Ichioka, "Study in Dualism," 53.

25. *Nichibei Shimbun*, 13 May 1930.

26. "Saburo Kido," in Kim, *Dictionary of Asian American History*, 348–49. Kido's column in the *Shin Sekai* began in November 1936. The editorial note announcing his column also stated that Kido was a Republican.

27. *Shin Sekai*, 23 Dec. 1936. For an insightful and concise overview of Asian Americans and labor, see Glenn Omatsu, "Asian Pacific American Workers and the Expansion of Democracy," *Amerasia Journal* 18 (1992): v–xix.

28. *Shin Sekai*, 14 June 1938.

29. *Doho*, 1 Sept. 1938. For details about labor issues among the Nisei, see Modell, *Economics and Politics*, chap. 6.

30. *Rafu Shimpo*, 15 Apr. 1937.

31. Daniels, *Politics of Prejudice*, 91–99, 105. For a sample of McClatchy's views, see *Four Anti-Japanese Pamphlets* (New York: Arno Press, 1978).

32. *Rafu Shimpo*, 4 May 1937; ibid., 6 May 1937. McClatchy got his information from a translation of an article from a Japanese newspaper, *Osaka Mainichi*,

19 Mar. 1937, that reported that Nisei attraction to things Japanese had resulted in more of them coming to Japan for educational purposes. McClatchy must have fabricated the number of Nisei (50,000); the article, according to the *Rafu* summary, had simply stated "hundreds" of Nisei.

33. *Nichibei Shimbun*, 19 Apr. 1937.

34. *Rafu Shimpo*, 16 May 1938.

35. In a further twist of irony, McClatchy and fellow publisher William Randolph Hearst had a long history of using their newspaper chains to fuel stereotypical and sensational coverage of Japanese Americans.

36. A Nisei magazine called *Current Life*, published by James Omura in San Francisco's Bay Area, did offer a more critical view of race relations as they affected Americans of Japanese ancestry but only began publishing toward the end of 1940 and shut down soon after the attack on Pearl Harbor. Omura will be discussed in chapter 5.

37. The press made its case for "racial responsibility" during an era marked by clearer racial divisions than those in place today. What I have characterized as "racial responsibility" formed the dominant—though by no means exclusive—perspective in the papers. Union organizer Dyke Miyagawa of Seattle expressed more radical views on race prejudice that appeared in the newspapers. See *Nichibei Shimbun*, 1 Jan. 1939.

38. Sucheng Chan, *Asian Americans: An Interpretive History* (Boston: Twayne, 1991), 59–61. See also Megumi Dick Osumi, "Asians and California's Anti-Miscegenation Laws," in *Asian and Pacific American Experiences: Women's Perspectives*, ed. Nobuya Tsuchida (Minneapolis: Asian/Pacific American Learning Resource Center and General College, University of Minnesota, 1982), 1–38.

39. Paul Spickard, *Mixed Blood: Intermarriage and Ethnic Identity in Twentieth-Century America* (Madison: University of Wisconsin Press, 1989), 50–52.

40. For helpful background on marriage in the context of kinship studies in anthropology, see Yanagisako, *Transforming the Past*, chap. 3.

41. The newspapers referred only to heterosexual relationships.

42. *Nichibei Shimbun*, 24 June 1930.

43. Louise Suski of the *Rafu Shimpo* enjoyed a long tenure as editor or coeditor of the English-language section from 1926 to 1942, but she wrote very little throughout her career. For some indication of her views on gender roles, see the 11 Nov. 1940 issue. See also her biography of the Suski family in JERS, T1.96. Evelyn Kirimura, on staff with the *Shin Sekai Asahi*, featured profiles of Nisei women in June and July 1938. Dr. Megumi Shinoda also authored an occasional medical column in the *Rafu Shimpo* (1939–41) that sometimes touched on women's issues/concerns (e.g., 21 Apr. 1940).

44. Anthropologist Micaela di Leonardo's study of Italian Americans in California has shown that women often held the responsibility for the "work of kinship." This "work" entailed a wide range of activities and decision making intended to maintain kinship networks. Di Leonardo's work does not speak directly to Nisei

women, but I found her research helpful in thinking about the broader contexts in which women have often carried on the work of kinship. See *The Varieties of Ethnic Experience: Kinship, Class, and Gender among California Italian-Americans* (Ithaca, N.Y.: Cornell University Press, 1984), chap. 6.

45. *Nichibei Shimbun,* 17 Feb. 1936; Spickard, *Mixed Blood,* 101. Spickard notes that Nisei did marry Issei in America. In Los Angeles during 1937–38, 19 percent of the Nisei (men and women) who married took immigrant spouses. This rate fell to 7 percent by 1941–42, largely because there were relatively few unmarried Issei. Nisei also had many other Nisei from which to choose a partner.

46. *Shin Sekai,* 27 Mar. 1930. The papers ran items suggesting that Nisei women outnumbered Nisei men and that this was one of the reasons for unmarried Nisei women. Census figures from 1940 show, however, the ratio of men to women for the second generation to be quite even, with men slightly more numerous than women. See U.S. Department of War, *Final Report: Japanese Evacuation from the West Coast, 1942* (Washington, D.C.: Government Printing Office, 1943), 403.

47. The debate ended on 12 Apr. 1930, when the editor stated that enough time had been spent on the issue despite continuing reader response.

48. *Shin Sekai,* 29 Mar. 1930. There is no explanation why Spanish pseudonyms are used, but it is interesting that they are not translated for the readers. This is one indicator of the multicultural context of the American West.

49. Ibid., 2 Apr. 1930.

50. *Shin Sekai Asahi,* 1 Jan. 1940.

51. Matsumoto, "Desperately Seeking 'Deirdre,' " 22–26. Matsumoto provides helpful background on Oyama and other Nisei women writers during the prewar period. From her article, it seems that literary pieces offered Nisei women greater access to the press that was not open to them in the male-dominated editorial and columnist positions. Unfortunately, literary sections or inserts appeared (in the papers I read) only on an occasional basis (e.g., New Year's special editions and sometimes on an intermittent weekly basis).

52. *Nichibei Shimbun,* 17 May 1936.

53. Spickard, *Mixed Blood,* 60–61. Some immigrant parents may have been more open to interracial relationships, but it seems relatively safe to suggest that most Issei wanted their children to marry people of Japanese descent.

54. Ibid., 47–52. Issei in Los Angeles (1924–33) outmarried extremely rarely— three out of every one hundred men and 1.7 percent of women. The European study looked at New York City for the years 1908–12. Spickard notes that the big jump in outmarriage by Sansei may be an indicator that the Nisei levels were artificially low. I found Spickard's discussion of terminology (e.g., "intermarriage" and "miscegenation") helpful; see especially his introduction. For further reading, see Russell Endo and Dale Hirokawa, "Japanese American Intermarriage," *Free Inquiry in Creative Sociology* 11 (Nov. 1983): 159–66; Akemi Kikumura and Harry Kitano, "Interracial Marriage: A Picture of Japanese Americans," *Journal of Social Issues* 29 (1973): 67–82; Larry Shinagawa and Gin Yong Pang, "Marriage Pat-

terns of Asian Americans in California, 1980," in *Income and Status Differences between White and Minority Americans*, ed. Sucheng Chan (Lewiston, N.Y.: Edward Mellen Press, 1990), 225–82; John N. Tinker, "Intermarriage and Assimilation in a Plural Society: Japanese Americans in the United States," *Marriage and Family Review* 5 (1982): 61–74.

55. *Shin Sekai Asahi*, 2 Feb. 1938; Eiichiro Azuma, "Walnut Grove: Japanese Farm Community in the Sacramento River Delta, 1892–1942" (master's thesis, University of California at Los Angeles, 1992), 176–79. Because of labor needs, farmers usually did not heed warnings to not hire laborers for more than two consecutive years.

56. Spickard, *Mixed Blood*, 103–6. Spickard discusses a hierarchy of choice among Japanese Americans and states that Filipinos fell among the "genuinely despised peoples" that also included: Okinawans, Burakumin, Mexicans, Puerto Ricans, and African Americans.

57. *Shin Sekai*, 25 Jan. 1930. In the late 1930s, the male-female ratio for Filipino Americans was twenty-one to one. See Spickard, *Mixed Blood*, 345.

58. *Shin Sekai*, 12 Jan. 1934.

59. The story did not say whether she survived.

60. *Rafu Shimpo*, 6 Jan. 1935.

61. Ibid., 15 Jan. 1938. This citation applies to the remaining paragraph of the Kurihara/Salsan story.

62. For background, see Yuji Ichioka, "Japanese Immigrant Nationalism: The Issei and the Sino-Japanese War, 1937–41," *California History* 69.3 (1990): 260–75.

63. For a sense of the coverage in *Doho*, see the following issues: 10 June 1938, 1 Aug. 1938, 15 Aug. 1939, 1 Mar. 1941. The convergence of left-wing and right-wing factions within the Japanese American community as the result of the attack on Pearl Harbor and America's entry into the war will be discussed in chapter 4.

64. Japanese Americans were indeed "victims" to the extent that they suffered on account of their ancestry for events out of their control. The issue here, however, is on how the press positioned the Nikkei as victims and why such a strategy might have been employed.

65. One can speak of "racial" issues sparked by the Sino-Japanese War because, I would argue, the Chinese and Japanese Americans viewed each other not simply as other Asians but as different races. Whether other Americans saw the two groups in this way is another matter.

66. The key difference is that the Nisei sought to portray themselves (not Japan) as victims and thereby distanced themselves from Japan. I assume that Chinese Americans focused more on China as victim rather than on themselves, since they benefited, by extension, from widespread American support of China.

67. *Shin Sekai Asahi*, 1 Jan. 1938. The American Institute of Public Opinion found that, in November 1937, 59 percent of Americans sided with China, 40 percent declared themselves neutral, and only 1 percent favored Japan (*Nichibei Shimbun*, 15 Nov. 1937).

68. *Nichibei Shimbun,* 1 Oct. 1937.

69. Ibid., 3 Oct. 1937.

70. Ibid., 5 Oct. 1937.

71. Ibid., 10 Dec. 1937.

72. Ibid., 14 Mar. 1938, 10 Dec. 1937.

73. Ibid., 14 Aug. 1937; *Rafu Shimpo,* 27 Nov. 1938.

74. *Rafu Shimpo,* 16 Mar. 1941, 9 Nov. 1941.

75. Ibid., 26 May 1940.

76. For a helpful study on the development of Nisei patriotism, see Hiroshi Yoneyama, "The Forging of Japanese American Patriotism, 1931–41" (master's thesis, University of Tsukuba [Japan], 1984).

77. JERS, **O10.16.

Chapter 4: The Firestorm of War and Incarceration

1. Yoshiko Uchida, *Desert Exile: The Uprooting of a Japanese American Family* (Seattle: University of Washington Press, 1982), 46. Uchida went on to a distinguished career as a writer of novels and nonfiction for young people and incorporated Japanese American history into some of her works.

2. Ibid., 47–48.

3. For background on the Asian American movement, see Gary Y. Okihiro, Shirley Hune, Arthur A. Hansen, and John M. Liu, eds., *Reflections on Shattered Windows: Promises and Prospects for Asian American Studies* (Pullman: Washington State University Press, 1988); William Wei, *The Asian American Movement* (Philadelphia: Temple University Press, 1993). On redress and reparations, see *Personal Justice Denied: Report of the Commission on Wartime Relocation and Internment of Civilians* (Washington, D.C.: Civil Liberties Public Education Fund; Seattle: University of Washington Press, 1997); Roger Daniels, Sandra C. Taylor, and Harry H. L. Kitano, eds., *Japanese Americans: From Relocation to Redress* (Seattle: University of Washington Press, 1991); Leslie T. Hatamiya, *Righting a Wrong: Japanese Americans and the Passage of the Civil Liberties Act of 1988* (Stanford, Calif.: Stanford University Press, 1993); William Hohri, *Repairing America* (Pullman: Washington State University Press, 1988); Glen Ikuo Kitayama, "Japanese Americans and the Movement for Redress: A Case Study of Grassroots Activism in the Los Angeles Chapter of the National Coalition for Redress/Reparations" (master's thesis, University of California at Los Angeles, 1993); Alice Yang Murray, " 'Silence No More': The Japanese American Redress Movement, 1942–1992" (Ph.D. diss., Stanford University, 1994); Takezawa, *Breaking the Silence.*

4. On the role of the camps and historical memory, see Takezawa, *Breaking the Silence;* Murray, " 'Silence No More.' " See also David Yoo, "Captivating Memories: Museology, Concentration Camps, and Japanese American History," *American Quarterly* 48.4 (Dec. 1996): 680–99.

5. A vast secondary literature continues to grow. Kim's *Asian American Studies*

is a good starting point for this literature, as are the annual bibliographies compiled by UCLA's *Amerasia Journal*.

6. In *Prisoners without Trial: Japanese Americans in World War II* (New York: Hill and Wang, 1993), Roger Daniels distills decades of research and writing on the topic into a concise and helpful overview.

7. While there will be some discussion of newspapers in this chapter, they will be the focus of chapter 5.

8. Richard Drinnon, *Keeper of Concentration Camps: Dillon S. Myer and American Racism* (Berkeley: University of California Press, 1987), 44.

9. *Pacific Citizen*, 11 June 1942; also quoted in Audrie Girdner and Anne Loftis, *The Great Betrayal* (New York: Macmillan, 1969), 3.

10. Bob Kumamoto, "The Search for Spies: American Counterintelligence and the Japanese American Community, 1931-1942," *Amerasia Journal* 6 (1979): 45-46, 69-70; Roger Daniels, *Concentration Camps, U.S.A.: Japanese-Americans and World War II* (New York: Holt, Rinehart and Winston, 1971), 34-35.

11. For insight into the decision-making process, see Daniels, *Prisoners*, chap. 2.

12. Scholars have established that internal military documents during the war determined that Japanese Americans on the West Coast did not pose danger to the United States. See Peter Irons, *Justice at War: The Story of the Japanese American Internment Cases* (New York: Oxford University Press, 1983).

13. For an analysis of interest groups that promoted and sought to profit from the woes of Japanese Americans, see Morton Grodzins, *Americans Betrayed: Politics and the Japanese Evacuation* (Chicago: University of Chicago Press, 1949).

14. On the test cases, see Irons, *Justice at War*.

15. Daniels, *Concentration Camps, U.S.A.*, 86-90. The WRA, under the U.S. Department of the Interior, came into existence on 18 March 1942 and took over administration of Japanese Americans from the WCCA in early November 1942.

16. JERS has been mentioned in previous chapters and will be discussed in some detail in chapter 6.

17. Fred Hoshiyama, "Tanforan: Population and Composition," Japanese [American] Evacuation and Resettlement Study (JERS), Bancroft Library, University of California at Berkeley, 67/14c, folder B8.23. A number of studies have examined the ethical dilemmas of several social scientific studies of Japanese Americans and the camps conducted during the war, including Starn, "Engineering Internment," 700-720; Ichioka, *Views from Within*.

18. Hoshiyama, JERS, B8.23.

19. Tamie Tsuchiyama, "A Preliminary Report on Japanese Evacuees at Santa Anita Assembly Center," JERS, B8.05.

20. Tamie Tsuchiyama, "Attitudes," JERS, B8.05. Tsuchiyama also noted that the JACL had come under attack for reportedly having turned in other Japanese Americans to the FBI. Rumors suggested that the informers had received cash payments for information, and many Japanese Americans quickly shunned JACL leaders "like lepers."

21. JERS, **B9.50.

22. Gary Y. Okihiro, "Japanese Resistance in America's Concentration Camps: A Re-evaluation," *Amerasia Journal* 2 (Fall 1973): 20–34.

23. The information on camouflage strikers is taken from Michi Weglyn, *Years of Infamy: The Untold Story of America's Concentration Camps* (New York: William Morrow and Co., 1976), 81. The riot is detailed in Arthur A. Hansen and David A. Hacker, "The Manzanar 'Riot': An Ethnic Perspective," in *Voices Long Silent: An Oral Inquiry into the Japanese American Evacuation,* ed. Arthur A. Hansen and Betty E. Mitson (Fullerton: Oral History Project, California State University, 1974), 47–79.

24. Unauthored reports, JERS, B8.34; Shibutani, Najima, and Shibutani, "The First Month at the Tanforan Assembly Center for Japanese Evacuees," JERS, B8.31.

25. JERS, B8.34.

26. Ibid. After quite a bit of reading of the various camp newspapers, I decided not to include analysis of them in this chapter, instead opting to devote chapter 5 to journalists and newspapers that operated outside the camps. Others have written on the camp newspapers, including John D. Stevens, "From Behind Barbed Wire: Freedom of the Press in World War II Japanese Centers," *Journalism Quarterly* 48 (Summer 1971): 279–87; Lauren Kessler, "Fettered Freedoms: The Journalism of World War II Japanese Internment Camps," *Journalism History* 15 (Summer–Autumn 1988): 70–79.

27. Henry Tani, "The Tanforan High School," JERS, B8.32; miscellaneous reports, JERS, B4.01; James, *Exile Within,* 27–33.

28. JERS, B8.32.

29. JERS, B4.01.

30. James, *Exile Within,* 38–42.

31. JERS, B8.31.

32. Ibid.

33. JERS, B8.05.

34. JERS, B8.17.

35. JERS, B8.05, B8.17.

36. Because of the policy regarding certain archival materials, names in quotes are fictitious.

37. "Diary," JERS, **B12.10.

38. Any number of works on the camps (e.g., Daniels, *Concentration Camps, U.S.A.;* Weglyn, *Years of Infamy*) detail this episode.

39. Although efforts were made to send "loyal" Japanese Americans to other camps once Tule Lake had been reclassified, some people chose not to leave.

40. The section on camp education addresses those who left the camps to continue their education. Chapter 6, in focusing on early resettlers in Chicago, touches on those who left the camps for work.

41. "Military Intelligence Service," in Niiya, *Japanese American History,* 230–31. For more on the MIS, see Joseph Harrington, *Yankee Samurai: The Secret Role*

of Nisei in America's Pacific Victory (Detroit: Pettigrew, 1979); Tad Ichinokuchi, ed., *John Aiso and the M.I.S.: Japanese American Soldiers in the Military Intelligence Service, World War II* (Los Angeles: Military Intelligence Service Club of Southern California, 1988).

42. Thomas D. Murphy, *Ambassadors in Arms* (Honolulu: University of Hawaii Press, 1946).

43. "442nd Regimental Combat Team," in Niiya, *Japanese American History,* 137–38. For more information, see Masayo Duus, *Unlikely Liberators: The Men of the 100th and 442nd* (Honolulu: University of Hawaii Press, 1987).

44. James, *Exile Within,* 38–42. For a portrait of camp administrators and the WRA, see Drinnon, *Keeper of Concentration Camps.*

45. Quoted in Jerome T. Light, "The Development of a Junior-Senior High School Program in a Relocation Center for People of Japanese Ancestry during the War with Japan" (Ed.D. diss., Stanford University, 1947), 49–50.

46. Robert Chipman Lee George, "The Granada (Colorado) Relocation Center Secondary School" (master's thesis, University of Colorado, 1944), 36–40.

47. Robert A. Mossman, "Japanese American War Relocation Centers as Total Institutions with Emphasis on the Educational Program" (Ed.D. diss., Rutgers University, 1978), 72–75.

48. I found Lane Ryo Hirabayashi's essay "The Impact of Incarceration on the Education of Nisei Schoolchildren" helpful in thinking about education during the camps. See *Japanese Americans: From Relocation to Redress,* ed. Roger Daniels, Sandra C. Taylor, and Harry H. L. Kitano (Seattle: University of Washington Press, 1991), 44–51.

49. George, "Granada (Colorado) Relocation Center," 36–37. Carole Katsuko Yumiba discusses the role of early resettlement in the educational programs at the Arkansas camps in "An Educational History of the War Relocation Centers at Jerome and Rohwer, Arkansas, 1942–45" (Ph.D. diss., University of Southern California, 1979), chaps. 4 and 5.

50. James, *Exile Within,* 43.

51. Yumiba, "Educational History," 74–75.

52. Ibid., 69–70, 78, 129.

53. James, *Exile Within,* 32–33, 43, 51–60.

54. The figure of nearly 30,000 students comes from William Zeller, "The Educational Program Provided the Japanese Americans during the Relocation Period, 1942–45" (Ph.D. diss., Michigan State University, 1963), introduction.

55. Yumiba, "Educational History," 61–62; Mossman, "War Relocation Centers," 108.

56. Yumiba, "Educational History," 88.

57. After graduate studies at UCLA, Afton Nance (1902–86) taught throughout southern California, including posts in which she instructed Nisei. Nance worked with the American Friends Service Committee during the war to protest

the incarceration of Japanese Americans. She also corresponded with Kusuda (hereafter cited by date of letter) and many other former students, sending along gifts and writing letters of recommendation and reference. The letters between Nance and her Nisei students are in the possession of Dr. Ruth Morpeth of Poway, California. Dr. Morpeth has kindly allowed me access to the unpublished letters and to unpublished biographical material about Nance. Nance served for many years as a curriculum consultant to the California State Department of Elementary Education.

58. Kusuda, 12 May, 18 May, and 20 May 1942.

59. Ibid., 25 May 1942.

60. Ibid., 27 May 1942.

61. James, *Exile Within*, 140–41.

62. Ibid., 142–55. James describes the Tule Lake situation in fuller detail.

63. For a overview of the NJASRC and its program, see Robert O'Brien, *College Nisei* (Palo Alto, Calif.: Pacific Books, 1949).

64. Ibid., 60–72.

65. Ibid., 54–55. The reasons for resisting resettlement are drawn from the personal camp papers (Tanforan and Topaz) of Tad Fujita of Berkeley, Calif. The figure of 18 percent is taken from James, *Exile Within*, 113.

66. Hundreds of letters have been deposited at the Hoover Institution Archives at Stanford University by Thomas Bodine, a field representative of the NJASRC and staff member of the American Friends Service Committee (hereafter cited as Bodine Papers).

67. Bodine Papers, box 7, folder 8, 7 Oct. 1942.

68. Ibid., folder 8, 7 Oct. 1942; folder 7, 10 Sept. 1942.

69. Ibid., folder 16, 8 July 1943.

70. Ibid., folder 13, 13 Apr. 1943.

71. Ibid., folder 18, 29 May 1944.

72. Historical Report No. 439, JERS, H2.07. Kitano received his Ph.D. in social welfare from the University of California at Berkeley, taught for many years at UCLA, and was the inaugural occupant of the endowed chair in Japanese American Studies at UCLA.

73. U.S. Department of the Interior, "Buddhism in the United States," 7. The total number of internees is listed as 111,170. I have not listed the various groups that fall under the category of "other." The statistical information is taken from this report.

74. Quoted in Toru Matsumoto, *Beyond Prejudice* (New York: Friendship Press, 1946), 23.

75. JERS, O2.75, O2.76, O2.78; **J6.25J.

76. Heihachiro Takarabe, ed., *Issei Christians* (Sacramento, Calif.: Issei Oral History Project, 1977), 51–52; Shizo Yoshina, ed., *Nisei Christian Journey* (Sacramento, Calif.: Nisei Christian Oral History Project, 1988), 26–30. The churches

also played the major role in the early resettlement of Japanese Americans to the Midwest and East during the war and of Japanese Americans after the war.

77. Smith, "Religion and Ethnicity," 1155–56. Smith recognizes that preoccupation with homogeneous communities tends to present static understandings of the relationship between ethnicity and religion.

78. Gary Y. Okihiro, "Religion and Resistance in America's Concentration Camps," *Phylon* 45 (1984): 220–33.

79. JERS, N1.68, N1.69.

80. Ibid., T5.03.

81. Ibid., Q2.67. Only a portion of the poem is quoted.

82. Ibid., T5.091.

83. The literature by and about the WRA is extensive. For a helpful analysis of the WRA, see Starn, "Engineering Internment." Starn specifically highlights the role of professional anthropologists and how they had a very real influence in the ways that internment was handled, presented, and justified. The role of education will be discussed more fully in the next section of this chapter. See also Sandra C. Taylor, "'Fellow-Feelers with the Afflicted': The Christian Churches and the Relocation of the Japanese during World War II," in Daniels et al., *Japanese Americans,* 123–29; idem, *Jewel of the Desert: Japanese American Internment at Topaz* (Berkeley: University of California Press, 1993).

84. Budd Fukei, *The Japanese American Story* (Minneapolis: Dillon Press, 1976), 133.

85. Lester Suzuki, "Ministry in the Wartime Relocation Centers," *Christian Century,* 12 Jan. 1972, 35–41; Suzuki interview, 17 Nov. 1989. Also helpful is Suzuki's *Ministry in the Assembly and Relocation Centers of World War II* (Berkeley, Calif.: Yardbird, 1979).

86. Yoshina, *Nisei Christian Journey,* 100. Other Japanese Americans criticized white Christians; see, for example, JERS, B12.00, K8.58, R21.03. Most Japanese Americans qualified their criticism of white Christians in recognizing that groups like the Society of Friends (Quakers) offered aid through the American Friends Service Committee. See *Friends Journal* 38 (Nov. 1992) for a commemorative issue regarding World War II.

87. JERS, H3.51.

88. Daisuke Kitagawa, *Issei and Nisei* (New York: Seabury Press, 1967), 67–71; JERS, **R20.86.

89. For Ito, see Thomas et al., *Salvage,* 209–10; "Judy Nishimura," tape-recorded interview by the author, San Francisco, Calif., 14 Nov. 1989.

90. JERS, O2.78.

91. Ibid., K8.58.

92. Ibid., B12.35.

93. Mitsue Kato, ed., *Our Recollections* (Tokyo: Art Printing, 1986), 63–77; JERS, J2.97B.

Chapter 5: Insiders on the Outside

1. *Nichibei Shimbun,* 19 June 1940; *Pacific Citizen,* 11 June 1942.

2. On the Asian American movement, see Karin Aguilar–San Juan, ed., *The State of Asian America* (Boston: South End Press, 1994), especially the essay by Glenn Omatsu; Okihiro et al., *Reflections;* and Wei, *Asian American Movement.*

3. Omura's campaign against the JACL did not include the Tajiris, whom he respected as leading journalists of the day (especially Larry); the unusual alliances that the war could foster is discussed later in the chapter.

4. During the war, government officials masked their actions in euphemistic language: for example, renaming American citizens of Japanese ancestry "non-aliens" who were carted off not to concentration camps but to "relocation centers." See Raymond Okamura, "The American Concentration Camps: A Cover-up through Euphemistic Terminology," *Journal of Ethnic Studies* 10 (1982): 95–109.

5. Togo Tanaka, "Journal," Japanese [American] Evacuation and Resettlement Study (JERS), Bancroft Library, University of California, Berkeley, no. 67/14C, folder A17.07. The JERS archive contains extensive documentation on the wartime experiences of Japanese Americans and includes a University of California sociological study of the camps headed by Dorothy Swaine Thomas; government documents from the War Relocation Authority; and other sets of papers related to the camps. For a detailed directory, see Barnhart, *Japanese American Evacuation.*

6. *Nichibei Shimbun,* 21 Feb. 1942.

7. JERS, A17.07.

8. James Omura, "Japanese American Journalism during World War II," in *Frontiers of Asian American Studies,* ed. Gail Nomura, Russell Endo, Stephen H. Sumida, and Russell C. Leong (Pullman: Washington State University Press, 1989), 71–80. Larry Tajiri also discusses censorship in "Nisei USA," *Pacific Citizen,* 4 Aug. 1945.

9. JERS, A17.07.

10. Togo Tanaka, "How to Survive Racism in America's Free Society," in *Voices Long Silent: An Oral Inquiry into the Japanese American Evacuation.* Ed. Arthur A. Hansen and Betty E. Mitson (Fullerton: Oral History Project, California State University, 1974), 93–94. I have woven facts from both Tanaka's journal (in the JERS archives) and from his article/address into this paragraph.

11. JERS, A17.07.

12. *Pacific Citizen,* 30 Dec. 1944; Bill Hosokawa, *JACL: In Quest of Justice* (New York: William Morrow and Co., 1982), 178.

13. Hosokawa, *JACL,* 64–71.

14. Circulation figures are only listed for 1945 (6,300) in N. W. Ayer and Son's *Newspaper Annual and Directory.* Searches for the years 1935–45 yielded no figures for the three other papers mentioned on pp. 9–10.

15. The paper changed its name from *Rocky Nippon* to the *Rocky Shimpo* in April 1943 without giving a reason for the change.

16. The microfilm edition of the paper for 1940–45 had sporadic missing issues. Frequently (and frustratingly) I could not clearly make out the dates of publication as the numbers were faded and partially missing. By context, months and years were easier to decipher than the actual day of publication.

17. *Rocky Nippon,* 19 Dec. 1941.

18. *Nichibei Shimbun,* 20 May 1931, 24 Oct. 1934. Tsuguyo Marion Tajiri, telephone interview by the author, Berkeley, Calif., 21 May 1992.

19. *Nichibei Shimbun,* 16 Oct. 1936.

20. See Takahashi, "Japanese American Responses," 29–57.

21. *Nichibei Shimbun,* 25 Feb. 1935, 25 Mar. 1937, 19 June 1940; *Pacific Citizen,* 11 June 1942; Tajiri interview, 21 May 1992.

22. Hosokawa, *JACL,* 71, 156–57.

23. *Pacific Citizen,* 13 Aug. 1942.

24. Tajiri often mentioned William Randolph Hearst and devoted a full column to him in the 28 Jan. 1943 issue of *Pacific Citizen.*

25. Ibid., 15 Apr. 1943.

26. Ibid., 7 Jan. 1943.

27. See Clayton R. Koppes and Gregory D. Black, *Hollywood Goes to War* (Berkeley: University of California Press, 1990); K. R. M. Short, ed., *Film and Radio Propaganda in World War II* (Knoxville: University of Tennessee Press, 1983).

28. Kumamoto discusses the Black Dragons in "Search for Spies," 45–75.

29. *Pacific Citizen,* 12 Nov. 1942.

30. Ibid., 21 Aug. 1943.

31. Ibid., 8 Jan. 1944, 21 Aug. 1943. Although images have not remained static over the years, Hollywood has continued its legacy of Asian American stereotypes. See Russell Leong, ed., *Moving the Image* (Los Angeles: Asian American Studies Center, University of California, and Visual Communications, 1991).

32. *Pacific Citizen,* 18 Feb. 1943.

33. Ibid., 16 July 1942.

34. Ibid., 25 Sept. 1943.

35. Ibid., 23 Oct. 1943, 12 Feb. 1944, 22 July 1944.

36. Ibid., 12 Feb. 1944, 28 Apr. 1945, 22 Sept. 1945.

37. Ibid., 4 Mar. 1943.

38. Ibid., 16 July 1942.

39. Ibid., 12 Feb. 1944.

40. Ibid., 15 Sept. 1945.

41. Ibid., 18 Nov. 1944.

42. Ibid., 3 Feb. 1945.

43. For an indication of Guyo Tajiri's involvement in the running of *Pacific Citizen,* see her correspondence regarding Nisei efforts on the home front in the Japanese American Research Project (JARP), Special Collections, University Research

Library, UCLA, no. 2010, box 48:1. The JACL did not pay the Tajiris much, given the war and the financial status of the organization, but it did pay Larry $75 per month, three times more than Guyo. The JACL also subsidized the Tajiris' rental home. The identity of "Ann Nisei" is revealed in Hosokawa, *JACL,* 223, 186–87, 156.

44. *Pacific Citizen,* 4 June 1942.

45. Ibid., 18 June 1942, 6 Aug. 1942, 24 June 1943, 3 July 1943, 18 Dec. 1943, 25 Mar. 1944.

46. Valerie J. Matsumoto, "Japanese American Women during World War II," *Frontiers* 8 (1984): 6–14. Although little scholarship has been devoted specifically to the experiences of Japanese American women, the extant documentation, oral histories, and theoretical perspectives within women's history allow for greater attention to issues of gender and how they affected the journeys of Japanese Americans. See Matsumoto's analysis of Nisei advice columns before the war in "Desperately Seeking 'Deirdre,'" 19–32; see also Nakano, *Japanese American Women.*

47. *Pacific Citizen,* 16 Oct. 1943, 25 Dec. 1943.

48. Ibid., 8 Apr. 1944.

49. Ibid., 4 Mar. 1944.

50. Ibid., 25 Dec. 1943, 1 July 1944, 6 Jan. 1945.

51. Ibid., 7 Jan. 1943.

52. For helpful background on the JACL, see Tanaka's manuscript history, JERS, T6.25. Hosokawa, *JACL,* gives an in-house history.

53. For a discussion of the convergence of the Left and the JACL, see Takahashi, *Nisei/Sansei.* I thank Scott Kurashige of UCLA for letting me read his unpublished paper on "Internment and the Japanese American Left."

54. Yoneda, *Ganbatte,* 123.

55. JERS, A17.07. The Central Japanese Association membership consisted of Issei community leaders.

56. On the rise of the JACL, see Paul Spickard, "The Nisei Assume Power: The Japanese Citizens League, 1941–42," *Pacific Historical Review* 52 (May 1983): 147–74.

57. Roger Daniels, *Concentration Camps: North America* (Malabar, Fla.: Robert Krieger, 1981), 74–81.

58. Many have pointed out the bloated figure of 20,000 members given by Masaoka. Actual membership figures were about 7,500. See Drinnon, *Keeper of Concentration Camps,* 70.

59. U.S. Congress, House, Select Committee Investigating National Defense Migration, *Hearings,* 77th Cong., 2d Sess., Pt. 29 (Washington, D.C.: Government Printing Office, 1942), 11137 (hereafter cited as *Hearings*).

60. Ibid., 11141.

61. Ibid., 11152.

62. Ibid., 11148.

63. JERS, **B12.41.

64. *Utah Nippo,* 29 Mar. 1943.

65. Spickard, "Nissei Assume Power," 147–48, 158–71. Many studies have documented the hostility directed toward the JACL. See, for example, Drinnon, *Keeper of Concentration Camps;* Weglyn, *Years of Infamy;* Thomas and Nishimoto, *Spoilage.*

66. *Hearings,* 11229. The testimonies of Iiyama and Kunitani appear on pp. 11220–29.

67. Ibid., 11223–32.

68. Omura, "Japanese American Journalism," 72–73.

69. *Rocky Nippon,* 31 Mar. 1943.

70. Ibid., 4 Jan. 1943.

71. Ibid., 7 Dec. 1942. The 22 Mar. 1943 issue lists James Omura as the executive director of the bureau.

72. Ibid., 19 Mar. 1943.

73. *Rocky Shimpo,* 31 Mar. 1944. Omura devoted some print space to the alleged investigation by the Dies Committee of Larry Tajiri, who, Omura pointed out, had been "rather sympathetic to Nisei Communists." It is clear from the article that Omura has a great deal of respect for Tajiri as a journalist. Tajiri's willingness to work for the JACL, however, made him subject to criticism. See *Rocky Shimpo,* 28 June 1943.

74. Daniels, *Concentration Camps,* 118–23.

75. Ibid., 124–26.

76. Ibid., 127–29. The seven were sentenced to two to four years in prison. There were other trials regarding draft resistance. See Douglas Nelson, *Heart Mountain: The History of an American Concentration Camp* (Madison: State Historical Society of Wisconsin, 1976).

77. Omura, "Japanese American Journalism," 73–74. The U.S. Attorney General's Office failed to charge Omura with sedition because of a lack of evidence.

78. Frank Seishi Emi, "Draft Resistance at the Heart Mountain Concentration Camp and the Fair Play Committee," in *Frontiers of Asian American Studies,* ed. Gail Nomura, Russell Endo, Stephen H. Sumida, and Russell C. Leong (Pullman: Washington State University Press, 1989), 41–69.

Chapter 6: Recording Nisei Experiences

1. See *Personal Justice Denied.* The number of oral history collections and works based on oral history continues to grow. One example is John Tateishi, ed., *And Justice for All: An Oral History of the Japanese American Detention Camps* (New York: Random House, 1984).

2. Thomas et al., *Salvage.*

3. Thomas and Nishimoto, *Spoilage,* xii.

4. Thomas et al., *Salvage,* 128.

5. Nagata argues for the lasting influence of the camps into the third generation (Sansei) in *Legacy of Injustice*.

6. Among the many works that emphasize this point, see Weglyn, *Years of Infamy*; Drinnon, *Keeper of Concentration Camps*.

7. Takagi, "Life History Analysis," 203. I thank Dana Takagi for discussing with me her interview with and impressions of Charles Kikuchi. Dana Takagi, telephone interview by the author, Santa Cruz, Calif., 15 Dec. 1997.

8. Charles Kikuchi, "Through the JERS Looking Glass: A Personal View from Within," in *Views from Within: The Japanese American Evacuation and Resettlement*, ed. Yuji Ichioka (Los Angeles: Asian American Studies Center, University of California, 1989), 179–95 (quote on 185).

9. Ichioka, *Views from Within*, 4–8. Ichioka's introduction includes greater detail and an overview of the JERS project. I have condensed and summarized information relevant for my purposes.

10. Ibid., 9–13; Kikuchi, "JERS Looking Glass," 190.

11. This analysis of W. I. Thomas and developments in American sociology are taken from Takagi, "Life History Analysis," 197–216.

12. Thomas et al., *Salvage*, 90–109. See this section for more details about the resettlement process.

13. Michael D. Albert, "Japanese American Communities in Chicago and the Twin Cities" (Ph.D. diss., University of Minnesota, 1980), 114–18, 177–94. For a comparative study of postwar Cleveland, see Thomas Linehan, "Japanese American Resettlement in Cleveland during and after World War II," *Journal of Urban History* 20 (Nov. 1993): 54–80.

14. Setsuko Matsunaga Nishi, "Japanese American Achievement in Chicago: A Cultural Response to Degradation" (Ph.D. diss., University of Chicago, 1963), 158–69. See also Masako K. Osako, "Japanese-Americans: Melting into the All-American Pot," in *Ethnic Chicago*, 4th ed., ed. Melvin G. Holli and Peter d'A. Jones (Grand Rapids, Mich.: Eerdmans, 1995), 409–37.

15. Kikuchi was a prolific diarist, and he continued to keep a journal for many years after the war. These diaries are part of the Charles Kikuchi Papers, Collection 1259, Special Collections, University Research Library, UCLA (hereafter cited as Kikuchi Papers). For a sense of Kikuchi's writing, see *The Kikuchi Diary: Chronicle from an American Concentration Camp*, ed. John Modell (Urbana: University of Illinois Press, 1993). The entries are from Kikuchi's time in the Tanforan Assembly Center and represent only a fraction of his total wartime and postwar diary keeping.

16. Kikuchi, "JERS Looking Glass," 190–91.

17. Louis Adamic, *From Many Lands* (New York: Harper and Bros., 1939), 184–234.

18. I thank Yuji Ichioka for sharing with me his unpublished paper " 'Unity within Diversity': Louis Adamic and Japanese-Americans."

19. After the war, Kikuchi moved to New York City, where he worked as a clinical social worker for the Veteran's Administration for over twenty years. He also served, unofficially, as a therapist to the Martha Graham Dance Company. His wife, Yuriko, danced for many years as a leading member of the company.

20. Kikuchi, "JERS Looking Glass," 180. Ichioka's *Views from Within* is based on presentations given at this conference and includes reminiscences by several of the other Japanese American JERS staff members.

21. Thomas et al., *Salvage,* 131–50. The life history outline is found in ibid., 136–44.

22. Kikuchi, "JERS Looking Glass," 191.

23. Thomas et al. note this process in *Salvage,* 144.

24. Dana Takagi, "Personality and History: Hostile Nisei Women," in *Reflections on Shattered Windows: Promises and Prospects for Asian American Studies,* ed. Gary Y. Okihiro, Shirley Hune, Arthur A. Hansen, and John M. Liu (Pullman: Washington State University Press, 1988), 184–92.

25. W. I. Thomas, "The Employment of the Behavior Document in the Social Sciences" (1943?), in Kikuchi Papers, box 53. The accompanying correspondence indicates that the essay was delivered as a lecture at the University of California at Berkeley and was being sent to Kikuchi for his reference.

26. Kikuchi Papers, box 53.

27. While some of the analysis may touch on the fifteen cases that Thomas excerpted (including some discussion of materials omitted), the focus of the chapter will be to highlight certain themes based on a more comprehensive reading of the life histories as a whole.

28. This is not to suggest that there were not those Nisei who were sincere in their beliefs in Buddhism and Christianity but rather to recognize the highly varied nature of religious affiliation.

29. Through the content analysis of life histories, my aim is to demonstrate how the documents reveal a far more nuanced picture of Nisei experience than might be assumed from the brief but suggestive frame that Thomas et al. introduce in the summary and prefatory remarks in *Salvage,* v–viii.

30. My reading is based on life history documents that are part of the JERS Collection in the Bancroft Library, University of California at Berkeley, and the life histories that are part of the Charles Kikuchi Papers at University of California at Los Angeles. I have gone through the complete set of life histories located at the Bancroft but found the Kikuchi Papers holdings at UCLA more revealing, since they included other documents such as correspondence, private journal entries that were not sent to JERS, and what I believe to be a full run of the personal diaries of Kikuchi. Developing the habit of recording his thoughts in a daily diary in the assembly center at Tanforan racetrack, Kikuchi continued the practice throughout the remainder of his life. According to Yuji Ichioka, Kikuchi wrote his diary out by hand before beginning his casework as a social worker in New York City. It should be noted that the Kikuchi Papers at UCLA contain only cases 1–50. Be-

cause I will be drawing from many cases, there will be no effort to sketch out the individual and family backgrounds of each case except as they might be relevant for the analysis at hand. Those interested in the full details are referred to the life histories themselves; the fifteen excerpted and published accounts in Thomas et al.'s *Salvage* are easily accessed.

31. To protect the anonymity of interviewees, pseudonyms were given to each individual.

32. Kikuchi Papers, box 49, CH-50, 39–49. Each case history (CH) was assigned a number.

33. Ibid., box 47, CH-22, 13–14.

34. Ibid., box 46, CH-14, 6–18a.

35. JERS, **R, CH-3, 9–15; Kikuchi Papers, box 46, CH-3, 68.

36. Kikuchi Papers, box 49, CH-48, 5.

37. Ibid., box 47, CH-27, 235. The section from which this quote is taken was not included in the version excerpted in Thomas et al., *Salvage*.

38. Kikuchi Papers, box 47, CH-23, 88–89.

39. Ibid., box 49, CH-48, 141–42.

40. Ibid., box 49, CH-50, 5, 75–76.

41. Ibid., box 48, CH-46, 28.

42. Ibid., box 47, CH-32, 43, 63–64. "White bastard" is an approximate translation of the Japanese word *keto*, which refers more literally to "foreign barbarian."

43. Ibid., box 48, CH-47, 48–49.

44. Ibid., CH-14, 14, 18a.

45. Ibid., box 46, CH-13, 48–57.

46. Ibid., 96–107; see also the section entitled "The Writer's Opinion and Unscientific Observations" appended to the life history and with new pagination. The departure for New York City is noted on pages 3–4.

47. Kikuchi Papers, box 47, CH-20, 17–18; JERS, **R, CH-20, summary sheet.

48. Kikuchi Papers, box 47, CH-22, 14. I found it interesting that a number of Nisei commented on other racial-ethnic groups—including Filipinos, African Americans, and Jews—and often in less than flattering ways. In some cases the views were those passed on by elders; in other cases they were drawn from personal experiences. In any event, the opinions expressed suggest that Nisei were no more immune than others in formulating racial attitudes toward others that smacked of prejudice and were based on stereotypes.

49. Ibid., CH-16, 17–18, 56.

50. Vicki Ruiz makes this point in her discussion of Latinas who changed their hair color or used particular facial creams. See " 'Star Struck': Acculturation, Adolescence, and Mexican-American Women, 1920–1950," in *Small Worlds: Children and Adolescents in America, 1850–1950*, ed. Elliot West and Paula Petrik (Lawrence: University Press of Kansas, 1992), 61–80.

51. Kikuchi Papers, box 46, CH-8, 14.

52. Ibid., box 47, CH-30, 20.

53. Ibid., box 48, CH-33, 17–18.

54. Ibid., box 46, CH-13, 32–38.

55. Ibid., 116–17. Katayama's statement to Kikuchi about his candor comes from Kikuchi's diary, 13 Oct. 1943, which can be found in the Kikuchi Papers, box 13.

56. Ibid., box 49, CH-48, 85–89.

57. Ibid., box 48, CH-35, 25–26.

58. Ibid., box 46, CH-13, 106–7.

59. Ibid., box 47, CH-32, 67.

60. Ibid., CH-16, 17–18, 55–56.

61. Ibid., box 48, CH-35, 19–20, 30–38; Thomas et al., *Salvage*, 341–67.

62. Kikuchi Papers, box 48, CH-35, 54–73. The pages listed here, appended to the life history, were taken from Kikuchi's diary, 29 May 1945, but were grafted into the interview itself, since pagination continued without a break. It is not clear why Thomas et al. chose not to include the material in the published version. The quote appears on page 67.

63. On the role of historical memory and the war, see Takezawa, *Breaking the Silence;* Yoo, "Captivating Memories," 680–99.

Epilogue

1. *"Endo, Ex Parte,"* in Niiya, *Japanese American History,* 134–35. For more background, see Irons, *Justice at War.*

2. Daniels et al., *Japanese Americans,* xxii; Niiya, *Japanese American History,* 65.

3. Sandra C. Taylor, "Evacuation and Economic Loss: Questions and Perspectives," in *Japanese Americans: From Relocation to Redress,* ed. Roger Daniels, Sandra C. Taylor, and Harry H. L. Kitano (Seattle: University of Washington Press, 1991), 166. The sum of $370 million represented the high end of an estimated figure, and the $2.5–6.2 billion (by 1983 dollars) figure allowed for a 3 percent interest rate adjusted for inflation.

4. Among a number of studies that address aspects of postwar Japanese America, see Roger Daniels, *Asian America: Chinese and Japanese in the United States since 1850* (Seattle: University of Washington Press, 1988); Tetsuden Kashima, "Japanese American Internees Return, 1945–1955: Readjustment and Social Amnesia," *Phylon* 41 (June 1980), 107–15; Takahashi, *Nisei/Sansei.*

5. Stanley I. Kutler, *American Inquisition: Justice and Injustice in the Cold War* (New York: Hill and Wang, 1982), 15, 29; Masayo Duus, *Tokyo Rose: Orphan of the Pacific* (Tokyo: Kodansha, 1979), 2, 109–16. Kutler discusses the role of radio personality Walter Winchell, who used his popularity to place pressure on the Truman administration to prosecute the case.

6. *Pacific Citizen,* 24 Sept. 1949.

7. *Newsweek,* 17 Sept. 1945; *San Francisco Chronicle,* 5 July 1949; *Pacific Citizen,* 10 Sept. 1949; Duus, *Tokyo Rose,* 40–49.

8. *Pacific Citizen,* 10 Sept. 1949.

9. Ibid., 20 Aug. 1949, 3 Sept. 1949, 10 Sept. 1949; *San Francisco Chronicle*, 16 Aug. 1949. D'Aquino began work on the Zero Hour program in late November 1943. Her participation dwindled after Cousens left the program because of a heart attack in June 1944. See Duus, *Tokyo Rose*, 90–96.

10. *San Francisco Chronicle*, 8 July 1943, 12 July 1943, 13 July 1949.

11. D'Aquino never received the $2,000 advance. See Niiya, *Japanese American History*, 126–27.

12. Kutler, *American Inquisition*, 3–4, 14, 17–20, 25–28. Lee worked for the International News Service and Brundidge was with *Cosmopolitan*, both part of the Hearst empire. Kutler documents the unsavory role that Brundidge played in the case, suborning perjured testimony. See also Duus, *Tokyo Rose*, 94–96. Iva and Felipe met at the radio station and were married on 19 April 1945. Felipe d'Aquino, a Portuguese citizen, was three-quarters Japanese.

13. Clifford Uyeda notes that Felipe and Iva d'Aquino's child died at birth in January 1948, adding to their tragic story. See *A Final Report and Review: The Japanese American Citizens League National Committee for Iva Toguri*, Occasional Monographs No. 1 (Seattle: Asian American Studies Program, University of Washington, 1980), 24.

14. *San Francisco Chronicle*, 6 July 1949; *Pacific Citizen*, 1 Oct. 1949, 15 Oct. 1949. D'Aquino was convicted under Overt Act 6: "said defendant . . . did speak into a microphone concerning the loss of ships." The eight counts are listed in the *San Francisco Chronicle*, 19 July 1949.

15. With the conviction, d'Aquino lost her U.S. citizenship. She left for the Federal Women's Reformatory at Alderson, West Virginia, on 15 November 1949. See *Pacific Citizen*, 19 Nov. 1949.

16. Duus, *Tokyo Rose*, 224–33; Niiya, *Japanese American History*, 126–27. Attorney Wayne Collins filed appeal after appeal, enabling d'Aquino to stay in the United States. Collins also filed the petition that eventually led to her pardon. The JACL, which had turned its back on d'Aquino during the trial, led a campaign for her pardon in the mid-1970s. Part of the many costs borne by d'Aquino was the loss of her marriage, as Felipe was barred from entry to the United States soon after the trial. As a stateless person, Iva would very likely be barred from returning to the United States if she left the country. See Clifford Uyeda, "The Pardoning of 'Tokyo Rose': A Report on the Restoration of American Citizenship to Iva Ikuko Toguri," *Amerasia Journal* 5 (Fall 1978): 69–84. After her release in 1956, d'Aquino lived in Chicago with the Toguri family. The latest records that I have found indicate that she is still alive and living in the Chicago area.

17. My comments are based on the coverage of the trial in the JACL newspaper, *Pacific Citizen*, from March to November 1949. Some articles carry the byline of Larry or Marion Tajiri, but other articles do not identify the reporter.

18. Apparently, the defense lawyers in the Kawakita treason case in Los Angeles had hoped to bring in race to gain the support of the African American and Japanese American jurors. The strategy did not appear to work. Tomoya Kawa-

kita, a Nisei, was convicted in 1948 for treason for his role as an interrogator of Allied POWs in Japan during the war. For more information on Kawakita and the trial, see Frank Chuman, *The Bamboo People: The Law and Japanese Americans* (Del Mar, Calif.: Publisher's Inc., 1976).

19. Quotes and interpretation based on Larry Tajiri's editorial in *Pacific Citizen,* 9 July 1949. Tajiri also expressed concern that d'Aquino herself seemed to be ignorant of race prejudice, based on comments she had made to the press stating that she had not been aware of its existence before the war.

20. Ibid., 16 July 1949, 6 Aug. 1949, 3 Sept. 1949, 10 Sept. 1949, 15 Oct. 1949.

21. "Community of memory" is taken from Takaki, *Strangers,* 10.

SELECTED BIBLIOGRAPHY

Archives and Personal Papers

Charles Kikuchi Papers, Special Collections, University Research Library, University of California at Los Angeles
Graduate Theological Union Library Archives, Berkeley, Calif.
Institute of Buddhist Studies (IBS), Berkeley, Calif.
Japanese [American] Evacuation and Resettlement Study (JERS), Bancroft Library, University of California at Berkeley
Japanese American Library, San Francisco, Calif.
Japanese American Research Project (JARP), Special Collections, University Research Library, University of California at Los Angeles
Pacific School of Religion Archives, Berkeley, Calif.
Pine United Methodist Church Archives, San Francisco, Calif.
Ruth Morpeth Personal Papers, Poway, Calif.
Ryo Munekata Personal Papers, Los Angeles, Calif.
San Francisco Theological Seminary Library Archives, San Anselmo, Calif.
Survey of Race Relations, Hoover Institution Archives, Stanford University, Stanford, Calif.
Tadashi Fujita Personal Papers, Berkeley, Calif.
Thomas Bodine Collection, Hoover Institution Archives, Stanford University, Stanford, Calif.

Interviews and Oral Histories

Dana Takagi, telephone interview by the author, Santa Cruz, Calif., 15 Dec. 1997
Judy Nishimura, tape-recorded interview by the author, San Francisco, Calif., 14 Nov. 1989
Lester and Seda Suzuki, tape-recorded interview by the author, Berkeley, Calif., 17 Nov. 1989 and 15 May 1993
Ryo Munekata, tape-recorded interview by the author, Los Angeles, Calif., 21 July 1995

Sol Cohen, Graduate School of Education, University of California at Los Angeles, 8 Jan. 1993

Togo Tanaka, tape-recorded interview by the author, Los Angeles, Calif., 18 May 1992

Tsuguyo Marion Tajiri, telephone interview by the author, Berkeley, Calif., 21 May 1992

Newspapers and Journals

Berkeley Bussei
Bhratri
Bussei Review
Campanile Review
Colorado Times
Current Life
Doho
Friends Journal
Hokubei Asahi
Japanese American Courier
Japanese Methodist Episcopal Church Weekly News
Japanese Student Bulletin
Kashu Mainichi (Japan-California Daily)
Nichibei Shimbun (Japanese American News)
Official Journal, Pacific Japanese Mission of the Methodist Episcopal Church
Osaka Mainichi
Pacific Citizen
Rafu Shimpo (Los Angeles Japanese Daily News)
Rocky Nippon
Rocky Shimpo
San Francisco Chronicle
Sangha
San Pedro High School Fore 'n Aft
Shin Sekai (New World)
Shin Sekai Asahi (New World–Sun Daily)
Tanforan Totalizer
Theodore Roosevelt High School Rough Rider
Utah Nippo

U.S. Government Documents

Commission on Wartime Relocation and Internment of Civilians. *Personal Justice Denied.* Washington, D.C.: Government Printing Office, 1982.

U.S. Congress, House, Select Committee Investigating National Defense Migration. *Hearings.* 77th Cong., 2d Sess., Pt. 29. Washington, D.C.: Government Printing Office, 1942.

U.S. Department of the Interior, War Relocation Authority. Community Analysis Section, Report No. 9: "Buddhism in the United States," 15 May 1944. Washington, D.C.

U.S. Department of the Interior, War Relocation Authority. *The Evacuated People: A Quantitative Description.* Washington, D.C.: Government Printing Office, 1946.

U.S. Department of War. *Final Report: Japanese Evacuation from the West Coast, 1942.* Washington, D.C.: Government Printing Office, 1943.

Other Sources

Adamic, Louis. *From Many Lands.* New York: Harper and Bros., 1939.

Aguilar–San Juan, Karin, ed. *The State of Asian America.* Boston: South End Press, 1994.

Akagi, Roy. *The Second Generation Problem: Some Suggestions toward Its Solution.* New York: Japanese Students' Christian Association in North America, 1926.

Albanese, Catherine. *America: Religions and Religion.* Belmont, Calif.: Wadsworth, 1981.

Albert, Michael D. "Japanese American Communities in Chicago and the Twin Cities." Ph.D. diss., University of Minnesota, 1980.

Allison, Gertrude M. "Japanese Unit of Study for Fourth and Third Grade." *Los Angeles School Journal* 13 (17 Mar. 1930): 11–14.

Almaguer, Tomas. *Racial Fault Lines: The Historical Origins of White Supremacy in California.* Berkeley: University of California Press, 1994.

Angevine, Michael J. Kimura, and Ryo Yoshida. "Contexts for a History of Asian American Presbyterian Churches: A Case Study of the Early History of Japanese American Presbyterian Churches." Ms., Dec. 1989. Author's files.

Azuma, Eiichiro. "Walnut Grove: Japanese Farm Community in the Sacramento River Delta, 1892–1942." Master's thesis, University of California at Los Angeles, 1992.

Barkan, Elazar. *The Retreat of Scientific Racism: Changing Concepts of Race in Britain and the United States.* Cambridge: Cambridge University Press, 1992.

Barnhart, Edward A. *Japanese American Evacuation and Resettlement: Catalog of Materials in the General Library.* Berkeley: General Library, University of California, 1958.

Beechert, Edward D. *Working in Hawaii: A Labor History.* Honolulu: University of Hawaii Press, 1985.

Bell, Reginald. *Public School Education of Second-Generation Japanese in California.* Stanford, Calif.: Stanford University Press, 1935.

Berrol, Selma Cantor. *Growing Up American: Immigrant Children in America Then and Now.* Boston: Twayne, 1995.

Blauner, Robert. *Racial Oppression in America.* New York: Harper and Row, 1972.

Bogardus, Emory. "Culture Conflicts in Relocation Centers." *Sociology and Social Research* 27 (May 1943): 381–90.

———. *Immigration and Race Attitudes.* Boston: D. C. Heath and Co., 1928.

———. "A Race-Relations Cycle." *American Journal of Sociology* 35 (Jan. 1930): 612–17.

———. "Some Causes of Prejudice." *Los Angeles School Journal* 12 (31 Dec. 1928): 16–17.

Bogardus, Emory, and Robert Ross. "The Second-Generation Race Relations Cycle: A Study in Issei-Nisei Relationships." *Sociology and Social Research* 24 (Mar.–Apr. 1940): 357–63.

Bottomley, Gillian. *From Another Place: Migration and the Politics of Culture.* Cambridge: Cambridge University Press, 1992.

Bryant, William, ed. *The Church's One Hundred Years in the Japanese American Community.* San Francisco: Christ United Presbyterian Church, 1988.

Cain, Leonard, Jr. "Japanese-American Protestants: Acculturation and Assimilation." *Review of Religious Research* 3 (Winter 1962): 113–21.

Cameron, James William. "The History of Mexican Public Education in Los Angeles, 1910–1930." Ph.D. diss., University of Southern California, 1976.

Chan, Sucheng. *Asian Americans: An Interpretive History.* Boston: Twayne, 1991.

Chang, Gordon H. "Asian Americans and the Writing of Their History." *Radical History Review* 53 (1992): 105–14.

———, ed. *Morning Glory, Evening Shadow: Yamato Ichihashi and His Internment Writings, 1942–45.* Stanford, Calif.: Stanford University Press, 1997.

Chansler, Horace. "The Assimilation of the Japanese in and around Stockton." Master's thesis, College of the Pacific, 1932.

Cheng, Lucie, and Edna Bonacich, eds. *Labor Immigration under Capitalism.* Berkeley: University of California Press, 1984.

Chijiwa, Saikichi. "A Social Survey of the Japanese Population in Palo Alto and Menlo Park." Master's thesis, Stanford University, 1933.

Chuman, Frank. *The Bamboo People: The Law and Japanese Americans.* Del Mar, Calif.: Publisher's Inc., 1976.

Cloud, Roy. *Education in California.* Stanford, Calif.: Stanford University Press, 1952.

Cohen, Ronald. "Review Essay: Education for Racial and Ethnic Communities." *Journal of American Ethnic History* 5 (Fall 1985): 73–79.

Connor, John. *Tradition and Change among Three Generations of Japanese Americans.* Chicago: Nelson-Hall, 1977.

Conroy, Hilary. *The Japanese Frontier in Hawaii, 1868–1898.* Berkeley: University of California Press, 1953.

Conzen, Kathleen Neils, David A. Gerber, Ewa Morawska, George E. Pozzetta, and Rudolph Vecoli. "The Invention of Ethnicity: A Perspective from the USA." *Journal of American Ethnic History* 12 (Fall 1992): 3–63.

Cremin, Lawrence. *The Transformation of the School: Progressivism in American Education, 1876–1957.* New York: Alfred A. Knopf, 1961.

Cronon, William, George Miles, and Jay Gitlin, eds. *Under an Open Sky.* New York: W. W. Norton, 1992.

Daniels, Roger. "American Historians and East Asian Immigrants." *Pacific Historical Review* 43 (Nov. 1974): 449–72.

———. *Asian America: Chinese and Japanese in the United States since 1850.* Seattle: University of Washington Press, 1988.

———. *Concentration Camps: North America.* Malabar, Fla.: Robert Krieger, 1981.

———. *Concentration Camps, U.S.A.: Japanese-Americans and World War II.* New York: Holt, Rinehart and Winston, 1971.

———. "The Japanese." In *Ethnic Leadership in America.* Ed. John Higham. 36–63. Baltimore: Johns Hopkins University Press, 1978.

———. "Japanese America, 1930–41: An Ethnic Community in the Great Depression." *Journal of the West* 24 (Oct. 1985): 35–49.

———. *The Politics of Prejudice: The Anti-Japanese Movement in California and the Struggle for Japanese Exclusion.* Berkeley: University of California Press, 1962.

———. *Prisoners without Trial: Japanese Americans in World War II.* New York: Hill and Wang, 1993.

———. "Westerners from the East: Oriental Immigrants Reappraised." *Pacific Historical Review* 35 (Nov. 1966): 373–84.

———, ed. *Japanese Immigration.* New York: Arno Press, 1978.

Daniels, Roger, Sandra C. Taylor, and Harry H. L. Kitano, eds. *Japanese Americans: From Relocation to Redress.* Seattle: University of Washington Press, 1991.

Degler, Carl. *In Search of Human Nature.* New York: Oxford University Press, 1991.

Di Leonardo, Micaela. *The Varieties of Ethnic Experience: Kinship, Class, and Gender among California Italian-Americans.* Ithaca, N.Y.: Cornell University Press, 1984.

Directory of the Japanese Students in North America, 1925–26. New York: Japanese Students' Christian Association in North America, 1925–26.

Dolan, Jay P. "The Immigrants and Their Gods: A New Perspective of American Religious History." *Church History* 57 (1988): 61–72.

Dower, John. *War without Mercy.* New York: Pantheon, 1986.

Drinnon, Richard. *Keeper of Concentration Camps: Dillon S. Myer and American Racism.* Berkeley: University of California Press, 1987.

Dumoulin, Heinrich, ed. *Buddhism in the Modern World.* New York: Macmillan, 1976.

Duus, Masayo. *Tokyo Rose: Orphan of the Pacific.* Tokyo: Kodansha, 1979.

———. *Unlikely Liberators: The Men of the 100th and 442nd.* Trans. Peter Duus. Honolulu: University of Hawaii Press, 1987.

Elder, Glen, Jr., John Modell, and Ross D. Parke, eds. *Children in Time and Place: Developmental and Historical Insights.* Cambridge: Cambridge University Press, 1993.

Emi, Frank Seishi. "Draft Resistance at the Heart Mountain Concentration Camp and the Fair Play Committee." In *Frontiers of Asian American Studies.* Ed. Gail Nomura, Russell Endo, Stephen H. Sumida, and Russell C. Leong. 41–69. Pullman: Washington State University Press, 1989.

Endo, Russell, and Dale Hirokawa. "Japanese American Intermarriage." *Free Inquiry in Creative Sociology* 11 (Nov. 1983): 159–66.

Espiritu, Yen Le. *Asian American Panethnicity.* Philadelphia: Temple University Press, 1992.

Fass, Paula. *Outside In: Minorities and the Transformation of American Education.* New York: Oxford University Press, 1989.

Fields, Barbara J. "Ideology and Race in American History." In *Region, Race, and Reconstruction: Essays in Honor of C. Vann Woodward.* Ed. J. Morgan Kousser and James M. McPherson. 143–78. New York: Oxford University Press, 1982.

Fowler, Ruth M. "Some Aspects of Public Opinion Concerning the Japanese in Santa Clara." Master's thesis, Stanford University, 1934.

Fuchigami, Takako. "Both Buddhism and Christianity Are Vitally Important to the Second Generation." *Bhratri* 2 (July 1934): 17–18.

Fuchs, Lawrence. *Hawaii Pono: A Social History.* New York: Harcourt, Brace, and World, 1961.

Fugita, Stephen S., and David J. O'Brien. *Japanese American Ethnicity: The Persistence of Community.* Seattle: University of Washington Press, 1991.

Fujita, Tadashi. "Biography of Rev. Suzunosuke Kato." Ms., n.d. Personal Papers of Tadashi Fujita, Berkeley, Calif.

Fujiyoshi, Donald. "A Study of the Educational Program of the Church School of the Japanese Christian Church and Institute of Los Angeles." Master's thesis, University of Southern California, 1942.

Fukei, Budd. *The Japanese American Story.* Minneapolis: Dillon Press, 1976.

Garcia, Mario T. *Mexican Americans: Leadership, Ideology, and Identity, 1930–60.* New Haven, Conn.: Yale University Press, 1989.

George, Robert Chipman Lee. "The Granada (Colorado) Relocation Center Secondary School." Master's thesis, University of Colorado, 1944.

Girdner, Audrey, and Anne Loftis. *The Great Betrayal.* New York: Macmillan, 1969.

Glazer, Nathan, and Daniel Moynihan, eds. *Ethnicity: Theory and Experience.* Cambridge, Mass.: Harvard University Press, 1975.

Glenn, Evelyn Nakano. *Issei, Nisei, War Bride: Three Generations of Japanese American Women in Domestic Service.* Philadelphia: Temple University Press, 1986.

Graff, Harvey J. *Conflicting Paths: Growing Up in America.* Cambridge, Mass.: Harvard University Press, 1995.

Grazier, Jean P., and Cecile Gaziano. "Robert Ezra Park's Theory of News, Public Opinion, and Social Control." *Journalism Monographs* n.v. (Nov. 1979): 1–47.

Gregory, Steven, and Roger Sanjek, eds. *Race.* New Brunswick, N.J.: Rutgers University Press, 1994.

Grodzins, Morton. *Americans Betrayed: Politics and the Japanese Evacuation.* Chicago: University of Chicago Press, 1949.

Guarneri, Carl, and David Alvarez, eds. *Religion and Society in the American West.* Lanham, Md.: University Press of America, 1987.

Hada, John Juji. "The Indictment and Trial of Iva Ikuko Toguri d'Aquino." Master's thesis, University of San Francisco, 1973.

Handlin, Oscar. *The Uprooted.* Boston: Little, Brown, 1951.

Hansen, Arthur A., ed. *Japanese American WWII Evacuation History Project.* 5 vols. Westport, Conn.: Greenwood Press, 1990–92.

Hansen, Arthur A., and David A. Hacker. "The Manzanar 'Riot': An Ethnic Perspective." In *Voices Long Silent: An Oral Inquiry into the Japanese American Evacuation.* Ed. Arthur A. Hansen and Betty E. Mitson. 47–79. Fullerton: Oral History Project, California State University, 1974.

Hansen, Arthur A., and Betty E. Mitson, eds. *Voices Long Silent: An Oral Inquiry into the Japanese American Evacuation.* Fullerton: Oral History Project, California State University, 1974.

Harrington, Joseph. *Yankee Samurai: The Secret Role of Nisei in America's Pacific Victory.* Detroit: Pettigrew, 1979.

Hartmann, Edward. *The Movement to Americanize the Immigrant.* New York: Columbia University Press, 1948.

Hashimoto, Hideo. "From University to Pastorate." Ms., n.d. Author's files.

Hatamiya, Leslie T. *Righting a Wrong: Japanese Americans and the Passage of the Civil Liberties Act of 1988.* Stanford, Calif.: Stanford University Press, 1993.

Hayashi, Brian Masaru. *"For the Sake of Our Japanese Brethren": Assimilation, Nationalism, and Protestantism among the Japanese of Los Angeles, 1895–1942.* Stanford, Calif.: Stanford University Press, 1995.

Hayashi, Kaori. "History of the *Rafu Shimpo*: Evolution of a Japanese American Newspaper, 1903–1942." Master's thesis, California State University at Northridge, 1990.

Hendrick, Irving. *California Education: A Brief History.* San Francisco: Boyd and Fraser, 1980.

———. "California's Response to the 'New Education' in the 1930s." *California Historical Quarterly* 53 (Spring 1974): 25–40.

———. *Public Policy toward the Education of Non-White Minority Group Children in California, 1849–1970.* Riverside: School of Education, University of California, 1975.

Hennings, Robert E. *James D. Phelan and the Wilson Progressives of California.* New York: Garland, 1985.

Herberg, Will. *Protestant-Catholic-Jew.* Garden City, N.Y.: Doubleday, 1955.

Herman, David. "Neighbors on Golden Mountain: The Americanization of Immigrants in California and Public Instruction as an Agency of Ethnic Assimilation, 1850 to 1933." Ph.D. diss., University of California at Berkeley, 1981.

Higginbotham, Evelyn Brooks. "African-American Women's History and the Metalanguage of Race." *Signs* 17.2 (Winter 1992): 251–75.

Hirabayashi, Lane Ryo. "The Impact of Incarceration on the Education of Nisei Schoolchildren." In *Japanese Americans: From Relocation to Redress.* Ed. Roger Daniels, Sandra C. Taylor, and Harry H. L. Kitano. 44–51. Seattle: University of Washington Press, 1991.

Hirohata, Paul, ed. *Orations and Essays by the Japanese Second Generation of America.* Los Angeles: Los Angeles Japanese Daily News, 1932.

Hohri, William. *Repairing America.* Pullman: Washington State University Press, 1988.

Horinouchi, Isao. "Americanized Buddhism: A Sociological Analysis of a Protestantized Japanese Religion." Ph.D. diss., University of California at Davis, 1973.

Hosokawa, Bill. *JACL: In Quest of Justice.* New York: William Morrow and Co., 1982.

——. *The Nisei: The Quiet Americans.* New York: William Morrow and Co., 1969.

Howe, Russell W. *The Hunt for Tokyo Rose.* Lanham, Md.: Madison Books, 1990.

Hune, Shirley. *Pacific Migrations to the United States: Trends and Themes in Historical and Sociological Literature.* RIIES Bibliographic Studies No. 2. Washington, D.C.: Research Institute on Immigration and Ethnic Studies, Smithsonian Institution, 1977.

Hunter, Louise H. *Buddhism in Hawaii: Its Impact on a Yankee Community.* Honolulu: University of Hawaii Press, 1971.

Ichihashi, Yamato. *Japanese in the United States: A Critical Study of the Problems of the Japanese Immigrants and Their Children.* Stanford, Calif.: Stanford University Press, 1932.

Ichinokuchi, Tad, ed. *John Aiso and the M.I.S.: Japanese American Soldiers in the Military Intelligence Service, World War II.* Los Angeles: Military Intelligence Service Club of Southern California, 1988.

Ichioka, Yuji. *A Buried Past.* Berkeley: University of California Press, 1974.

——. "Coming of Age." *Amerasia Journal* 13 (1986–87): ix–xiii.

——. *The Issei: The World of First Generation Japanese Immigrants, 1885–1924.* New York: Free Press, 1988.

——. "Japanese Immigrant Nationalism: The Issei and the Sino-Japanese War, 1937–41." *California History* 69.3 (1990): 260–75.

——. "*Kengakudan:* The Origin of Nisei Study Tours of Japan." *California History* 73.1 (Spring 1994): 30–43.

———. "The Meaning of Loyalty: The Case of Kazumaro Buddy Uno." *Amerasia Journal* 23 (Winter 1997–98): 45–72.

———. "A Study in Dualism: James Yoshinori Sakamoto and the *Japanese American Courier*, 1928–42." *Amerasia Journal* 13 (1986–87): 49–81.

———. "'Unity within Diversity': Louis Adamic and Japanese Americans." Ms., n.d. Author's files.

———, ed. *Views from Within: The Japanese Evacuation and Resettlement Study.* Los Angeles: Asian American Studies Center, University of California, 1989.

Irons, Peter. *Justice at War: The Story of the Japanese American Internment Cases.* New York: Oxford University Press, 1983.

Ishikawa, Michiji. "The Japanese in California." Master's thesis, Columbia University, 1928.

James, Thomas. *Exile Within: The Schooling of Japanese Americans, 1942–45.* Cambridge, Mass.: Harvard University Press, 1987.

Janowitz, Morris. *The Community Press in an Urban Setting.* 2d ed. Chicago: University of Chicago Press, 1967.

Japanese American Citizens' League, National Committee for Iva Toguri. *Iva Toguri (d'Aquino): A Victim of a Legend.* San Francisco: Japanese American Citizens' League, 1975.

Kagiwada, George. "The Assimilation of Nisei in Los Angeles." In *East across the Pacific: Historical and Sociological Studies of Japanese Immigration and Assimilation.* Ed. Hilary Conroy and T. Scott Miyakawa. 268–78. Santa Barbara, Calif.: ABC-Clio Press, 1972.

Kanda, Shigeo. "Recovering Cultural Symbols: A Case for Buddhism in the Japanese American Communities." *Journal of the American Academy of Religion* 44 (Dec. 1978): 445–75.

Kashima, Tetsuden. *Buddhism in America.* Westport, Conn.: Greenwood Press, 1977.

———. "Japanese American Internees Return, 1945–1955: Readjustment and Social Amnesia." *Phylon* 41 (June 1980): 107–15.

Kato, Mitsue, ed. *Our Recollections.* Tokyo: Art Printing, 1986.

Kawai, Kazuo. "Three Roads, and None Easy: An American-Born Japanese Looks at Life." *Survey Graphic* 9 (May 1926): 164–66.

Kennedy, Ruby Jo Reeves. "Single or Triple Melting-Pot? Intermarriage Trends in New Haven, 1870–1940." *American Journal of Sociology* 49 (Jan. 1944): 331–39.

Kessler, Lauren. "Fettered Freedoms: The Journalism of World War II Japanese Internment Camps." *Journalism History* 15 (Summer–Autumn 1988): 70–79.

Kiefer, Christie W. *Changing Culture, Changing Lives.* San Francisco: Jossey-Bass, 1974.

Kikuchi, Charles. *The Kikuchi Diary: Chronicle from an American Concentration Camp.* Ed. John Modell. Urbana: University of Illinois Press, 1993.

———. "Through the JERS Looking Glass: A Personal View from Within." In

Views from Within: The Japanese Evacuation and Resettlement Study. Ed. Yuji Ichioka. 179–95. Los Angeles: Asian American Studies Center, University of California, 1989.

Kikumura, Akemi, and Harry Kitano. "Interracial Marriage: A Picture of Japanese Americans." *Journal of Social Issues* 29 (1973): 67–82.

Kim, Hyung-chan. *Asian American Studies: An Annotated Bibliography.* Westport, Conn.: Greenwood Press, 1989.

———. *Dictionary of Asian American History.* Westport, Conn.: Greenwood Press, 1986.

Kimura, Yukiko. *Issei: Japanese Immigrants in Hawaii.* Honolulu: University of Hawaii Press, 1988.

Kitagawa, Daisuke. *Issei and Nisei.* New York: Seabury Press, 1967.

Kitagawa, Joseph M., and Mark H. Cummings, eds. *Buddhism and Asian History.* New York: Macmillan, 1987.

Kitano, Harry H. L., and Roger Daniels. *Asian Americans: Emerging Minorities.* 2d ed. Englewood Cliffs, N.J.: Prentice-Hall, 1995.

Kitayama, Glen Ikuo. "Japanese Americans and the Movement for Redress: A Case Study of Grassroots Activism in the Los Angeles Chapter of the National Coalition for Redress/Reparations." Master's thesis, University of California at Los Angeles, 1993.

Kivisto, Peter, and Dag Blanck, eds. *American Immigrants and Their Generations.* Urbana: University of Illinois Press, 1990.

Koga, Sumio, ed. *A Centennial Legacy: History of the Japanese Christian Missions in North America, 1877–1977.* Chicago: Nobart, 1977.

Koppes, Clayton R., and Gregory D. Black. *Hollywood Goes to War.* Berkeley: University of California Press, 1990.

Kumamoto, Bob. "The Search for Spies: American Counterintelligence and the Japanese American Community, 1931–1942." *Amerasia Journal* 6 (1979): 45–75.

Kurashige, Lon Yuki. "Made in Little Tokyo: Politics of Ethnic Identity and Festival in Southern California, 1934–1994." Ph.D. diss., University of Wisconsin at Madison, 1994.

Kurashige, Scott. "Internment and the Japanese American Left." Ms., n.d. Author's files.

Kutler, Stanley I. *American Inquisition: Justice and Injustice in the Cold War.* New York: Hill and Wang, 1982.

Larson, Ronald C. "*Doho:* The Japanese American 'Communist' Press, 1937–1942." Ms., 1975. Author's files.

LaViolette, Forrest E. *Americans of Japanese Ancestry: A Study of Assimilation in the American Community.* Toronto: Canadian Institute of International Affairs, 1945.

Layman, Emma McCloy. *Buddhism in America.* Chicago: Nelson-Hall, 1976.

Leong, Russell, ed. *Moving the Image.* Los Angeles: Asian American Studies Center, University of California, and Visual Communications, 1991.

Levine, Gene, and Colbert Rhodes. *The Japanese American Community: A Three-Generation Study.* New York: Praeger, 1981.

Light, Jerome T. "The Development of a Junior-Senior High School Program in a Relocation Center for People of Japanese Ancestry during the War with Japan." Ed.D. diss., Stanford University, 1947.

Limerick, Patricia Nelson, Clyde A. Milner II, and Charles E. Rankin, eds. *Trails: Toward a New Western History.* Lawrence: University Press of Kansas, 1991.

Linehan, Thomas. "Japanese American Resettlement in Cleveland during and after World War II." *Journal of Urban History* 20 (Nov. 1993): 54–80.

Lippy, Charles H., and Peter W. Williams. *Encyclopedia of American Religious Experiences.* 3 vols. New York: Scribner's, 1988.

Lipton, Dean. "Wayne M. Collins and the Case of Tokyo Rose." *Journal of Contemporary Studies* 8 (1985): 25–41.

Lowe, Lisa. *Immigrant Acts: On Asian American Cultural Politics.* Durham, N.C.: Duke University Press, 1996.

Lyman, Stanford. *Asians in North America.* Santa Barbara, Calif.: ABC-Clio Press, 1970.

———. "Generation and Character: The Case of the Japanese-Americans." In *East across the Pacific: Historical and Sociological Studies of Japanese Immigration and Assimilation.* Ed. Hilary Conroy and T. Scott Miyakawa. 279–314. Santa Barbara, Calif.: ABC-Clio Press, 1972).

Maffly-Kipp, Laurie. "Eastward Ho! American Religion from the Perspective of the Pacific Rim." In *Retelling U.S. Religious History.* Ed. Thomas A. Tweed. 127–48. Berkeley: University of California Press, 1997.

Mannheim, Karl. "The Problem of Generations." In *Essays in the Sociology of Knowledge.* Ed. and trans. Paul Kecskmeti. 286–312. New York: Oxford University Press, 1952.

Marty, Martin. "Ethnicity: The Skeleton of Religion in America." *Church History* 41 (Mar. 1972): 5–21.

Masaoka, Mike, with Bill Hosokawa. *They Call Me Moses Masaoka.* New York: William Morrow and Co., 1987.

Matsumoto, Toru. *Beyond Prejudice.* New York: Friendship Press, 1946.

Matsumoto, Valerie J. "Desperately Seeking 'Deirdre': Gender Roles, Multicultural Relations, and Nisei Women Writers of the 1930s." *Frontiers* 12.1 (1991): 19–32.

———. *Farming the Home Place: A Japanese American Community in California, 1919–1982.* Ithaca, N.Y.: Cornell University Press, 1993.

———. "Japanese American Women during World War II." *Frontiers* 8 (1984): 6–14.

———. "Redefining Expectations: Nisei Women in the 1930s." *California History* 73.1 (Spring 1994): 44–53.

Matthews, Fred H. *Quest for an American Sociology: Robert E. Park and the Chicago School.* Montreal: McGill-Queen's University Press, 1977.

McClatchy, Valentine Stuart, ed. *Four Anti-Japanese Pamphlets.* New York: Arno Press, 1978.

McClymer, John F. "Gender and the 'American Way of Life': Women and the Americanization Movement." *Journal of American Ethnic History* 10 (Spring 1991): 3–20.

McKenna, Alice Osborne. "Americanizing the Foreign Home." *Los Angeles School Journal* 9 (28 Sept. 1925): 13–14.

Mears, Elliot. *Resident Orientals on the Pacific Coast.* Chicago: University of Chicago Press, 1928.

Melton, Gordon. *The Encyclopedia of American Religion.* 3d ed. Detroit: Gale Research, 1989.

Michio, Araki. "The Schools of Japanese Buddhism." In *Buddhism and Asian History.* Ed. Joseph M. Kitagawa and Mark H. Cummings. 267–75. New York: Macmillan, 1987.

Miller, Sally M., ed. *The Ethnic Press in the United States: A Historical Analysis and Handbook.* Westport, Conn.: Greenwood Press, 1987.

Milner, Clyde A., II, ed. *A New Significance: Re-envisioning the History of the American West.* New York: Oxford University Press, 1996.

Milner, Clyde A., II, Anne M. Butler, and David R. Lewis, eds. *Major Problems in the History of the American West.* 2d ed. New York: Houghton Mifflin, 1997.

Milner, Clyde A., II, Carol O'Connor, and Martha Sandweiss, eds. *The Oxford History of the American West.* New York: Oxford University Press, 1994.

Miyamoto, S. Frank. "Problems of Interpersonal Style among Nisei." *Amerasia Journal* 13 (1986–87): 29–45.

———. *Social Solidarity among the Japanese in Seattle.* 1939. Rpt., Seattle: University of Washington Press, 1984.

Modell, John. "Class or Ethnic Solidarity: The Japanese American Company Union." *Pacific Historical Review* 38 (May 1969): 193–206.

———. *The Economics and Politics of Racial Accommodation: The Japanese of Los Angeles, 1900–1942.* Urbana: University of Illinois Press, 1977.

———. *Into One's Own: From Youth to Adulthood in America, 1920–1975.* Berkeley: University of California Press, 1989.

———. "The Japanese American Family: A Perspective for Future Investigations." *Pacific Historical Review* 37 (Feb. 1968): 67–81.

———. "Tradition and Opportunity: The Japanese Immigrant in America." *Pacific Historical Review* 40 (May 1971): 163–82.

Montalto, Nicholas. "The Intercultural Education Movement, 1924–41: The Growth of Tolerance as a Form of Intolerance." In *American Education and the European Immigrant, 1840–1940.* Ed. Bernard J. Weiss. 142–60. Urbana: University of Illinois Press, 1982.

Montero, Darrel. *Japanese Americans: Changing Patterns of Ethnic Affiliation over Three Generations.* Boulder, Colo.: Westview Press, 1980.

Moore, Deborah Dash. *At Home in America: Second Generation New York Jews.* New York: Columbia University Press, 1981.

Mori, Toshio. "Sweet Potato." In *The Chauvinist and Other Stories.* Los Angeles: Asian American Studies Center, University of California, 1979.

Morimoto, Toyotomi. "Language and Heritage Maintenance of Immigrants: Japanese Language Schools of California, 1903–1941." Ph.D. diss., University of California at Los Angeles, 1989.

Mossman, Robert A. "Japanese American War Relocation Centers as Total Institutions with Emphasis on the Educational Program." Ed.D. diss., Rutgers University, 1978.

Mullins, Mark R. "The Organizational Dilemmas of Ethnic Churches: A Case Study of Japanese Buddhism in Canada." *Sociological Analysis* 49 (1988): 217–33.

Munekata, Ryo, ed. *Buddhist Churches of America: 75 Year History, 1899–1974.* Chicago: Nobart, 1974.

Murphy, Thomas D. *Ambassadors in Arms.* Honolulu: University of Hawaii Press, 1946.

Murray, Alice Yang. "'Silence No More': The Japanese American Redress Movement, 1942–1992." Ph.D. diss., Stanford University, 1994.

Myer, Dillon. *Uprooted Americans.* Tucson: University of Arizona Press, 1971.

Nagata, Donna K. *Legacy of Injustice: Exploring the Cross-Generational Impact of the Japanese American Internment.* New York: Plenum Press, 1993.

Nakamaki, Hirochika. "The History of the Japanese Christian Churches and the Consciousness of Japanese Christians in Sacramento, California." In *Japanese Religions in California.* Ed. Keiichi Yanagawa. 241–85. Tokyo: Department of Religious Studies, University of Tokyo, 1983.

Nakamura, Hajime. "The Basic Teachings of Buddhism." In *Buddhism in the Modern World.* Ed. Heinrich Dumoulin. 000–00. New York: Macmillan, 1976.

Nakano, Mei. *Japanese American Women: Three Generations, 1890–1990.* Berkeley, Calif.: Mina Press, 1990.

Nelson, Douglas. *Heart Mountain: The History of an American Concentration Camp.* Madison: State Historical Society of Wisconsin, 1976.

Newspaper Annual and Directory. Philadelphia: N. W. Ayer and Son, various years.

Niiya, Brian, ed. *Japanese American History: An A to Z Reference from 1868 to the Present.* New York: Facts on File, 1993.

Nishi, Setsuko Matsunaga. "Japanese American Achievement in Chicago: A Cultural Response to Degradation." Ph.D. diss., University of Chicago, 1963.

Nishimoto, Richard S. *Inside an American Concentration Camp: Japanese American Resistance at Poston, Arizona.* Ed. Lane Ryo Hirabayashi. Tucson: University of Arizona Press, 1995.

Nodera, Isamu. "A Survey of the Vocational Activities of the Japanese in the City of Los Angeles." Master's thesis, University of Southern California, 1936.

Noriyoshi, Tamaru. "Buddhism in Japan." In *Buddhism and Asian History.* Ed.

Joseph M. Kitagawa and Mark H. Cummings. 159–74. New York: Macmillan, 1987.

O'Brien, Robert. *College Nisei*. Palo Alto, Calif.: Pacific Books, 1949.

Ogawa, Dennis. *From Japs to Japanese Americans*. Berkeley, Calif.: McCutchan, 1971.

———, ed. *Kodomo No Tame Ni—For the Sake of the Children: The Japanese Experience in Hawaii*. Honolulu: University of Hawaii Press, 1977.

Ogura, Kosei. "A Sociological Study of the Buddhist Churches in North America with a Case Study of Gardena, California, Congregation." Master's thesis, University of Southern California, 1932.

Okamura, Raymond. "The American Concentration Camps: A Cover-up through Euphemistic Terminology." *Journal of Ethnic Studies* 10 (1982): 95–109.

Okihiro, Gary Y. *Cane Fires: The Anti-Japanese Movement in Hawaii, 1865–1945*. Philadelphia: Temple University Press, 1991.

———. "Japanese Resistance in America's Concentration Camps: A Re-evaluation." *Amerasia Journal* 2 (Fall 1973): 20–34.

———. *Margins and Mainstreams: Asians in American History and Culture*. Seattle: University of Washington Press, 1994.

———. "Religion and Resistance in America's Concentration Camps." *Phylon* 45 (1984): 220–33.

———. *Storied Lives: Japanese American Students and World War II*. Seattle: University of Washington Press, 1999.

Okihiro, Gary Y., and Julie Sly. "The Press, Japanese Americans, and Concentration Camps." *Phylon* 44 (1983): 66–83.

Okihiro, Gary Y., Shirley Hune, Arthur A. Hansen, and John M. Liu, eds. *Reflections on Shattered Windows: Promises and Prospects for Asian American Studies*. Pullman: Washington State University Press, 1988.

Omatsu, Glenn. "Asian Pacific American Workers and the Expansion of Democracy." *Amerasia Journal* 18 (1992): v–xix.

Omi, Michael, and Howard Winant. *Racial Formations in the United States*. New York: Routledge, 1986.

Omura, James. "Japanese American Journalism during World War II." In *Frontiers of Asian American Studies*. Ed. Gail Nomura, Russell Endo, Stephen H. Sumida, and Russell C. Leong. 71–80. Pullman: Washington State University Press, 1989.

Osako, Masako K. "Japanese-Americans: Melting into the All-American Pot." In *Ethnic Chicago*. 4th ed. Ed. Melvin G. Holli and Peter d'A. Jones. 409–37. Grand Rapids, Mich.: Eerdmans, 1995.

Osumi, Megumi Dick. "Asians and California's Anti-Miscegenation Laws." In *Asian and Pacific American Experiences: Women's Perspectives*. Ed. Nobuya Tsuchida. 1–38. Minneapolis: Asian/Pacific American Learning Resource Center and General College, University of Minnesota, 1982.

Park, Robert E. "Behind Our Masks." *Survey Graphic* 9 (May 1926): 135–39.

———. *The Immigrant Press and Its Control.* New York: Harper and Bros., 1922.

———. "Our Racial Frontier on the Pacific." *Survey Graphic* 9 (May 1926): 192–96.

———. *Race and Culture.* Glencoe, Ill.: Free Press, 1950.

Pascoe, Peggy. "Miscegenation Law, Court Cases, and Ideologies of 'Race' in Twentieth-Century America." *Journal of American History* 83 (June 1996): 44–69.

———. "Race, Gender, and Intercultural Relations: The Case of Interracial Marriage." *Signs* 12.1 (1991): 5–18.

Personal Justice Denied: Report of the Commission on Wartime Relocation and Internment of Civilians. Washington, D.C.: Civil Liberties Public Education Fund; Seattle: University of Washington Press, 1997.

Persons, Stow. *Ethnic Studies at Chicago, 1905–45.* Urbana: University of Illinois Press, 1987.

Prebish, Charles. *American Buddhism.* North Scituate, Mass.: Duxbury Press, 1979.

Quinn, D. Michael. "Religion in the American West." In *Under an Open Sky.* Ed. William Cronon, George Miles, and Jay Gitlin. 145–66. New York: W. W. Norton, 1992.

Raftery, Judith. *Land of Fair Promise: Politics and Reform in Los Angeles Schools, 1885–1941.* Stanford, Calif.: Stanford University Press, 1992.

Ratanamani, Minimai. "History of Shin Buddhism in the United States." Master's thesis, College of the Pacific, 1960.

Regan, Lucile. "Nisei: The Second Generation." *Los Angeles School Journal* 19 (1 June 1936): 15, 48–51.

Reynolds, Frank E., and Charles Hallisey. "Buddhist Religion, Culture, and Civilization." In *Buddhism and Asian History.* Ed. Joseph M. Kitagawa and Mark H. Cummings. 3–28. New York: Macmillan, 1987.

Rosaldo, Renato. *Culture and Truth.* Boston: Beacon Press, 1989.

Ruiz, Vicki. "'Star Struck': Acculturation, Adolescence, and Mexican-American Women, 1920–1950." In *Small Worlds: Children and Adolescents in America, 1850–1950.* Ed. Elliot West and Paula Petrik. 61–80. Lawrence: University Press of Kansas, 1992.

Rust, William C. "The Shin Sect of Buddhism in America: Its Antecedents, Beliefs, and Present Condition." Ph.D. diss., University of Southern California, 1951.

Sanchez, George J. *Becoming Mexican American: Ethnicity, Culture, and Identity in Chicano Los Angeles, 1900–1945.* New York: Oxford University Press, 1993.

San Juan, E., Jr. *Racial Formations/Critical Transformations.* Highlands, N.J.: Humanities Press, 1992.

San Miguel, Guadalupe, Jr. *Let Them All Take Heed: Mexican Americans and the Campaign for Educational Equality in Texas, 1910–1981.* Austin: University of Texas Press, 1987.

Saxton, Alexander. *The Indispensable Enemy: Labor and the Anti-Chinese Movement in California*. Berkeley: University of California Press, 1971.

———. "Nathan Glazer, Daniel Moynihan, and the Cult of Ethnicity." *Amerasia Journal* 4 (1977): 141–50.

———. *The Rise and Fall of the White Republic*. London: Verso Press, 1990.

Shafer, Harry M. "Tendencies in Immigrant Education." *Los Angeles School Journal* 9 (5 Oct. 1925): 9–11.

Shikamura, Alice. "The Vocational Intentions of the Second-Generation Japanese Students in Three California Universities." Master's thesis, Stanford University, 1948.

Shinagawa, Larry, and Gin Yong Pang. "Marriage Patterns of Asian Americans in California, 1980." In *Income and Status Differences between White and Minority Americans*. Ed. Sucheng Chan. 225–82. Lewiston, N.Y.: Edward Mellen Press, 1990.

Shoho, Alan. "Americanization through Public Education of Japanese Americans in Hawaii, 1930–41." Ed.D. diss., Arizona State University, 1990.

Short, K. R. M., ed. *Film and Radio Propaganda in World War II*. Knoxville: University of Tennessee Press, 1983.

Smith, M. G. "Ethnicity and Ethnic Groups in America: The View from Harvard." *Ethnic and Racial Studies* 5 (Jan. 1982): 1–22.

Smith, Timothy L. "Religion and Ethnicity in America." *American Historical Review* 83 (Dec. 1978): 1155–75.

Smith, William C. *Americans in Process: A Study of Our Citizens of Oriental Ancestry*. Ann Arbor, Mich.: Edward Bros., 1937.

Sollors, Werner, ed. *The Invention of Ethnicity*. New York: Oxford University Press, 1989.

Spencer, Robert F. "Japanese Buddhism in the United States, 1940–46." Ph.D. diss., University of California at Berkeley, 1946.

Spickard, Paul. *Japanese Americans: The Formation and Transformation of an Ethnic Group*. Boston: Twayne, 1996.

———. *Mixed Blood: Intermarriage and Ethnic Identity in Twentieth-Century America*. Madison: University of Wisconsin Press, 1989.

———. "The Nisei Assume Power: The Japanese Citizens League, 1941–42." *Pacific Historical Review* 52 (May 1983): 147–74.

Starn, Orin. "Engineering Internment: Anthropologists and the War Relocation Authority." *American Ethnologist* 13 (Nov. 1986): 700–720.

Starr, Kevin. *Americans and the California Dream, 1850–1915*. New York: Oxford University Press, 1973.

Steinberg, Stephen. *The Ethnic Myth*. Boston: Beacon Press, 1981.

———. *Turning Back: The Retreat from Racial Justice in American Thought and Policy*. Boston: Beacon Press, 1995.

Stephan, John J. "Hijacked by Utopia: American Nikkei in Manchuria." *Amerasia Journal* 23 (Winter 1997–98): 1–44.

Stevens, John D. "From Behind Barbed Wire: Freedom of the Press in World War II Japanese Centers." *Journalism Quarterly* 48 (Summer 1971): 279–87.

Strong, Edward K. *Japanese in California.* Stanford, Calif.: Stanford University Press, 1933.

———. *The Second-Generation Japanese Problem.* Stanford, Calif.: Stanford University Press, 1934.

———. *Vocational Aptitudes of Second-Generation Japanese in the United States.* Stanford, Calif.: Stanford University Press, 1933.

Stroup, Dorothy A. "The Role of the Japanese-American Press in Its Community." Master's thesis, University of California at Berkeley, 1960.

Susman, Warren. "Communication and Culture: Keynote Essay." In *Mass Media between the Wars.* Ed. Catherine L. Covert and John D. Stevens. xi–xxiii. Syracuse, N.Y.: Syracuse University Press, 1984.

Suzuki, Lester. *Ministry in the Assembly and Relocation Centers of World War II.* Berkeley, Calif.: Yardbird, 1979.

———. "Ministry in the Wartime Relocation Centers." *Christian Century,* 12 Jan. 1972, 35–41.

———. "The Significance of the NCYPCC." Ms., n.d. Author's files.

Suzuki, Robert H. "Asian Americans as the 'Model Minority': Outdoing the Whites? or Media Hype?" *Change* 21 (Nov.–Dec. 1989): 13–19.

———. "Education and the Socialization of Asian Americans: A Revisionist Analysis of the 'Model Minority' Thesis." *Amerasia Journal* 4 (1977): 23–52.

Szasz, Ferenc M., and Margaret Connell Szasz, "Religion and Spirituality." In *The Oxford History of the American West.* Ed. Clyde A. Milner II, Carol O'Connor, and Martha Sandweiss. 356–91. New York: Oxford University Press, 1994.

Taft, William H. *Newspapers as Tools for Historians.* Columbia, Mo.: Lucas Bros., 1970.

Tajiri, Larry. "Nisei USA." *Pacific Citizen,* 4 Aug. 1945.

Takagi, Dana. "Life History Analysis and JERS: Re-evaluating the Work of Charles Kikuchi." In *Views from Within: The Japanese Evacuation and Resettlement Study.* Ed. Yuji Ichioka. 197–216. Los Angeles: Asian American Studies Center, University of California, 1989.

———. "Personality and History: Hostile Nisei Women." In *Reflections on Shattered Windows: Promises and Prospects for Asian American Studies.* Ed. Gary Y. Okihiro, Shirley Hune, Arthur A. Hansen, and John M. Liu. 184–92. Pullman: Washington State University Press, 1988.

Takahashi, Jerrold. "Japanese American Responses to Race Relations: The Formation of Nisei Perspectives." *Amerasia Journal* 9 (1982): 29–57.

———. *Nisei/Sansei: Shifting Japanese American Identities and Politics.* Philadelphia: Temple University Press, 1997.

Takahashi, Kyojiro. "A Social Study of Japanese Shinto and Buddhism in Los Angeles." Master's thesis, University of Southern California, 1937.

Takaki, Ronald, ed. *From Different Shores.* New York: Oxford University Press, 1987.

———. *Strangers from a Different Shore: A History of Asian Americans.* Boston: Little, Brown, 1989.

Takarabe, Heihachiro, ed. *Issei Christians.* Sacramento, Calif.: Issei Oral History Project, 1977.

Takezawa, Yasuko I. *Breaking the Silence: Redress and Japanese American Ethnicity.* Ithaca, N.Y.: Cornell University Press, 1995.

Tamura, Eileen H. *Americanization, Acculturation, and Ethnic Identity: The Nisei Generation in Hawaii.* Urbana: University of Illinois Press, 1994.

———. "The English-Only Effort, the Anti-Japanese Campaign, and Language Acquisition in the Education of Japanese Americans in Hawaii, 1915–40." *History of Education Quarterly* 33.1 (Spring 1993): 37–58.

Tanaka, Togo. "How to Survive Racism in America's Free Society." In *Voices Long Silent: An Oral Inquiry into the Japanese American Evacuation.* Ed. Arthur A. Hansen and Betty E. Mitson. 93–94. Fullerton: Oral History Project, California State University, 1974.

Tateishi, John, ed. *And Justice for All: An Oral History of the Japanese American Detention Camps.* New York: Random House, 1984.

Taylor, Sandra C. "Evacuation and Economic Loss: Questions and Perspectives." In *Japanese Americans: From Relocation to Redress.* Ed. Roger Daniels, Sandra C. Taylor, and Harry H. L. Kitano. 163–67. Seattle: University of Washington Press, 1991.

———. " 'Fellow-Feelers with the Afflicted': The Christian Churches and the Relocation of the Japanese during World War II." In *Japanese Americans: From Relocation to Redress.* Ed. Roger Daniels, Sandra C. Taylor, and Harry H. L. Kitano. 123–29. Seattle: University of Washington Press, 1991.

———. *Jewel of the Desert: Japanese American Internment at Topaz.* Berkeley: University of California Press, 1993.

Thernstrom, Stephan, Ann Orlov, and Oscar Handlin, eds. *The Harvard Encyclopedia of American Ethnic Groups.* Cambridge, Mass.: Harvard University Press, 1980.

Thomas, Dorothy S., Charles Kikuchi, and James Sakoda. *The Salvage.* Berkeley: University of California Press, 1952.

Thomas, Dorothy S., and Richard S. Nishimoto. *The Spoilage: Japanese-American Evacuation and Resettlement during World War II.* Berkeley: University of California Press, 1946.

Tinker, John N. "Intermarriage and Assimilation in a Plural Society: Japanese Americans in the United States." *Marriage and Family Review* 5 (1982): 61–74.

Toyama, Chotoku. "The Japanese Community in Los Angeles." Master's thesis, Columbia University, 1926.

Tuck, Donald. *Buddhist Churches of America.* Lewiston, N.Y.: Edwin Mellen Press, 1987.

Tuthill, Gretchen. "Study of the Japanese in the City of Los Angeles." Master's thesis, University of Southern California, 1924.

Tweed, Thomas A. *The American Encounter with Buddhism, 1844–1912.* Bloomington: Indiana University Press, 1992.

———, ed. *Retelling U.S. Religious History.* Berkeley: University of California Press, 1997.

Tyack, David B. *The One Best System.* Cambridge, Mass.: Harvard University Press, 1974.

Tyack, David B., and Elisabeth Hansot. *Public Schools in Hard Times.* Cambridge, Mass.: Harvard University Press, 1984.

Uchida, Yoshiko. *Desert Exile: The Uprooting of a Japanese American Family.* Seattle: University of Washington Press, 1982.

Uono, Kiyoshi. "The Factors Affecting the Geographical Aggregation and Dispersion of Japanese Residences in the City of Los Angeles." Master's thesis, University of Southern California, 1927.

Utsuki, Nishi. *The Shin Sect: A School of Mahayana Buddhism.* Kyoto, Japan: Publication Bureau of Buddhist Books, 1937.

Uyeda, Clifford. *A Final Report and Review: The Japanese American Citizens League National Committee for Iva Toguri.* Occasional Monographs No. 1. Seattle: Asian American Studies Program, University of Washington, 1980.

———. "The Pardoning of 'Tokyo Rose': A Report on the Restoration of American Citizenship to Iva Ikuko Toguri." *Amerasia Journal* 5 (Fall 1978): 69–84.

Vecoli, Rudolph. "From *The Uprooted* to *The Transplanted:* The Writing of American Immigration History, 1951–1989." In *From "Melting Pot" to Multiculturalism: The Evolution of Ethnic Relations in the United States and Canada.* Ed. Valeria Gennaro Lerda. 25–53. Rome: Bulzoni Editore, 1990.

Wacker, R. Fred. *Ethnicity, Pluralism, and Race.* Westport, Conn.: Greenwood Press, 1983.

Wakamatsu, Jack. *Silent Warriors: A Memoir of America's 442nd Regimental Combat Team.* New York: Vantage Press, 1995.

Wang, Ling-chi. "Asian American Studies." *American Quarterly* 33 (1981): 339–54.

Waters, Mary. *Ethnic Options.* Berkeley: University of California Press, 1990.

Waugh, Isami Arifuku. "Hidden Crime and Deviance in the Japanese-American Community, 1920–1946." D.Crim. diss., University of California at Berkeley, 1978.

Weber, Donald. "Reconsidering the Hansen Thesis: Generational Metaphors and American Ethnic Studies." *American Quarterly* 43 (June 1991): 320–32.

Weglyn, Michi. *Years of Infamy: The Untold Story of America's Concentration Camps.* New York: William Morrow and Co., 1976.

Wei, William. *The Asian American Movement.* Philadelphia: Temple University Press, 1993.

West, Elliot, and Paula Petrik, eds. *Small Worlds: Children and Adolescents in America, 1850–1950.* Lawrence: University Press of Kansas, 1992.

Williams, Peter. *America's Religions: Traditions and Cultures*. 1990. Rpt., Urbana: University of Illinois Press, 1998.

Williams, Raymond Brady. *Religions of Immigrants from India and Pakistan*. Cambridge: Cambridge University Press, 1988.

Wirth, Louis. "Consensus and Mass Communication." *American Sociological Review* 13 (1948): 1–15.

Woldring, Henk E. S. *Karl Mannheim: Philosophy, Sociology, and Social Ethics, with a Detailed Biography*. Assen, The Netherlands: Van Gorcum, 1986.

Wollenberg, Charles. *With All Deliberate Speed: Segregation and Exclusion in California Schools, 1855–1975*. Berkeley: University of California Press, 1976.

Yamamoto, Eriko. "Miya Sannomiya Kikuchi: A Pioneer Nisei Woman's Life and Identity." *Amerasia Journal* 23 (Winter 1997–98): 73–102.

———. "Struggle of a Frontier Nisei: A History of Japanese-Americans through Mrs. Kikuchi's Words." Master's thesis, Claremont Graduate School, 1982.

Yanagisako, Sylvia. *Transforming the Past: Tradition and Kinship among Japanese Americans*. Stanford, Calif.: Stanford University Press, 1985.

Yans-McLaughlin, Virginia, ed. *Immigration Reconsidered*. New York: Oxford University Press, 1990.

Yoneda, Karl. *Ganbatte: Sixty-Year Struggle of a Kibei Worker*. Los Angeles: Asian American Studies Center, University of California, 1983.

Yoneyama, Hiroshi. "The Forging of Japanese American Patriotism, 1931–41." Master's thesis, University of Tsukuba [Japan], 1984.

Yoo, David. "Captivating Memories: Museology, Concentration Camps, and Japanese American History." *American Quarterly* 48.4 (Dec. 1996): 680–99.

Yoshida, Ryo. "A Socio-historical Study of Racial/Ethnic Identity in the Inculturated Religious Expression of Japanese Christianity in San Francisco, 1877–1924." Ph.D. diss., Graduate Theological Union, Berkeley, Calif., 1989.

Yoshii, Michael. "The Young People's Christian Conference: The Formation and Development of a Nisei Christian Youth Movement." Ms., May 1985. Author's files.

Yoshina, Shizo, ed. *Nisei Christian Journey*. Sacramento, Calif.: Nisei Christian Oral History Project, 1988.

Young, Robert J. C. *Colonial Desire: Hybridity in Theory, Culture, and Race*. London: Routledge, 1995.

Yumiba, Carole Katsuko. "An Educational History of the War Relocation Centers at Jerome and Rohwer, Arkansas, 1942–45." Ph.D. diss., University of Southern California, 1979.

Yun, Grace, ed. *A Look beyond the Model Minority Image: Critical Issues in Asian America*. New York: Minority Rights Group, 1989.

Zeller, William. "The Educational Program Provided the Japanese Americans during the Relocation Period, 1942–45." Ph.D. diss., Michigan State University, 1963.

Zunz, Olivier. "American History and the Changing Meaning of Assimilation." *Journal of American Ethnic History* 4.2 (Spring 1985): 53–85.

INDEX

Collins, Wayne, 177
Colorado Times, 129–31, 145
Columbia Foundation, 153
Concentration camps, 6, 93; camp life, 103–6; economic loss from, 174; Gila River, 121, 176–78; Heart Mountain, 146–47; Jerome, 108, 117; Manzanar, 96, 109, 116, 134; Minidoka, 110; Poston, 96; Topaz, 120; Tule Lake, 104, 110, 150, 173
Congress of Industrial Organizations, 75
Cremin, Lawrence, 20
Cubberley, Ellwood, 22
Cult of ethnicity, 9
Culture. *See* Nisei subculture
Current Life, 130, 144

Daniels, Roger, 7
d'Aquino, Felipe, 176
d'Aquino, Iva Toguri, 174–79
Dating (by Nisei), 78–86
Democracy, 103; critique of, 151–52, 160, 168–70
Denver, Colo., 154–55
Depression, 21
de Wolfe, Tom, 175, 178
"Disloyals," 150
Doho, 70–71

Economic loss (from concentration camps), 174
Education, 8, 11, 17, 94, 99–101, 106–13, 122; and curricular issues, 107–8; and employment, 28; progressive, 11, 18, 20–21
Employment, 3, 27; and agriculture, 3–4; and job discrimination, 50; and nonagricultural fields, 3–4
Endo, Mitsuye, 122, 173
Endogamy, 83
Ethnicity, 2, 9; cult of, 9
Ethnic press. *See* Newspapers
Executive Order 9066, 95, 126

Fair Play Committee of One, 146. *See also* Concentration camps: Heart Mountain
Fass, Paula, 20
Federal Bureau of Investigation (FBI), 92, 95, 101, 118, 126–27, 141
Filipino Americans, 84–85
First Japanese Presbyterian Church of San Francisco, 55

Ford, Gerald, 177
442d Regimental Combat Team. *See under* U.S. Army
Fowler, Ruth, 24
Frazier, E. Franklin, 154
Fruit and Vegetable Workers Union, 126
Fuchigami, Takako, 38
Fujii, Sei, 87, 131
Fujita, Haruko, 31
Fujita, Tad, 58, 64
Fujiyoshi, Donald, 55
Fukuda, Manabu, 50, 54
Funakoshi, Florence, 52

Gender role expectations, 79–83
Gentlemen's Agreement, 3
Giannini Foundation, 153
Gibson, Rev. Otis, 55
Gila River, Ariz., camp at. *See under* Concentration camps
Gospel Society, 55
Grange, 76

Hanna, Paul, 106–7
Hartmann, Edward, 22
Hashimoto, Rev. Hideo, 60, 114–15
Hata, Bill, 65
Hawaii, 6
Hearst, William Randolph, 133
Heart Mountain, Wyo., camp at. *See under* Concentration camps
Heart Mountain Sentinel, 147
Hendrick, Irving, 21
Herberg, Will, 39–40
Hirabayashi, Gordon, 96, 122
Hirabayashi, Lane, 107
Hirano, Nisaburo, 42
Hirasawa, Mae, 130
Hirohata, Paul, 30
Historical agency, 2, 171
Hollywood (film industry), 134–35
Home Front Commandos, 135
Honen, 45. *See also* Buddhism
Hori, Tashi, 121
Horikoshi, Rev. Y. Caspar, 55
Horinouchi, Isao, 44
Horiuchi, Wilfred, 27
Hosokawa, Bill, 6, 33, 132

Ichioka, Yuji, 6, 16
Identity: American, 2, 152, 160; formation, 1–2, 5–6, 8, 51–53, 69, 179; and

DAVID K. YOO is an associate professor of history at Claremont McKenna College. He is the the editor of *New Spiritual Homes: Religion and Asian Americans.*

The Hood River Issei: An Oral History of Japanese Settlers in Oregon's
Hood River Valley   *Linda Tamura*
Americanization, Acculturation, and Ethnic Identity: The Nisei Generation
in Hawaii   *Eileen H. Tamura*
Sui Sin Far/Edith Maude Eaton: A Literary Biography
Annette White-Parks
Mrs. Spring Fragrance and Other Writings   *Sui Sin Far; edited by
Amy Ling and Annette White-Parks*
The Golden Mountain: The Autobiography of a Korean Immigrant,
1895–1960   *Easurk Emsen Charr; edited and with an introduction by
Wayne Patterson*
Race and Politics: Asian Americans, Latinos, and Whites in a Los Angeles
Suburb   *Leland T. Saito*
Achieving the Impossible Dream: How Japanese Americans Obtained
Redress   *Mitchell T. Maki, Harry H. L. Kitano, and S. Megan Berthold*
If They Don't Bring Their Women Here: Chinese Female Immigration
before Exclusion   *George Anthony Peffer*
Growing Up Nisei: Race, Generation, and Culture among Japanese
Americans of California, 1924–49   *David K. Yoo*

Typeset in 10/13 Sabon
with Sabon display
Designed by Dennis Roberts
Composed by Celia Shapland
for the University of Illinois Press
Manufactured by Braun-Brumfield, Inc.

University of Illinois Press
1325 South Oak Street
Champaign, IL 61820-6903
www.press.uillinois.edu